YANQUI POLITICS
AND THE
ISTHMIAN CANAL

A RIDER COLLEGE PUBLICATION

RIDER COLLEGE
Trenton, New Jersey

YANQUI POLITICS AND THE ISTHMIAN CANAL

Lawrence O. Ealy

THE PENNSYLVANIA STATE
UNIVERSITY PRESS
University Park and London

Standard Book Number: 271–01126–2
Library of Congress Catalog Card Number: 74–127385
Copyright © 1971 by The Pennsylvania State University
All Rights Reserved
Printed in the United States of America
Designed by Pamella Gecan

To Arthur Preston Whitaker
Professor of Latin American History
University of Pennsylvania (1936–1965)

In grateful recognition of those formative years
when he was teacher, counsellor, and friend.

Contents

Preface

During the course of several years of research into the history of Panama and of writing about the isthmus and the canal, I have been intrigued by the frequency with which the subject of an interoceanic canal became a matter of political action and controversy in the United States. The dream of an American "bridge of water" between the Atlantic and Pacific Oceans was not finally realized until after an intense partisan battle had been waged by the advocates of two competing routes. In recent years the combined issues of Panamanian nationalism and the need for a new waterway to replace or supplement the present outmoded Panama Canal have reactivated political controversy not only in the United States but also in the Republic of Panama. Consequently, I decided to pursue the political theme which unites the story of the various interoceanic canal projects, past and present. This is a fresh approach to a subject which has inspired an almost endless mass of published material.

For nearly three centuries before the American Revolutionary War, the possibility of an interoceanic canal in the New World aroused the interest of European leaders. Such a project also attracted the attention of post-Revolutionary American political figures including Franklin and Jefferson. This ambitious scheme was not realized, however, until the United States had taken its place as a world power— and then only after the necessary technological and material resources had united with a favorable political climate. And now, decades after the realization of a centuries-old dream, momentous problems still revolve around the Panama Canal. The pressing need for a new canal and the surge of Panamanian nationalism have initiated still another cycle of political crises which have not yet been resolved.

The main purpose of this book is to provide a comprehensive chronology of the political issues surrounding the Panama Canal without, however, delving into tedious detail of interest only to the most dedicated and specialized scholars. (For instance, one debate alone about the canal occupied more than three hundred pages of the *Congressional Record*; another argument was featured in books, newspapers, and magazines for the better part of a year.) This book attempts to tie the political story together, providing a framework of reference for those who may be interested in the details or in some particular phase of the general account.

Due apologies are offered to any readers, friends, or colleagues from below the Mason-Dixon Line who may feel outraged by the all-inclusive use of the term "Yanqui" in this book. I hasten to explain that "Yanqui" is a peculiarly Latin American word which is not at all synonymous with "Yankee." Even though a large majority of the U.S. citizens who have worked in Panama have come from the Southern states, whether he hails from Maine or Georgia every citizen of the United States is, to the Latin American, a "Yanqui." I shall also use the term "North American" when speaking of the United States and its policies, actions, and people. It is quite inaccurate to say "American" in this respect, since *all* inhabitants of the Western Hemisphere are Americans.

Most of the books published about the Panama Canal have been concerned with the epic story of its construction, with engineering technicalities, or with the diplomacy surrounding the building of the Canal. The numerous secondary works often refer to the North American political scene, but the basic source for this aspect of research is the massive collection of governmental publications. The *Congressional Record* and many House and Senate reports and documents published by the Government Printing Office are invaluable sources. The folio files of the Mahan Library at the Naval War College contain many valuable periodical clippings which pertain to the problem. The late Mr. Edward Schuster of New York generously allowed me to use his excellent private collection of Latin American materials. Panamanian friends supplied me with a quantity of published information on the Canal and opinions from isthmian sources, as well as many helpful observations and suggestions. The late Professor Arthur C. Bining of the History Department at the University of Pennsylvania, teacher and friend, offered many excellent criticisms on the first six chapters. Finally, I am indebted to Dr. Thomas R. Goethals (nephew of General George Goethals) who read the entire manuscript and made valuable recommendations.

Lawrence O. Ealy

Lawrenceville, New Jersey
January, 1971

1

Party Attitudes Prior to the Mexican War

The impact of the Panama Canal upon the economic, commercial, scientific, and diplomatic history of the Western Hemisphere is almost impossible to measure. Hundreds of books and articles have been written about the vital role which the concept of a canal has played in the history of the United States, and the matter has also been a major force in U.S. foreign relations. Furthermore, there have been several periods in history when the subject of an isthmian canal caused a major political controversy in the United States. The choice of the Panamanian route in preference to the originally considered Nicaraguan route was largely a result of this partisan struggle and its outcome. As we shall see, the problems involved have always been complicated, and today new issues are aggravating the unresolved difficulties of the past.

The dream of an isthmian canal dates almost from the time when Europeans reached the Pacific shores of the New World.[1] Balboa, the first to carry the white man's banners across the isthmus, planned various ways to create a commercial route. He actually moved dismantled ships along a tortuous path through jungle swamp, across the continental divide, and reassembled them on the Pacific side. Numerous other surveys were made by the Spanish during the sixteenth and seventeenth centuries. While many perceptive men were convinced that the job could and should be done, Philip II of Spain dismissed a detailed recommendation to build a canal, proclaiming that such a project was manifestly against the will of God, since the Almighty had imposed the isthmus as a land barrier to shipping.

The first U.S. politician to show an interest in constructing a canal was Benjamin Franklin. In 1779, while he was serving as minister to France, he received an unusual letter from Pierre-André Gargáz, a convict, who was confined at that time in the French penal galleys at Toulon. Enclosed with the letter was a manuscript advocating canals both at Suez and at Panama as a means of promoting world trade and international peace. Franklin, then very deeply involved with the American Revolutionary War and its diplomacy, laid the manuscript aside. The fighting had ended when Gargáz was released from prison. The former convict then visited Franklin and persuaded him to print the manuscript on his private press at Passy. Ironically, the copies which were circulated received very little attention until an English language version of this treatise was published in 1922.[2] Only then did the pathetic Gargáz gain his rightful place among the legion of men whose great ideas achieved recognition and success long after they themselves had died.

For some years after U.S. independence, an isthmian canal was merely an intellectual concept to the leaders of the young republic. The nation at that time was confined to a region with seaports only along the Atlantic coastline—the Gulf of Mexico being controlled exclusively by the Spaniards. Because the commercial trade interests of the United States were still oriented toward the Atlantic, there was little incentive for the building of a canal which would link the Atlantic and the Pacific.

However, in 1787, when Thomas Jefferson was the U.S. minister to France, he read a copy of the Gargáz thesis which Franklin had published. As a result, he became wary of the more-than-passing British interest in a canal. U.S. relations with Great Britain were still strained, and Jefferson found the Parisian atmosphere very condusive to his own feelings of antipathy toward London. Every move the British made was watched carefully. This anti-British sentiment, was later to become a cornerstone of the Democratic-Republican party opposition to the Federalist regimes of George Washington and John Adams.

Throughout the winter of 1787–88 Jefferson corresponded with William Carmichael, acting U.S. chargé d'affaires in Madrid, urging him to try to obtain details of the report of a rumored Spanish expedition allegedly sent to the isthmus in 1779–81 to survey a possible canal route. "I am assured," Jefferson wrote, "that a survey was made, that a canal appeared very practicable, and that the idea was suppressed for political reasons altogether . . . This report is to me a vast desideratum, for reasons political and philosophical. I cannot help suspecting the Spanish squadron to be gone to South America, and that some disturbances have been excited there by the British."[3]

Jefferson was right about British interest in the great idea. William Pitt, the Younger, was intrigued by a report from a South American patriot, Francisco Miranda, who set forth a plan for a canal at Panama. Although the London cabinet seriously considered the plan,[4] their attention was diverted to the Continent, where Napoleon Bonaparte was creating much more pressing problems for the British.

The Napoleonic Wars in Europe caused a trade crisis for the United States. Caught between British Orders in Council, Napoleon's Berlin and Milan decrees, Mr. Jefferson's embargo, and Mr. Madison's Non-Intercourse and Macon Bills, some frustrated shipowners turned to the China trade and to a small but flourishing commerce around the Horn with Chile. The great need for a canal to eliminate the long and tortuous trip around South America was becoming increasingly important.

About 1803, the writings of Alexander von Humboldt, a German scientist, stirred more speculation in the United States about the possibility of an interoceanic canal. Suggesting nine possible routes for a waterway, von Humboldt's study tended to tie together more than two centuries of survey, speculation, and writing about a canal. Over the years numerous routes through Tehuantepec, Honduras, Nicaragua, and Panama had been proposed. Von Humboldt, however, favored the Darién route in the Atrato River region of New Granada.[5]

When Thomas Jefferson read von Humboldt's *Political Essay on the Kingdom of New Spain*, he was so interested that early in 1809 he entered into correspondence with the German scientist. By that time Jefferson had retired from the presidency and could return wholeheartedly to his scholarly activities. For the United States, however, the Napoleonic Wars were about to become the War of 1812. Although many men read and discussed von Humboldt's essay, the war was naturally the overriding national concern.

This War brought out a new group of leaders for the United States, the "war hawks" such as Clay, Jackson, Calhoun, and Crawford. Members of the dominant Democratic-Republican Party, they were the nationalists and expansionists of the day. Henry Clay, in particular, was interested in the lands to the south. He accepted a view which Jefferson had been expounding in letters to von Humboldt and others,[6] "that America has a hemisphere to itself, and . . . must have a separate system of interest which must not be subordinated to those of Europe . . ." But Clay also envisaged the United States as the core of the Western Hemisphere, a view which would be disputed in short order by Latin American statesmen who, of course, favored a Pan-Latin order for the New World.

In any case, events in Europe gave considerable impetus to the new surge of nationalism in the United States, which was reaching out for hemispheric leadership. Concurrently, Latin American independence movements were beginning in 1810 as a nominal defiance of the Old World by "loyal" subjects of Ferdinand VII of Spain, who was then Napoleon's prisoner. However, the restoration of King Ferdinand after the fall of Napoleon soon made it necessary for the Latin American states to cast off their proclaimed "loyalty" to the Bourbons so that they could continue to enjoy the benefits of local political control and of trade with the entire world (particularly Britain). The alternative would have been a restoration of Spanish colonial mercantilism and a return to the political stagnation of the *ancien régime*.

In the United States there was immediate sympathy for the Latin American move for complete separation from Old World governments. Even so, this sympathy did not produce material assistance for the revolutionaries nor even moral support in the form of diplomatic recognition for the newly proclaimed governments primarily because a coalition of farmers and planters dominated the Democratic-Republican majorities in Congress. This coalition within Madison's own party exerted enough restraint upon the administration to thwart the ideas of Secretary of State Monroe and Secretary of the Treasury Gallatin (a more recent convert to the dynamic policy of "hemispheric leadership"). Professor Arthur P. Whitaker has commented that ". . . the fumbling and irresolute course of Madison's Administration in its early years was not due, as some writers hold, to his personal defects of character, such as lack of courage and firmness, but to the fact that his party was suffering from an acute case of schizophrenia."[7] The opposition Federalists offered no clear alternative because they, too, were stifled by commercial and agrarian power blocs.

Henry Clay was understandably concerned with the inertia which seemed to characterize governmental circles. He expressed alarm when the Spanish Cortes passed a decree in the name of the restored King Ferdinand VII to build a canal across Nicaragua. Rumors circulating in Ghent while Mr. Clay was one of the United States commissioners negotiating the peace treaty with Great Britain told of the formation of the Holy Alliance and of the possibility that it might give aid to Ferdinand in crushing the rebellion in his American colonies. In fact, forces of the royal government were said to be already at the mouth of the San Juan River in Nicaragua constructing fortifications for a huge base (which of course was also to be used to protect the canal-digging operations). Upon his return from Ghent, Mr. Clay spoke out strongly in an attempt to rally the United States against the supposed danger to the hemisphere.[8] But his efforts were to no avail.

Meanwhile in Central America and Northern South America, the forces of revolt were sweeping to triumph. The Spanish canal project in Nicaragua ceased when the newly proclaimed Emperor Augustín of Mexico accepted the proferred allegiance of the Central American leaders and extended his authority over most of the isthmus. Farther south, the other likely sites for a canal had come under the sway of Simon Bolívar's Gran Columbia.

The Spanish plan for a canal in Nicaragua had envisaged a waterway capable of carrying the largest ships of the time by utilizing the San Juan River and the deep waters of Lake Nicaragua as the major portion of the interoceanic route. When Emperor Iturbide was overthrown in 1824, the Central Americans seceded from Mexico and set up the Federal Republic of the United Provinces of Central America. The new government, realizing the importance of a canal, passed a law on June 16, 1825, providing for a waterway to be built along the old Spanish route which traversed the river and the lake.[9]

By this time Henry Clay was secretary of state in the administration of John Quincy Adams. The Central American minister in Washington, Antonio José Canaz, proposed in a letter to Secretary Clay that North American merchants be invited to contribute capital for the enterprise. Clay, replying that he agreed with the proposal, instructed the U.S. chargé d'affaires in Central America, John Williams, to compile a complete report upon which the Washington government would base its decision. For some reason Mr. Williams never followed these instructions. The Central American government, impatient with the delay, entered into private negotiations with de Witt Clinton and Aaron Palmer of New York. As a result, a syndicate which included two members of Congress was formed and an attempt was made in both England and the United States to raise a total investment of $5,000,000. All of these efforts ended in failure.[10]

The scene now shifted southward. The Isthmus of Panama had been incorporated into Simon Bolívar's new state of Gran Columbia, later called New Granada. Bolívar had always been conscious of the tremendous importance of Panama as the "crossroads of the World." His famous "Jamaica Letter" (1815) had suggested that the Isthmus of Panama might possibly become for America what Corinth had been for ancient Greece: a seat "for a Congress of representatives of kingdoms, republics, and empires that will discuss peace and war with the nations of the World." Although it has often been said that Bolívar did not advocate an association of Latin peoples with the United States in any "hemispheric" effort and was, in fact, thinking in even narrower terms of a Pan-Hispanic–American hegemony of some sort, nevertheless, one of his earliest diplomatic moves was to sign a twelve-year treaty of amity, commerce, and navigation with the North Americans in October, 1824. Furthermore, Article Two of the treaty provided that all transactions with other nations in commerce or navigation would be mutually beneficial, thus guaranteeing that the United States would have a share in *any* future canal venture across the Gran Colombian segment of the isthmus.

When Gran Colombia issued a call for a conference of nations to meet at Panama the next year, the canal enterprise was naturally included in the agenda. The United States was among the nations invited, although it was Santánder, Bolívar's vice president, who actually tendered the invitation. Secretary Clay was much more enthusiastic about attendance on the part of the United States than was President Adams, who had taken the "Black Legend" seriously. The "Black Legend" or *La Leyenda Negra* held that everything cruel, repressive, stupid, backward, and ignorant was integral to the way of life in Spain, Portugal, and their colonies. Circulated by enemies of the Iberian nations during the eighteenth century, this myth was an outgrowth of hatreds engendered during the wars of the Reformation and Counter-Reformation. Mr. Adams came from a background of New England Puritanism and thus almost automatically harbored doubts about the value of any agreements with Spanish-American peoples.

Once he had finally convinced the president, Mr. Clay then had to face the task of dealing with a hostile Congress. Unfortunately, the Adams administration and the National Republican party which had been formed to support it were continuously at odds with the Congress for four long years, and it was this same schism that contributed to the failure of the United States to attend the international gathering at Panama.[11]

The circumstances of Adams' election by the House of Representatives in 1824 had produced bitter recriminations on the part of the Jacksonian Democrats against both him and Henry Clay. Thus the charge of the "Corrupt Bargain" seemed to haunt every administrative proposal, however genuine. The Jacksonians, in their determination to destroy Adams and set things aright for the election of 1828, were ready to oppose anything which might reflect credit upon the president—as a successful hemispheric meeting at Panama might do.

To compound the problem, another burning issue in North American politics now emerged. The Missouri Compromise had only temporarily blunted a growing antislavery movement, and the proslavery men in Congress in 1826 feared that the Panama meeting might adopt an antislavery resolution. Bolívar's aversion to human slavery was well known, and there was little doubt that he would have the most potent voice at the conference. The expected attendance of representatives from the Negro kingdom of Haiti was another factor contributing to the strong opposition by Southern members of Congress to participation by the United States. The Southern Representatives argued that sitting at a conference table with black diplomats would be some kind of backhanded "recognition of Negro equality."

As if the odds were not already bad enough, the formal invitation to the conference arrived late and some felt that it was offered with little grace, coming as it did from Bolívar's second in command, and after the basic plans for the conference were set. These considerations served to amplify the raucous voice of the opposition. A prolonged debate (not quite a "filibuster") ensued in the Senate when the president proposed that two men go to Panama as "Ministers Plenipotentiary and Envoys Extraordinary." Richard Anderson, the U.S. minister at Bogotá, and John Sergeant, a former Pennsylvania congressman, were the chosen ministers, but it was May before a vote finally approved the proposal by a narrow margin.

Nonetheless, the conference at Panama was a fiasco for the United States. Shortly after the Congress opened at Panama City on June 22, 1826, Anderson died en route from Bogotá. Then, before he had even left Philadelphia, Sergeant received word that the negotiations had adjourned. Thus, because of domestic political bickering, the United States was deprived of the opporunity to participate in the first attempt to hold a Pan-American conference.

Sergeant's instructions, received from Secretary Clay on May 8, 1826, make interesting reading. Sergeant was told to refrain from committing the United States to a position on virtually any question but one—the construction of an isthmian canal! The secretary of state wrote:

> A cut or canal for purposes of navigation somewhere through the isthmus that connects the two Americas, to unite the Pacific and Atlantic Oceans, will form a proper subject for consideration at the Congress. If the work should ever be executed as to admit of the passage of sea vessels from ocean to ocean, the benefits ought not to be exclusively appropriated to any one nation, but should be extended to all parts of the globe upon the payment of a just compensation or reasonable tolls.[12]

Note here that Clay advanced the idea of a truly *international* canal. Although he might have been affecting a tone of high altruism to relieve himself and Mr. Adams of strong Congressional opposition, the legislative branch of the U.S. government was not to concur in the idea of an internationally beneficial interoceanic canal project until more than a decade later.

In the course of the Congressional debates in Washington, a number of speakers derided the Panama meeting as a "foreign association composed of states with whom we have no natural connection." The influence of the "Black Legend" upon North Americans was evident in remarks made by the congressmen who cast aspersions upon all Latin American states and peoples. James Buchanan of Pennsylvania attacked participation in the conference as an unjustifiable departure from Washington's admonition in his Farewell Address against entangling alliances. John Randolph of Virginia and Daniel Webster of Massachusetts both saw no possible community of interest with South America. Even the Monroe Doctrine came under widespread criticism. While it is possible that these outbursts were really intended to discredit Adams and Clay more than to disparage Latin America, it can well be imagined how such remarks were read and received in the states in the southern part of the hemisphere. Thus Mr. Clay in proposing an international canal, may very well have felt that *somebody* had to make some reassuring proposals to the representatives of Latin states with whom the United States expected to deal at the Panama conference.

Interestingly enough, the German philosopher Goethe had a premonition of the ultimate "go it alone" action by the United States. On February 21, 1827, he wrote:

> But I should wonder if the United States were to let an opportunity escape of getting such a work into their own hands. It may be foreseen that this young state, with its decided predilection to the West, will, in thirty or forty years, have occupied and peopled the large tract of land beyond the Rocky Mountains. . . . In such a case it would be not only desirable but almost necessary that a more rapid communication should be maintained between the Eastern and Western shores of North America, both by merchant ships and men-of-war, than has been possible hitherto with the tedious, disagreeable, and expensive voyage around Cape Horn. I therefore repeat that it is absolutely indispensable for the United States to effect a passage from the Mexican Gulf to the Pacific Ocean and I am certain that they will do it.[13]

When the Democratic party came to power with General Jackson, Clay's concept of a universal canal was reaffirmed, despite the rather nationalistic speeches which Democrats had made during the Adams administration. In 1830 when the Netherlands gained a concession from the Central American government and organized the Nicaraguan Canal Company, Secretary of State Edward Livingston instructed the minister in Guatemala City to insist that the United States "must have equal advantages in the use of any canal facilities." Subsequently the Dutch company collapsed as a result of the Belgian revolt against the House of Orange, and the "threat" from the Netherlands was soon forgotten.[14]

The swing of the political pendulum and the obligations of national leadership were making the Democratic leaders much more conscious of a growing "new nationalism" in the United States. The times demanded an active foreign policy, and the steady westward drift of boundaries and populations brought the Pacific coast and the long voyage around the Horn into greater focus—along with a more pressing compulsion to bisect the isthmus. In March of 1835, the United States Senate requested that President Jackson consider a treaty with Central America providing for the protection of possible canal rights. As a result, Charles Biddle was sent to investigate routes in Panama and Nicaragua. He never went to Nicaragua, but in a surprise move traveled to Bogotá. There he threw off his official role and, as a private citizen, exacted a concession for canal-building in Panama from the president of New Granada. This patent was transferred to Biddle from Baron de Thierry, a French speculator, who had received it some years earlier. De Thierry had exasperated the Bogotá government with his procrastination and fumbling efforts to finance the canal project. Naturally, Secretary of State John Forsyth was furious, denouncing this violation of instructions and repudiating Biddle's mission altogether. President Jackson then reported to the Senate that the time was not expedient "for further negotiations about an isthmian canal."[15]

Pressure was next brought to bear in Washington by a group of New York and Philadelphia commercial interests. Mayor Aaron Clark of New York led a delegation to the capital to urge Congress to take action "as a matter of national importance." The House of Representatives, sufficiently impressed to pass a resolution, requested that President Van Buren negotiate with the newly separated Central American republics and with New Granada.[16] This time John L. Stephens was sent to the area. His report recommended a Nicaraguan route at an estimated cost of $25,000,000.[17] However, this sum was too great to even think about, for the Van Buren administration not only was facing an election but was also suffering the political consequences of the Panic of 1837. In 1840 the Democrats became the first U.S. political party to formulate a platform when they promulgated a statement expounding their positions on the issues and claiming credit for past accomplishments. With reference to the problem of public expenditures they declared, ". . . it is the duty of every branch of the government to enforce and practice the most rigid economy in conducting our affairs, and no more revenue ought to be raised than is required to defray the necessary expenses of government."

The Democratic party lost the election. But the death of President William Henry Harrison brought many of its basic principles of government back into power. The succeeding president, John Tyler, made no secret of the fact that he had always been a "Jeffersonian." He had run for vice president on the Whig ticket only because a personal antipathy toward Andrew Jackson had led him to join a movement which seemed to have a chance of defeating Jackson's organization as represented by Van Buren. The new administration was frankly expansionistic. President Tyler's last secretary of state, John C. Calhoun, pushed the annexation of Texas through many ups and downs to final success.

The shifting of the nation's attention toward Texas promoted North American interest in Mexico, and a new discussion of the Isthmus of Tehuantepec as a route for an interoceanic canal began. The Mexican dictator, General de Santa Anna, had given the concession for possible canal construction to one of his own subjects, José de Garay, in March of 1842.[18]

De Garay had commissioned Gaetano Moro, an Italian engineer, to survey the possibilities for both a canal and a railroad. Moro proved to be unenthusiastic about attempting to dig a canal across Tehuantepec, but did recommend going ahead with a railroad. While de Garay was in the process of trying to finance this venture, war broke out between the United States and Mexico. During the aftermath of the conflict, while North American troops occupied much of Mexico, agitators both in Washington and in Tehuantepec itself demanded that the isthmus be annexed to the United States. De Garay appears to have reckoned upon the likelihood of annexation and to have concluded that his concession from Santa Anna might be worthless under such a change of political administration. In any case he decided to sell his patent to a group of New York financiers and they proceeded to take out a charter in New Orleans for the new Company of Tehuantepec, as they named it.

When the peace treaty was negotiated at Guadalupe-Hidalgo in 1848, an effort was made by President Polk's emissary, Nicholas P. Trist, to confirm the canal and railroad rights across Tehuantepec for United States interests, but the Mexican negotiators demurred and nothing was decided about the issue at the time. After the peace treaty was ratified and United States troops were withdrawn from Mexico, President José Joáquin de Herrera repudiated the transfer of de Garay's patent to the North Americans. Many years later, Mexico granted the concession to build a Tehuantepec railway to British investors who completed the project.

During the decade after the Mexican War, the more southerly routes for a possible canal in Nicaragua and in Panama received renewed attention from both Great Britain and the United States. A conflict between British policies of expansion in the Central American area, and efforts, generally supported by the United States, to prevent further development of American holdings by Old World powers began to reach serious and threatening proportions. According to the United States, British canal building would be in direct violation of the Monroe Doctrine.

Fortunately an altercation between the two English-speaking powers over Central America was averted by the Clayton-Bulwer Treaty. This compromise agreement was to create a kind of partnership situation in which the United States and Great Britain promised to undertake any future canal-building project as a joint enterprise.

2

The Clayton-Bulwer Treaty

The decade of the 1840's saw a new philosophy of expansionist nationalism sweep the United States. "Manifest destiny" had its roots in the Calvinist theory of Predestination. God had demonstrated his favor for the North American Republic, its institutions, and its people. This was the "Chosen Land" and nothing could stop its progress throughout a virgin hemisphere set apart by the Almighty for His children. The nobility of their way of life had been proven. Had they not gone from triumph to triumph since the hour of national birth? What better proof could there be of the favor of Heaven?

This was heady stuff for the politicians. The Democratic party, ever responsive to the reactions of the masses, was ready to exploit the new imperialism. Gone was the day when a Buchanan would arise in Congress to urge adherence to a doctrine of national isolation. Mr. Buchanan, as secretary of state, had agreed with President Polk's announcement in 1845 limiting the coverage of the Monroe Doctrine to North America.[1] But it must be remembered that the Monroe Doctrine at its inception had been a *unilateral* statement of policy aimed at Europe. It had never meant any renunciation of U.S. ambitions. When he was secretary of state, John Quincy Adams made an unforgettable statement on the matter to an English diplomat. Adams said, in effect, that the United States would have no objection to Old World retention of territories already held but that "the rest of North America must be left for us!" Gone from the Democratic camp of the 1840s was the type of hostile attitude expressed by John Randolph during the Congressional debate over the Panama Congress of 1826. The new party enthusiasm was well stated by a speaker at the Democratic State Convention in New Jersey in 1844:

Make way I say for the young American 'Buffalo'—he has not yet got land enough; he wants more land as his cool shelter in summer—he wants more land as his beautiful pasture grounds. I tell you, we will give him Oregon for his summer shade, and the region of Texas as his winter pasture. Like all of his race he wants salt too. Well, he shall have the use of two oceans—the mighty Pacific and turbulent Atlantic shall be his. He shall not stop his career until he slakes his thirst in the frozen oceans![2]

The Polk presidential campaign in 1844 made a very clever pitch for the annexation of Texas and the "reannexation" of Oregon to both Northern and Southern expansionists. Interestingly enough Clay, the Whig presidential candidate, tried to straddle the expansionist issues and may have lost the election because he did. It is an ironic commentary on one of the most eloquent of the war hawks, but it does illustrate a feature of North American politics which had become a fixture by this time. Often a political party and a political candidate would be pressured into questionable positions because their opponents moved swiftly to take the more popular stand. Because of this situation the Whig Party became identified in the public mind with a less aggressive foreign policy than the Democrats.

During Polk's administration the subject of an isthmian canal held attention in spite of the excitement over the Mexican War. Because both the British and the French were showing an interest in Nicaragua and Panama, businessmen and politicians in the United States were apprehensive lest the great project come into being without their having a stake in it. The activities of the British in Nicaragua aroused particular concern. A number of North Americans seeking possible canal concessions had been frustrated by the British support of the Mosquito Indians in their effort to maintain a native state independent of the Central American republics. British forces occupied both Greytown at the mouth of the San Juan River and the River itself all the way up to Lake Nicaragua. The authority of the "King" of the Mosquito nation was proclaimed up and down the coast for miles, and the Nicaraguan authorities were expelled.[3]

These events aroused great excitement in Washington, New York, and Philadelphia. Not only was the Nicaraguan canal route apparently falling into British hands, but the most flagrant flaunting of the Monroe Doctrine was clear in the British action. Polk and Secretary Buchanan dealt with this matter by charging Elijah Hise, the U.S. representative in Guatemala, to attempt to reunite the disbanded Central American Confederation, which might more effectively resist the British encroachments. Buchanan instructed Hise to point out that the United States could do little to resist European interference while the Central American states continued to weaken themselves by division and civil war, thus depriving themselves of the ability to take any measure for their own protection.

Hise was successful in negotiating a treaty at Guatemala City on June 21, 1849. Nicaragua granted to the United States, or to a company that might be organized by its citizens, the exclusive right to build a canal, road, or railway over its territories from sea to sea. In return the United States guaranteed the independence of Nicaragua.[4]

This treaty might well have caused a head-on clash between Britain and the United States. The Polk administration had also moved to establish another U.S. position in the isthmian region at Bogotá. There on December 12, 1846, U.S. chargé d'affaires in New Granada, Benjamin A. Bidlack, signed a treaty with Manuel Mallarino, the Granadine foreign secretary. Here too the United States made an absolute guarantee of Granadine sovereignty over the Isthmus of Panama. In return U.S. citizens were to have free transit of the isthmus, on a basis of equality with Granadines, whether by road, railroad or canal.[5] This treaty was all the more significant in view of New Granada's failure to get similar guarantees from the British.

The Bidlack-Mallarino Treaty was ratified before the Polk Administration left office, but the Hise agreement with Nicaragua was not. Hise had proceeded at Guatemala City under his general authority from Polk, but his concession was not signed until June of 1849 and by then there had been a change of administration at home.

The election of 1848 at long last brought the Whig Party to power. As the party out of power during the years of the surge of "manifest destiny," this party had been almost forced to advocate a less bellicose foreign policy. The new president, Zachary Taylor, and his secretary of state, John M. Clayton, were determined not to have war with Britain over the canal areas. The Whig administration was quite ready to adopt the policy enunciated in Henry Clay's instructions to John Sergeant. This policy stated that the notable benefits which would accrue from an interoceanic canal should not be the property of any one nation. Taylor and Clayton were ready not only to head off a quarrel with Britain over the isthmus, but also to accept her as a partner in any canal building enterprise.

The new administration therefore repudiated the Hise treaty on the ground that he had exceeded his instructions. The treaty was never submitted to the Senate for ratification. Hise himself was recalled from his mission and was succeeded by Ephraim G. Squier. This emissary was warned not to commit the United States either to a political alliance or any commercial ventures. He was to make a treaty which would allow the American Atlantic and Pacific Ship Canal Company, a private company owned by Cornelius Vanderbilt, to secure a canal concession. The project would be open to the ships of all nations.

Squier arrived in Central America in the summer of 1849 and remained until early fall. When he saw the extent of the British penetrations, he essentially repeated the course of conduct pursued by his predecessor. He tried to form a union of Costa Rica, Honduras, and Nicaragua. When he negotiated the treaty with Nicaragua for the Vanderbilt company's concession, he included a guarantee of Nicaraguan independence. He then brought the crisis with Britain to a decided climax by negotiating a treaty with Honduras. This treaty gave the United States a naval base on the Pacific coast at the Gulf of Fonseca. When a British naval commander in the Pacific landed a party to occupy Tigre Island, Squier ordered them out!

Secretary Clayton eased tensions by immediately repudiating Squier's actions and his treaties.[6] However, the Vanderbilt company did get its concession from the government of Nicaragua for building a canal, a railroad, and a highway. When it was unable to secure the capital for a canal-building venture, the company organized subsidiary associates such as the Accessory Transit Company to operate steamers on the San Juan River and across Lake Nicaragua. From there pack mules carried passengers over the continental divide to ships on the Pacific coast. The great trek to California, produced by the discovery of gold there, made this operation a veritable bonanza for Vanderbilt and his associates.[7] The California migration also gave an enormous impetus to discussion of a canal and to schemes for its construction.

The California gold rush brought untold thousands of people to the American isthmus. Vanderbilt's sidewheelers and pack trains offered the safest, most comfortable, and also the most expensive route. In consequence persons of limited means struggled over the Tehuantepec, Panama, and Chiriquí routes. Panama in particular attracted many because of the short distance involved in crossing it. But at that time there was neither highway nor railroad and the tortuous passage was made by boat along the Chagres River and then overland through dense jungle.[8] Ships on the final run to San Francisco picked up passengers very spasmodically at Panama City. There were often hundreds of North Americans stranded in that steaming town for months on end. They endured many hardships, but probably no group of people better exemplified the all-pervasive spirit of "manifest destiny" which permeated those years. Some among this group were enterprising enough to begin publication of an English language newspaper. This was the *Panama Star* and it continues to this day as an English language paper of very high calibre, the *Panama Star and Herald*. A number of stories in the first issue, dated February 24, 1849,[9] merit some mention here. The following is an account of Washington's birthday on the isthmus:

> The assemblage of American citizens on this morning of the 22nd, temporarily residing in this city, to celebrate the return of the birthday of Washington, the father of his country affords a strong proof, that although far distant from their homes in a foreign land, the same spirit which animated their fathers in '76 have not degenerated in their offspring, but burns with the same patriotic spirit which is the boon of all Americans. The procession numbering several hundred formed in front of the American Hotel, at 6 o'clock A.M., marched to the Governor's house, fired a salute, gave him three cheers, and then proceeded to the East Battery, fronting the harbor, raised the American flag, fired a grand volley as it floated to the breeze—marched to the American Consul's house, gave him three cheers—passed the French Consul's house, and gave three cheers for the French Republic—marched to the American Hotel and dismissed . . .
>
> The following toasts were delivered at the table:
> 1. The birthday of Washington—not only a national, but a universal anniversary, welcomed with joy wherever civilization has extended her sway, or liberty erected an altar. The sons of Columbia here assembled are proud to acknowledge and celebrate it as the glory of their country.
> 2. The California Emigrants—Their character and general intelligence, their leaving their native homes from choice, and not from necessity, giving a faithful guarantee that their future course will present a brilliant page in their country's history.

3. California—Ere long destined to be one of the greatest growing and most enterprising States of the American Union.
4.–9. The President, states Governors, the Ladies, etc.
10. The Star Spangled Banner
    "Around the Globe, through every clime,
    Where commerce wafts or man hath trod,
    It floats aloft unstained by crime,
    But hallowed by heroic blood."

On the front page a letter from Major General Persifer F. Smith,
Commander of the Pacific Military Division (California) warns that
he intends to enforce vigorously the laws of the United States and that
he will impose numerous and severe penalties upon those (aliens)
who unlawfully occupy the public land. He continues, "nothing can
be more unjust and unmeasureable than for persons not citizens of the
United States to direct their companies in pursuit and to dig the gold
. . . in California."

On the last page a letter from a "reader" obviously was timed
to underline the hearty endorsement of the General's stand by the
local colony of expatriates:

Messrs. Editors: I understand there will be published in your
paper a copy of the proclamation of Gen. Persifer F. Smith,
declaring that none but American citizens can dig or work at our
gold mines in California . . . all our countrymen in California and
those on the road bound to the gold regions will, if true to themselves, support our government to the last extremity in carrying
out so just a law; for after the toil, expense, and misery we pass
through to get to the gold regions, we are not willing to be over-
run by the outcasts of the world, who, if permitted, would select
the best spots and leave us the refuse. If foreigners come let them
till the soil, and make roads, or do any other work that may suit
them, and they may become properous; but the gold mines were
preserved by Nature for Americans only, who possess noble
hearts and are willing to share with their fellow men more than
any other race of men on earth! But they still do not wish to
give all. I ask of them who have left their homes—their comforts,
their wives and children and other dear relatives, if they would
be willing to share all the hopes with the millions who might be
shipped from the four quarters of the globe? I will answer for

them and say no. We will share our interest in the gold mines with none but American citizens. J.A.K.

During this period Great Britain was represented in Washington by Sir Henry Bulwer, a most able diplomat. Sir Henry had been sent to the United States in December, 1849, for the specific purpose of negotiating a treaty which would protect British interests in Central America while at the same time lessening tensions caused by the rivalries developing in that area between the two nations. He had a thorough understanding of North American politics. He knew that the practical Whigs, heavily supported by business circles in Eastern cities, would be much more interested in the commercial advantages of a transisthmian canal than in carrying a jingoistic torch for the rights of Central American republics against the claims of the Mosquito Indians. A partnership between the United States and Great Britain might bring the long-dreamed-of engineering feat to reality. The discovery of gold in California, the settlement of the Oregon question, and the swelling tide of western migration was convincing evidence that the United States had reached that phase of its "manifest destiny" which ordained it to be a Pacific power. Not even the Whigs could ignore the growing potentialities of a canal which would link the Atlantic with the Pacific.

Because the Whigs saw little beyond the commercial advantages to be gained from the projected waterway, the astute Bulwer was quick to grasp the narrow limitations of their viewpoint and turn it to the legalistic advantage of Great Britain. Now was the time to commit the United States, formally, to the position that any isthmian canal should *not* belong exclusively to one nation.

News of the British landings in the Gulf of Fonseca and of Minister Squier's tub-thumping diplomacy in Central America had now reached the press. The opponents of the administration were castigating it for Clayton's rebuff of Squier. Democrats in Congress demanded that the president release the full text of Squier's dispatches. When Taylor refused to do so he was accused of supinely standing aside while the Monroe Doctrine was being flaunted.[10] Bulwer was alarmed over the trend of events and feared that the jingoistic elements, now raising a hue and cry against the administration, might destroy all hope of compromise. The Whigs in electing Taylor had not won control of Congress. A Free Soil bloc held the balance of power between Whigs and Democrats in the House of Representatives. The Democrats were taking advantage of both "manifest destiny" and anti-British feeling ever latent in the United States during the nineteenth century. On March 19, 1850, Secretary Clayton bowed to the uproar and submitted the Squier portfolio to the Senate, which has the constitutional right to participate in the conduct of foreign relations. The Democrats had organized the Senate, but its deliberative processes could be expected to allay the tempest for a time while diplomatic negotiations proceeded.

In the meantime Bulwer had recommended to Lord Palmerston that the London cabinet disavow the actions of the British naval commanders and also disclaim any plans for taking over Costa Rica, which was rumored to be the next aggression in the blueprint of "perfidious Albion." These recommendations were followed by Palmerston. Minister Bulwer then had a long interview with President Taylor and Clayton who absolutely disavowed any U.S. ambitions to acquire territory in Central America or to control exclusively a canal.[11]

The question of the "Mosquito Kingdom" had been a vexing one in relations between the United States and Great Britain. It was going to be difficult to work out any solution likely to be accepted by the Congress and the North American people—unless some formula of words could be found to assuage Britain's apparent violation of the Monroe Doctrine. The Whig leaders were willing enough to overlook the "Mosquito" matter. They realized that the whole episode had been a move to secure a British hegemony along the canal route. They knew that no hearts were bleeding in London for the cause of "independence" for the Mosquito Indians. Now that the United States and Britain were to be partners, the need for the "Mosquito Kingdom" device was over. If the British would formally renounce any plan to "occupy, fortify, colonize, or assume, or exercise any dominion over Nicaragua, Costa Rica, the Mosquito Coast, or any part of Central America" the United States of course would do the same. The extremists in the United States thus would be deprived of their complaints. On April 19, 1850, Bulwer was able to take such a draft, approved and signed by Lord Palmerston, to Clayton. From this draft the two men composed and signed the famous Clayton-Bulwer Treaty. It was ratified by the Senate on May 22, 1850,[12] and went into effect on July 5, 1850.

The Clayton-Bulwer treaty pointed toward a Nicaraguan canal as the one most likely to be built, but its eighth article extended the treaty's provisions to "any other practical communications, whether by canal or railway, across the isthmus which connects North and South America; and equally to the interoceanic communications should the same prove to be practicable, whether by canal or railway, which are now proposed to be established by the way of Tehuantepec or Panama. The canal shall be open to the citizens and subjects of the parties on equal terms."

Not only was the canal to be under the joint patronage of Britain and the United States, but also it was to be neutral. No fortifications were to be allowed, and even in case of war between the signatories, vessels flying their flags were to have unhampered passage.

The choice of such amiable phraseology proved to be very helpful in steering the treaty through the Senate. Still, North American nationalists had not lost their suspicions of England.

The expansionists had another problem on their hands in the summer of 1850. The Wilmot Proviso had raised the ugly issue of slavery in the territories recently won from Mexico, and Henry Clay's compromise was facing a doubtful fate in Congress. Southern radicals were again muttering of secession. The "Little Giant" from Illinois, Stephen A. Douglas, arose in opposition to ratification of the Clayton-Bulwer pact and declared in an eloquent speech that the United States should have "no partnership with Britain . . . but exclusive control of canals." There were enough members of his party, however, to join with the Whigs to pass the treaty. These Democrats felt that the nation's clouded future would be brightened a little by eliminating the threat of war with Great Britain.

It might be asked why the opposition did not prove more potent. It is hard to reconcile the Clayton-Bulwer Treaty with the Monroe Doctrine. Surely the United States had conceded valuable rights which were not indisputably Britain's beforehand. This couldn't be consistent with the "non-colonization" clause of the Doctrine. The best answer seems to be that the flaming domestic political scene occupied the attention of most North Americans during the summer of 1850.

As for the "partnership" between the United States and England —it was a firm which never did any business. One writer has suggested that it even retarded rather than stimulated the building of a canal. Either party conceivably might have gone ahead alone. Now each felt constricted by the terms of this treaty. Even the dispute over the Mosquito Coast dragged on for another decade before it was resolved. This was due to differing interpretations of the extent of the boundaries around the long-held British settlements near Belize.

The Democrats in Congress still used the canal question to embarrass the administration, even though the Clayton-Bulwer Treaty had effected a settlement of the international crisis which had threatened North American relations with England. The House of Representatives now demanded the files on the abortive Hise mission and launched into an examination of Clayton's handling of that affair.[13] The issue of national expansion was thus kept alive. It undoubtedly played some part in the midterm elections of 1850 which resulted in a general disaster for the Whigs and widespread Democratic gains. These results foreshadowed the great Democratic victory in the presidential election of 1852 and the disappearance of the Whig Party after Scott's defeat in that year.

3

From Buchanan to Cleveland

During the mid-fifties popular interest in an isthmian canal was stimulated by the great success of the Panama Railroad. This first transcontinental railway in the Western Hemisphere was built by three New York financiers, Henry Aspinwall, John Lloyd Stephens, and Henry Chauncey. They took over a railroad concession given by New Granada to a French concern which had failed to raise sufficient capital to proceed. These North American promoters were encouraged by the Bidlack-Mallarino treaty negotiations to believe that they might get financial aid from the United States government. At one time a House committee did recommend a yearly subsidy of $250,000 but Congress never appropriated the money. The Panama Railroad Company nevertheless went ahead on its own by slow stages and opened for business on January 28, 1855, when the first train crossed the isthmus.[1]

The railroad was so successful that within a short time it was paying sensational dividends to its shareholders. The great migration to California showed little sign of abating and by far the safest and most comfortable way to make the trip was by this railroad, with ship connections to and from New York and San Francisco. But it was quite clear that a canal would be even better. Legislative bodies, trade associations, and canal conventions were among the many organizations which poured petitions and resolutions into Congress in an attempt to speed the work. All of these developments had been prophetically visualized by a French diplomat in Bogotá during the construction of the railroad. He had been attempting to stir his government to some action which might head off North American monopoly in transisthmian communication. "The road which the United States is trying to construct at its own expense across the isthmus will so modify the present state of things that, when the day comes that public opinion in the Union abandons its present indifference and takes an active interest in the matter it will be irresistible,"[2] he wrote to Paris.

Actually it was not indifference but an overpowering preoccupation with the domestic issues which were driving toward the Civil War that relegated the canal question to secondary interest during these years. Time could not be found for such interests in Washington. All efforts to take the public mind off slavery and the sectional problem were failures. The Know-Nothing movement was a transitory diversion. The "Young America" advocates of an aggressive foreign policy led the Democrats to a setback in the mid-term elections of 1854. In January, 1855, Edward Everett wrote that the adventurers such as William Walker who had made so many headlines with his guerilla expeditions in Central America, were now attracting very little attention in the nation's capital.[3]

During these years the Democratic party was regarded by many thoughtful persons as the only vehicle capable of saving the Union. It had grass roots in both North and South. But it strove to avoid the free soil issue which would surely split it asunder.[4] The canal was a matter of obvious importance, and a project which could still arouse interest in many quarters. Political parties striving to bury one embarrassing issue may be depended upon to trot forth anything to distract public attention from the original issue. This is probably the explanation for the rather long statement on the isthmian canal which was written into the Democratic platform for the presidential election of 1856:

> Resolved, that the great highway which nature, as well as the assent of the United States most immediately interested in its maintenance, has marked out for a free communication between the Atlantic and the Pacific oceans, constitutes one of the most important achievements realized by the spirit of modern times and the unconquerable energy of our people. That result should be secured by a timely and efficient exertion of the control which we have the right to claim over it, and no power on earth should be suffered to impede or clog its progress by any interference with the relations it may suit our policy to establish between our Government and the Governments of the States within whose dominions it lies. We can, under no circumstances, surrender our preponderance in the adjustment of all questions arising out of it . . .

Resolved: That, in view of so commanding an interest, that people of the United States cannot but sympathize with the efforts which are being made by the people of Central America to regenerate that portion of the continent which covers the passage across the Interoceanic Isthmus.

Despite Mr. Buchanan's narrow victory, it is doubtful whether many votes were won by the foregoing platform plank. The new president found that the Kansas-Nebraska issue caused almost everything else to pale into insignificance. Even the North American adventurer, William Walker, twice bailed out of disaster by the United States Navy, found his countrymen waving different flags than those of "manifest destiny" imperialism when he failed for the third time in an expedition against Honduras. No particular uproar was aroused in the United States when British naval forces aided the Honduran authorities to defeat him. He was subsequently executed in Honduras by the government which he had attempted to overthrow. By the time of his death in September, 1860, public attention in the United States was centered on far more dynamic issues—the threat of secession and the pending presidential election.

Under these circumstances certain European canal schemers felt that the times favored their moving into Central America while the Yanqui republic was otherwise engaged. One of these was a Frenchman, Felix Belly, who was apparently on a secret mission for Napoleon III. The emperor himself had cherished dreams of a Nicaraguan canal—ten years before he had even written a treatise on the subject. Belly came into Central America and played upon local apprehension about the Yanqui aim of "manifest destiny" which had been intensified by the expeditions of William Walker. The versatile and brilliant promotor succeeded in getting Costa Rica and Nicaragua to accept his mediation of their old boundary dispute and secured from them a ninety-nine–year concession to build and operate a canal. They also agreed to the stationing of French warships on the San Juan River and Lake Nicaragua.[5]

This news produced quite a stir in the United States, not only because of the Monroe Doctrine but also because Commodore Vanderbilt and others still held concessions in Nicaragua. There might have been more excitement if North American newspapers had not reported that Belly had no funds to carry on his projects. The Frenchman confirmed this by coming to the United States in the summer of 1858 in an attempt to interest North American capital in backing him.

No investors could be found, however, and he had no better success in England. It is probable that the Clayton-Bulwer Treaty, the Monroe Doctrine, and the specter of Louis Napoleon's warships all contributed to the cool reception given to Belly's plan in both countries.

He was a remarkably persistent man, and finally managed to raise a considerable sum in France and elsewhere on the continent. A small expedition sailed and established its base at Felicia, where the Rio Frío flows into Lake Nicaragua, and at San Carlos. The reaction from Washington was swift. Secretary of State Lewis Cass instructed the U.S. minister, Mirabeau B. Lamar, to make every effort to induce the Nicaraguans to reduce Belly's concession. Lamar did get changes made by the Nicaraguan Congress which had the effect of vitiating Costa Rica's ratification. Then there were quarrels among the engineers, technicians, and Belly's associates back home, who were supposed to be supervising public relations and the raising of capital. But these associates proved to be a strange coterie of scamps, incompetents, visionaries, and obstructionists. The end of this ill-fated enterprise came when yellow fever struck the canal encampment with decimating results. Subsequently bankruptcy proceedings were instituted against Belly and his associates. He was still trying to raise money for another Nicaraguan adventure shortly before he died.

At the same time that Belly was planning his Nicaraguan canal, another Frenchman was planning to cross the isthmus further south in Costa Rica on a route running from the Gulf of Dulce on the Pacific to Boca del Toro on the Atlantic. This was Gabriel Lafond, formerly the French consul at San José. He planned a combination of macadamized road and railroad or canal to effect the crossing. His efforts to raise money in Europe failed because of the unsettled conditions there due to the Crimean War, and his prospects of patronage on the isthmus were dimmed by the great success of the Panama Railroad. But Ambrose W. Thompson, a Yanqui, dealt a mortal blow to Lafond's hopes. Thompson claimed that Lafond's concession from Costa Rica was transferred to him in 1854. This claim was recognized by important Costa Rican statesmen and by the administration of President James Buchanan in Washington.[6]

Jingoistic nationalism was still an important influence in the United States despite the gathering clouds of imminent Civil War. President Buchanan's attention was attracted by navy surveys showing coal deposits in Chiriquí and recommendations that an additional transisthmian railroad be built, with naval stations at each terminus.

Such a project would insure North American military control in the entire isthmian region and provide safe passage for commerce as well. The Chiriquí Improvement Company was now organized by Thompson and a preliminary contract made with Secretary of the Navy Isaac Toucey for coal, transit rights, and naval station sites.

Most of this Chiriquí area was in dispute at this time between Costa Rica and New Granada, the latter claiming it for its Province of Panama. New Granada proceeded to invalidate the Thompson-Toucey contract. It seems that the Panama Railroad did some lobbying at Bogotá to help bring this about. The U.S. Congress of 1860 could not be persuaded to take its attention away from the domestic crisis to sift out these claims and counterclaims. It did not ratify the contract, but the recognition which the Buchanan administration had given to Thompson placed him in a good practical position for future negotiations with the government of the United States.[7]

From 1861 to 1865 the Civil War in the United States caused the isthmian canal issue to be relegated to a topic of minor consideration in both governmental and private circles. Even the Panama Railroad faltered as the gold rush subsided and private capital found isthmian schemes and plans less attractive. Such interest as there was arose when foreign canal plans came to the surface. There was concern when it was learned that Napoleon III (Louis Napoleon) had sent a French engineering party to survey the Nicaraguan route.[8] In view of the French intervention in Mexico, it was feared that the successful establishment of a Maximilian empire might lead to an absorption of Nicaragua, which the Mexican emperor Iturbide also had ruled. A reassertion of Mexican sovereignty there seemed even more possible when the childless Maximilian adopted Iturbide's grandson. A future "Augustín II" (General Iturbide had become Augustín I when he assumed the Mexican crown in 1823) might pose a difficult problem one day. Louis Napoleon had a grant carefully filed away for just such a contingency. Nicaragua had given him this grant in 1845 to construct "The Napoleon Canal."[9]

There had been a certain complacency about the French interest in the isthmus since the collapse of the Belly enterprise. President Buchanan had advised Congress in his last message in December, 1860, that the isthmian situation was entirely favorable to U.S. interests.[10] In 1862 Mr. Seward had remarked calmly that U.S. concern about any canal project across the isthmus of Panama was really no different from that of any of the other maritime powers. Now, because of French activity in Latin America, he made a show of convincing the Old World that the U.S. interest was indeed a special one. In March, 1865, marines landed in Panama City, ostensibly to guard the U.S. consulate there during an outbreak of "local lawlessness."[11] In 1867 Secretary Seward instructed the U.S. ministers in Paris and London to inquire whether those governments would not join with the United States in guaranteeing the safety of the Panama route and the authority of the government of New Granada on the isthmus. He said in his message that "the United States would not permit a public enemy of the American Continent the use or advantages of a work executed by the nations of the New World."[12]

During this same year French troops were withdrawn from Mexico in response to Washington's demand, and execution of the fallen Emperor Maximilian showed, as had nothing before, that the Monroe Doctrine *did* have teeth. The fiasco in Mexico probably marked the turning point in Louis Napoleon's career.

Aside from canal building schemes, the isthmus drew attention during the Lincoln administration because of another intriguing problem. President Lincoln was concerned with the disposition of the American Negroes after their emancipation. He seems to have tentatively accepted the idea that the readjustment of three million former slaves to the society, economy, and politics of another race which had been holding them in bondage might pose nearly insurmountable problems. From the time he assumed office, Abraham Lincoln toyed with the idea of resettling American Negroes in some tropical land. When the Lafond-Thompson concession in Chiriquí was brought to his attention, he studied the descriptions of this area and concluded that this was the ideal place. A contract was drawn with Thompson by the Secretary of the Interior, Caleb B. Smith. Negro leaders were called to the White House on August 14, 1862. President Lincoln then unfolded the plan and urged them to back it. They were unenthusiastic and some of them expressed understandable bewilderment.

When the president sent a message to Congress informing it of the Thompson contract and of his plan "Respecting the Transportation of Persons of the African Race," a storm broke out in both houses of the national legislature. Mr. Lincoln had a constant conflict with the Radical Republican leadership on Capitol Hill. Thaddeus Stevens, whose common-law wife was black, was an especially enthusiastic champion of the Negro. He railed eloquently and persuasively against the plan, as a scheme which would forever sully North American honor in the pages of history. Opposition came from still a different quarter when the government of Costa Rica announced that it would refuse to countenance the immigration. Costa Rica had and still has the largest Caucasian population of any of the Central American states, so it can be imagined what the prospect of this mass settlement did to opinion there. In the face of such formidable opposition, Mr. Lincoln quietly put the plan aside. There will always be some doubt as to whether or not he clung to some hope of returning to a colonization project once the war had ended.[13] Because of his untimely death he never had the opportunity.

With the end of the war the canal issue came into its own once more. On March 19, 1866, a Senate resolution called upon the secretary of the navy to submit a study of all practicable canal routes across the isthmus. Seward told the Colombian minister that he believed the time was now propitious for construction of a canal. This was so not only for technical reasons and for the need to counter the French moves in Nicaragua and Mexico, but also because the government at Bogotá was in dire financial straits and would probably welcome the prospect of canal revenues.

The administration of President Andrew Johnson entered into negotiations with Colombia which dragged on for more than a year and a half. The Johnson administration was embroiled in an intense conflict with the Congressional Radicals. Thus it may be forgiven for fumbling diplomacy in sending unclear and at times bewildering instructions to its negotiators at Bogotá and for its failure to deal effectively with British interests which were trying to impair the whole effort. These mistakes belie Mr. Seward's usually brilliant record in office, but it must be remembered that he too was involved with the domestic political struggle in Washington and was devoting most of his time and energy to helping President Johnson in the impeachment proceedings instigated against him by the Radical Republicans.

In time a canal treaty did emerge and was submitted to the Senate on February 15, 1869. That body was not disposed to consider favorably any act that might reflect credit upon the administration of Andrew Johnson. The treaty did contain provisions that would have been decidedly unfavorable to the United States—limiting U.S. defense of the canal zone to a token force, providing Colombia with twenty-five percent of the net income from canal operations, and setting a time limit on the preliminary survey of the site and also on the construction period. The Senate Republicans denounced the work as another piece of "incompetence" by the Tennessee tailor and the treaty was rejected.[14] They felt that this was no real setback for the canal in any event. Johnson was a political "lame duck." Their man, Ulysses S. Grant, was due to assume the Presidency within a month. Let a Republican administration get the credit for bringing the long-dreamed-of canal into being.

Many of the old-time Whigs had found their way into the Republican Party. But the "partnership" and "good of the whole world" tones of the ante bellum Whig policy and the Clayton-Bulwer Treaty did not come into Republican policy. In 1869 President Grant's new secretary of state, Hamilton Fish, wrote to the U.S. minister at Bogotá, "The President is disinclined to enter into any entanglement in participation of control over the work with other powers; he regards it as an American enterprise, which he desires to be carried out under American auspices, to the benefit of which the whole commercial world should be fully admitted."[15] In his annual message to Congress on the State of the Union in December, 1869, President Grant said: "The subject of an interoceanic canal to convert the Atlantic and Pacific Oceans through the isthmus of Darien is one in which commerce is greatly interested. Instructions have been given to our Minister to the Republic of the United States of Colombia to endeavor to obtain authority for a survey by this government, in order to determine the practicability of such an undertaking, and a charter for the right of way to build, by private enterprise, such a work, if the survey proves it to be practicable."[16]

Following this a considerable number of surveys were undertaken, most of them by the United States navy, some by the army, and one by a mixed commission of army, navy, and civilian engineers. A canal treaty was even consummated with Colombia but the Senate pigeonholed it because an argument developed over whether or not the Panama route was the superior one.[17] In the spring of 1872 the Senate asked President Grant to review the work of all the survey parties and to recommend a route. The President then appointed the Isthmian Canal Commission, the first of a number of official bodies to bear that name. It contained army, navy, and civilian engineers. This commission unanimously recommended the Nicaragua route in its report of February 7, 1876.[18]

The selection of a route was as far as action concerning the canal went. The completion of the transcontinental railroad to California had taken the pressure off the need for a canal to speed domestic shipments to the west coast. There were those who felt that the United States should be the sole canal builder and should delay its operations until it could secure a release from the Clayton-Bulwer partnership with Britain. Besides, a presidential election was at hand. The election of 1876 proved to be the most exciting in U.S. history because of its disputed result. Few people could turn their minds to any other subject until it was resolved. At virtually the last moment the dispute was decided in favor of Rutherford B. Hayes who was inaugurated in March, 1877.

The Hayes administration showed no interest in the isthmian canal until it became disturbed by that old specter of North American politics—the fear of European intervention. Ferdinand de Lesseps, builder of the Suez Canal, was in Panama in December, 1879, with a ninety-nine-year canal concession obtained in Bogotá the previous year. A company had been formed in France and was raising money. It was obvious that de Lesseps meant to go ahead. The reaction came quickly in the United States. The old cry of the Monroe Doctrine went up from a hundred editorial pages. President Hayes turned out the files of the old Ambrose Thompson concessions and ordered secret surveys of the Chiriquí Lagoon and the naval sites and coaling stations along the Gulf of Dulce. The press was full of the stories of North American naval vessels moving in Chiriquí waters to checkmate French influence. On March 8, 1880, the president sent a message to Congress:

> . . . the policy of this country is a canal under American control. The United States cannot consent to the surrender of this control to any European power or to any combination of European powers . . .
>
> An interoceanic canal across the American isthmus will essentially change the geographical relations between the Atlantic and Pacific coasts of the United States, and between the United States and the rest of the world. It will be the great ocean thoroughfare between our Atlantic and our Pacific shores and virtually a part of the coast line of the United States. Our merely commercial interest in it is greater than that of all other countries, while its relation to our means of defense, our unity, peace, and safety, are matters of paramount concern to the people of the United States. No other great power would under similar circumstances fail to assert a rightful control over a work so closely and vitally affecting its interest and welfare.

Without urging further the grounds of my opinion, I repeat—that it is the right and duty of the United States to assert and maintain such supervision and authority over any interoceanic canal . . . as will protect our national interests.[19]

Secretary of State William Evarts reinforced this presidential declaration by delivering a protest to Colombia for granting the canal concession to de Lesseps' associate, M. Bonaparte-Wyse, in 1878. The fact that M. Wyse was related to the French imperial family conjured up all sorts of apprehensions in the United States. The memory of Louis Napoleon's incursion into Mexico and of his dreams of an isthmian canal could not fail to incur North American disapproval of the activities of his distant relative. Secretary Evarts declared that the interests of the United States could not condone the granting of rights for canal projects to "imperialist interests," and his note of April 19, 1880, to Colombia continued:

This Government cannot consider itself excluded by an arrangement between other powers or individuals, to which it is not a party from a direct interest, and, if necessary, a positive supervision and interposition in the execution of any project which, by completing an interoceanic connection through the isthmus, would materially affect its commercial interests, change the territorial relations of its own sovereignty, and impose upon it the necessity of a foreign policy, which, whether in its feature of warlike preparations or entangling alliance, has been hitherto sedulously avoided.[20]

Ferdinand de Lesseps came to the United States in a personal effort to allay these fears. He was, after all, a private citizen and his canal company a private concern. The French government had no official connection with his enterprise. He traveled all over the United States making speeches. He set aside a considerable block of shares in his company for North American investors. But he could not get any American stockbroker to handle the issue.[21] It seems likely that they were pressured by Washington. Secretary Evarts was particularly truculent in his attitude upon the matter:

Our Pacific Coast is so situated that with our railroad connections time would always be allowed to prepare for its defense. But with a canal through the isthmus the same advantage would be given to a hostile fleet which would be given to friendly commerce;

its line of operations and the time in which warlike demonstrations could be made, would be enormously shortened. All the treaties of neutrality in the world might fail to be a safeguard in time of a great conflict.[22]

Ferdinand de Lesseps was an inveterate optimist. He was either unable to appraise his reception in the United States correctly or was determined to ignore its unfavorable omens for his enterprise. As a world renowned engineer he was of course given courteous hearings. More than eight thousand people are said to have come to banquets, symposiums, and lectures to hear him. He was the builder of one successful canal and few doubted his abilities to build another, although the press did carry ill-natured and uncharitable attacks upon his idea of a sea level canal and his choice of the Panama route.

The Frenchman even mistook the charm and courtesy which President Hayes displayed in a personal interview for approval of his canal project and persisted in interpreting the President's message to Congress, quoted above, as intended only to assure the security of the waterway. He sent off messages to his associates telling of the "enthusiastic and unanimous adherence to our cause" which he found in the United States. André Siegfried says, "When one has studied the United States, and particularly the part they have played in this matter (of an isthmian canal), one can easily understand their attitude. Ferdinand de Lesseps either could not or would not appreciate it."[23]

It was probably the uncompromising disapproval of U.S. officials which finally chilled all hope of persuading the French government to give direct financial backing to de Lesseps when his company failed because of yellow fever and the rock of the Culebra Cut. He had managed to do less than one-fourth of the job. There seems to have been no reason why he would not have finished it if he had been able to get the backing of the French government. His failure was one of the tragedies of history.

So long as the de Lesseps operation remained a private enterprise the United States could do little more than frown with disapproval. Many newspapers did just that. There were sarcastic editorials about the folly, inefficiency, and poor promise of the Panama project. But, just in case it *should* by some mischance succeed, most of the editors urged that the United States balance such French achievement and its influence by building its own Nicaraguan canal. Circles outside the government moved faster than those inside. The Maritime Canal Company of Nicaragua obtained a ninety-nine–year concession from the Nicaraguan Congress on May 22, 1880. Its list of incorporators included such distinguished names as Ulysses S. Grant, George B. McClellan, and Levi P. Morton.[24]

The policy, which Rutherford B. Hayes adopted, of seeking a pathway to a canal built and operated by the United States was continued by his successors, James A. Garfield and Chester A. Arthur, and their Secretaries of State, James G. Blaine and Frederick T. Frelinghuysen. Garfield announced in his inaugural address that he would follow the Hayes canal policy and would be motivated by a constant purpose to assure a "thorough protection of American interests."[25] In order to move in the direction of a go-it-alone course the United States had to extricate itself somehow from the commitments of the Clayton-Bulwer Treaty. Blaine opened negotiations with a rather brusque note to London. He was well known for his anti-British utterances in North American election campaigns. The British foreign minister, Lord Granville, quietly replied that his government expected the "observance of all engagements." Two better reasoned and moderately phrased notes from Blaine still failed to budge the British from this position. His successor, Secretary Frelinghuysen, had no better results and dropped the matter in 1883.[26]

In 1883 the French were still at work in Panama and seemed to be nearing ultimate success even though they were encountering many difficulties. This made it imperative for the United States to move to combat in some way the psychological impact of the de Lesseps operation. Nicaragua was the obvious point of counterattack. On December 1, 1884, Secretary Frelinghuysen signed a canal treaty with the Nicaraguan representative, Joaquin Zavala, providing for the construction of a canal by the United States. The canal would then be held in joint ownership with Nicaragua, and the United States would guarantee Nicaraguan independence.[27]

This treaty was submitted to the United States Senate on December 10, 1884. It was an unfortunate time. A political overturn was impending. The Democratic Party was about to regain power with newly elected Grover Cleveland. Important legislation languished during the "lame duck" session, and although President Arthur and Secretary Frelinghuysen labored to get the treaty ratified, they too were only "lame ducks" with little influence. The Senate adjourned March 3, 1885, without taking final action on the agreement.[28]

4

The Abrogation of the Clayton-Bulwer Treaty

For half a century the Clayton-Bulwer Treaty was to plague the super-nationalists in the United States who could not concede that the Monroe Doctrine would countenance a European power establishing such an interest in the Western Hemisphere as the "partnership" in an isthmian canal would give to Great Britain. At the time the treaty was negotiated it was the Democrats who largely held this view. Then in the post–Civil War days the Republicans adopted the nationalistic position which the Democrats had held before the war, with Grant, Hayes, Garfield, and Arthur all advocating a canal built and controlled by the United States alone. The practice of North American politics which usually requires the opposition to take a position contrary to that elected by the incumbent party impelled the Democrats essentially to reject the views of Polk and Stephen A. Douglas. Two basic principles now crystalized and competed for supremacy:

(1) The Clayton-Bulwer Treaty is voidable at the option of the United States, and must be voided to assure exclusive United States hegemony over any canal project.

(2) The canal must be for the benefit of the whole world, not just the United States, and must be held in trust for mankind without domination by any single power. If the United States is to be sole "trustee" for the world the British must release

her from the binding restrictions of the Clayton-Bulwer Treaty.[1]

After the rebuff of efforts to modify the Clayton-Bulwer Treaty Arthur and Frelinghuysen had accepted principle (1). They had negotiated the Frelinghuysen-Zavala Treaty on the theory that the United States could take unilateral action to escape its commitments under the Clayton-Bulwer pact. President Arthur had kept the Frelinghuysen-Zavala Treaty before the "lame duck" session of the Senate after a preliminary test on January 29, 1885, had shown that it lacked only one vote of the two-thirds majority required for its passage. Since the Senate is a continuing body, the convention was therefore still technically before it when Cleveland took office. One of his first acts was throw the new Democratic administration's support behind principle (2). On March 5, 1885, he withdrew the Frelinghuysen-Zavala Treaty from consideration before the Senate.[2]

President Cleveland declared that he favored an isthmian canal, but that he felt private enterprise should build it and not the government. He said the Frelinghuysen-Zavala Treaty's guarantee of Nicaragua constituted an entangling alliance in violation of the now historic policy stated in Washington's Farewell Address. His secretary of state, Thomas F. Bayard, was strongly convinced that any transisthmian canal should be an international project and that the Clayton-Bulwer Treaty was a valuable guarantee of that end by the two most powerful states with interests in the New World.

Cleveland's idea of a privately constructed canal now bore fruit. The Maritime Canal Company of Nicaragua had just been chartered. Among its incorporators was James Roosevelt,[3] father of the future President Franklin D. Roosevelt. Mr. Roosevelt had been closely associated with the now President Cleveland in New York politics and he was also a friend of Senator John T. Morgan of Alabama, the Democratic Party's leading Senate advocate of a Nicaragua canal. This company actually began construction work near Greytown, at the mouth of the San Juan River in June, 1890. The Panic of 1893 ended its financial support. Efforts were made to get Congress to appropriate money to save the project, which already had made an impressive start. Several appropriation bills were delayed by legislative committees. The company had only been given a ten-year concession by Nicaragua and this had now expired.[4]

The Republicans reacted in a partisan way to Mr. Cleveland's canal policies, as might well have been expected. The Republican National Convention in 1888 adopted the following declaration in its platform:

> The conduct of foreign affairs by the present administration has been distinguished by its inefficiency and its cowardice. Having withdrawn from the Senate all pending treaties effected by Republican administrations . . . it has neither effected nor proposed any others in their stead. Professing adherence to the Monroe Doctrine it has seen with idle complacency the extension of foreign influence in Central America and of foreign trade everywhere among our neighbors. It has refused to charter, sanction, or encourage any American organization for contstruction of the Nicaraguan Canal, a work of vital importance to the maintenance of the Monroe Doctrine and of our National influence in Central and South America, and necessary for the development of trade with our Pacific territory, with South America, and with the islands and further coasts of the Pacific Ocean.

The Democratic platform was silent on the matter. It will be recalled that Mr. Cleveland was defeated in this election because he lost the key state of New York. His foreign policy played a large role in losing the campaign in that commercial state, particularly his alleged favoring of the British at the "expense of the North American industrial worker."[5]

The Republicans under Benjamin Harrison took office for a four year term unique in American political history, coming as it did between the two administrations of President Cleveland. It was during this administration that the debacle of de Lesseps became complete. In 1889 the French company had come to the verge of utter bankruptcy because of a combination of factors: mismanagement, unpredictably harsh physical terrain along the canal route, and the plague of yellow fever which carried off hundreds of workers, skilled and unskilled, every year. In response to an appeal from de Lesseps and his associates, the French government was debating whether or not to guarantee the bonds of the company.[6] There was an earnest desire to save this magnificent enterprise under the direction of French technology. In retrospect, almost all writers concerned with this sad episode agree that with such backing Ferdinand de Lesseps could have finished his canal, although at much greater cost than he had ever envisaged. But at this point, Yanqui nationalism asserted itself against the penetration of the hemisphere by a foreign government. There was impressive bipartisan support for a resolution, introduced in Congress in 1889, stating that the United States would look with "serious concern and disapproval" on *any* connection of a European government with the Panama Canal project.[7] President Harrison announced his support of the resolution. The French government, remembering Napoleon III and Mexico, retreated. The company collapsed and all work halted on the isthmus. The jungle crept over machinery and unfinished construction to reclaim its own.

The Democratic support of this question represented a shift in that party's viewpoint from the high altruism of Bayard to the direction of exclusive American control. The Democratic platform of 1892 reflects this:

> For purposes of national defense and the promotion of commerce between the states, we recognize the early construction of the Nicaragua canal and its protection against foreign control as of great importance to the United States.

The Republicans used almost identical language:

> The construction of the Nicaragua canal is of the highest importance to the American people, both as a measure of National defense and to build up and maintain American commerce, and it should be controlled by the United States government.

When Grover Cleveland came back for his second term he had a new secretary of state, Richard Olney. Olney believed in full U.S. control over the canal. But he and Cleveland still recognized the validity of the Clayton-Bulwer Treaty and considered that the consent of Britain must be obtained before the United States could proceed alone to build the canal, either in its own exclusive interest or as "trustee" for the rest of the commercial nations of the world.

In a memorandum written in 1896, Secretary of State Olney characterized the Monroe Doctrine as a fixed policy of the United States, but one which could be waived in a given instance. He held that the Clayton-Bulwer Treaty had been such a waiver and not a departure from the Doctrine itself. In view of the fact that Stephen A. Douglas denounced the treaty in 1850 this statement by a Democratic secretary of state becomes increasingly interesting:

> The United States is *estopped* [my italics] from denying that the treaty (Clayton-Bulwer) is in full force and vigor. If changed

conditions now make stipulations which were once deemed advantageous either inapplicable or injurious the true remedy is not in ingenious attempts to deny existence of the treaty or to explain away its provisions, but in a direct and straightforward application to Great Britain for a reconsideration of the whole matter.[8]

During Cleveland's second administration there was a well-defined cleavage between his party and the Republican party over foreign policy with particular respect to overseas expansion. The situation foreshadowed the turn of the century when the Republicans would ride the wave of jingoistic imperialism and the Democrats would beat the forlorn drums of national restraint. President Cleveland signaled this demarche on his first day in office by deciding to withdraw the treaty for the annexation of Hawaii which the outgoing Harrison administration had sent to the Senate. The revolution there which had overthrown the Kamehameha Dynasty and paved the way for the "republic" which negotiated the treaty had succeeded because of both covert and overt assistance from the United States.[9] When Cleveland withdrew the treaty on March 9, 1893, a storm of partisan invective swirled about his head. His policy toward the Clayton-Bulwer Treaty further irritated those Republicans who had accepted the Blaine proposition that the United States take unilateral action to abrogate the pact of 1850. Among those supporting such action was young Theodore Roosevelt who had once been a supporter of Cleveland when the President was governor of New York. On October 27, 1894, Mr. Roosevelt wrote to his friend Henry Cabot Lodge, "I am surprised all the time to receive new proofs that every man, even every Southerner who lives outside the country, has gotten to have a perfect hatred and contempt for Cleveland's administration because of its base betrayal of our interests abroad. I do wish our Republicans would go in avowedly to annex Hawaii and build an oceanic canal with the money of Uncle Sam."[10]

Nevertheless, Secretary Olney opened discussions with the British on the subject of changing the treaty. He had not gotten beyond the stage of polite inquiry before the British-Venezuelan boundary controversy put every other topic of Anglo-American relations aside. Then time ran out on the Cleveland administration and the Republicans came back with William McKinley.

Interestingly enough, the return of the Republicans did not mean a return to the Blaine principle of unilateral abrogation. The new secretary of state, John Hay, was a moderate and seasoned statesman who saw that the United States would be saving its moral reputation in international affairs and better serving its own ultimate best interests by seeking a new arrangement with Britain. President McKinley opened the way by declaring in his annual message to Congress in December, 1898, that the isthmian canal had now become a national necessity.[11] The long voyage of the U.S.S. *Oregon* around South America during the recent Spanish-American War had driven this point home very graphically to all segments of North American opinion. In England public opinion was also changing. The British were embroiled in the Boer War and had been alarmed by the growing animosity of the Germany of Wilhem II. It seemed to London that the time had come to look for new ties. English control of the Suez Canal had lessened the feeling that interests of the world empire required some control of an American canal. Seemingly in reply to President McKinley's message of five days earlier, the *London Spectator,* in its issue of December 10, 1898, aptly summarized the situation:

> The force of circumstances is often the most ironical of goddesses, but sometimes she brings about things which are curiously fitting and appropriate. When one half of the Anglo-Saxon race holds the waterway between the Mediterranean and the Indian Ocean, what could be more appropriate than that the other half should hold that between the Atlantic and the Pacific? . . . It is not for us to delay but to hasten that auspicious hour.

The United States suggested to the British government that the British ambassador in Washington represent his country in the negotiations. This was Lord Julian Pauncefote who was very popular in the United States. Such an arrangement also enabled Mr. Hay personally to represent the United States. The British agreed and the talks began.[12]

Many Republicans who had accepted the Blaine principle of unilateral abrogation were quite impatient about the slow pace of diplomacy. The Republican platform of 1896 had pledged the party to a government built, owned, and operated canal in Nicaragua. They felt that it was time to begin the project. When Congress reconvened in December, 1899, the Hepburn Bill was introduced. It provided for the construction of a canal and entirely ignored the Clayton-Bulwer Treaty.[13] A considerable number of Democrats in both houses supported the measure including Senator John T. Morgan of Alabama, chairman of the Senate Committee on Interoceanic Canals. Senator Morgan had been chairman of this committee when the Democrats controlled the Senate and had been so identified with the subject of the isthmian canal that the Republicans as a courtesy had retained him as chairman of the committee. He was the leader of a group of congressional Democrats who were anxious to have the project begun at any price. They were, of course, committed to the Nicaragua waterway. The Hepburn Bill was delayed in the Senate because of a disagreement over the Panama and Nicaragua routes. Secretary Hay deplored the passage of the Hepburn Bill in this form and accurately foretold that it would complicate the negotiations with Britain. But Theodore Roosevelt was in complete accord with the bill. He was now governor of New York and about to become his party's vice-presidential nominee. He wrote to Hay, ". . . as for treaties . . . I do not admit the 'dead hand' of the treaty making power in the past. A treaty can always be honorably abrogated."[14]

The first Hay-Pauncefote Treaty had been sent to the Senate on February 5, 1900. It provided that the United States should build, own, and operate the canal, but the waterway was to be neutralized and under no circumstances was the United States to ever fortify it.[15]

It was a mistake to put such a treaty before the country just before a presidential election. Senator Morgan at once denounced it as a surreptitious British move to dominate the canal indirectly. Governor Roosevelt said the pact might be fraught with very great mischief and expressed a wish to Hay "that you and the President would drop the treaty and push through a bill to build and fortify our own canal."[16] The Democratic party held its national convention and adopted a plank in its platform condemning the Hay-Pauncefote Treaty "as a surrender of American rights and interests not to be tolerated by the American people." In view of the generally anti-imperialistic tone of this platform and the anti-imperialistic campaign later put on by the nominee, Mr. Bryan, and in the light of Secretary Olney's policy in the latest Democratic administration, this 1900 Democratic plank has a double interest for the reader. About the canal itself the platform stated:

> We favor the immediate construction, ownership, and control of the Nicaraguan Canal by the United States, and we denounce the insincerity of the plank in the Republican National Platform for an Isthmian Canal in the face of the failure of the Republican majority to pass the bill pending in Congress [the Hepburn Bill had passed the House but was being held up in the Senate].

The Republican platform favored ". . . the construction, ownership, control and protection of an isthmian canal by the Government of the United States."

The silver Republican party, which supported Bryan mainly on the money issue, was also critical of the administration in its platform declaration about the treaty and the canal:

> We believe the Monroe Doctrine to be sound in principle and a wise national policy, and we demand a firm adherence thereto. We condemn acts inconsistent with it that tend to make us parties to the interest and to involve us in the controversies of European nations and to recognition by pending treaty, of the right of England to be considered in the construction of an interoceanic canal. We declare that such a canal when constructed ought to be controlled by the United States in the interests of American nations.

Professor Thomas A. Bailey speaks of the incredible ramifications of this election-year vendetta against the treaty:

> The Irish-Americans, who deplored the recent friendliness with the Mother Country, added their voices to the outcry. They were joined by the German-Americans, who had been greatly aroused by the killing of their fellow Teutons in the Boer War. These "hyphenated Americans" were the real "idiots" wrote John Hay when they demanded that he show his Americanism by crying "To Hell with the Queen" at every breath.[17]

It is interesting to note how many newspapers of the supernationalistic point of view, who otherwise supported the administration, took occasion to lambaste poor Mr. Hay. He cried out in anguish against the "filthy newspaper abuse," but comforted himself with the thought that it would pass away, and that he was right in his negotiations.[18]

After the election, the Senate took up the treaty and ratified it with three substantial amendments—there was to be no obstacle to the United States fortification of the canal, the invitation of other powers to adhere to the pact was eliminated, and a direct statement that the Clayton-Bulwer Treaty was now superseded was to be included. These amendments caused a resentful storm in the British press and the London government refused to accept them. The entire negotiation lapsed in March, 1901, when the seven month period allowed for the exchange of ratifications had expired.[19]

Secretary Hay was very bitter at first over the collapse of his efforts. He submitted his resignation but McKinley pressed him to stay on and try again. The next time around a number of factors led to success. Hay submerged his sense of outrage which had led him to brand the Senate as a forum of "ignorance and spite, acting upon cowardice" upon a matter in which "no one out of a madhouse could fail to see that the advantages were all on our side."[20] He bolstered himself to cultivate the Senate leaders and consult with them during the negotiations. Then suddenly McKinley was assassinated and Mr. Roosevelt became President. The new chief executive had, of course, been most unenthusiastic about the treaty and his coolness had helped to strengthen its opponents. Now with full responsibility suddenly dropped into his lap he gave the situation more objective appraisal, requested Hay to stay in the cabinet, and put his full support behind a treaty.

On the other side of the Atlantic the British had come to a more realistic understanding of North American politics. Above all they wanted U.S. friendship in the face of swiftly deteriorating relations with Germany. If possible they hoped to get something more than friendship —some sort of understanding, diplomatic collaboration among the world powers, even an alliance. Lord Pauncefote returned to London with word that North American public opinion would not be denied, that the London cabinet must accede the point of fortification or lose the entire undertaking in the face of a *fait accompli* which would be a diplomatic loss of face for Britain and a terrible obstacle to further Anglo-American collaboration.

The result of all of these factors was a new Hay-Pauncefote Treaty, signed on November 18, 1901, ratified by the Senate on December 16th, and proclaimed in effect on February 22, 1902.[21] The instrument gave the United States a free hand to construct, control, and police a canal, the only condition being that it should be open to merchantmen and warships of all nations, without discrimination or unequable toll charges.

Domestically, the atmosphere was now cleared for one of the bitterest battles of North American political history. This was the struggle between adherents of the rival Panama and Nicaragua routes which had already begun. The canal was to be built, and it was to be under the absolute control of the United States—but *where*?

5

Nicaragua or Panama?

The choice of the Panama route is one of the amazing stories of American history—a tale of fanatical determination, of starry-eyed idealism, of the employment of every type of financial and economic pressure, of the exercise of political power and influence where it might count. It is the story of a group that fought with brass knuckles and no holds barred to turn assured defeat into victory.

Prior to 1900 there was little question but that the North American public considered the Nicaragua route the national objective. Many surveys of the isthmus were made—as many as nine routes had been under consideration at one time or another. But discussion narrowed to Panama and Nicaragua. The Nicaragua route had been the choice of the Isthmian Canal Commission. Ex-President Grant had written articles in support of it and had headed a Nicaragua Canal Company.[1] The advantage of this route lay in its projected use of the San Juan River and deep Lake Nicaragua. The terrain was also considered more favorable for digging the balance of the waterway.

In 1875, Ferdinand de Lesseps had made what purported to be the most careful survey of the Panama route up to that time. Through the Societé Geographique of Paris he arranged an International Congress of Geographic Sciences which assembled in Paris May 15, 1879.[2] The United States was represented officially by Rear Admiral Ammen and Chief Engineer Menocal of the navy. Seven feasible routes were discussed by this conference. De Lesseps was convinced of the priority of the Panama route and he had committed himself personally by taking the concessions obtained the year before from Colombia by his associate Bonaparte-Wyse. The ultimate failure of his effort to bring the

Panama Canal into existence tended to convince many people that the Nicaragua route was the superior of the two.[3]

But in spite of the assumption that the United States was committed to the Nicaragua route there was always a latent, if at times silent, predilection for the Panama route on the part of certain navy engineers. There were civilians in places of influence who felt the same way. Among them was the former ambassador to France, John Bigelow, who had known de Lesseps. He was impressed that de Lesseps had favored Panama. Despite its unfortunate failure the French company *had* left the project about one-third of the way completed. Why not take over from there and finish the job? His influence with President McKinley is generally given as the reason why the president avoided the term "Nicaragua canal" in his message to Congress in December, 1898.[4] It is interesting, too, that Bigelow was a Democrat.

Sentiments such as these were influential enough to cause Congress to appropriate $1,000,000 in 1899 to make one final investigation of the relative merits of the canal sites in Panama and Nicaragua. An earlier commission headed by Admiral Walker had surveyed the Nicaraguan line but had not visited Panama. Pursuant to the congressional action President McKinley appointed the second Walker Commission on March 3, 1899.[5] Its report recommended Nicaragua but probably did so because the French company still held the Panama concession and it was anticipated that there would be difficulties in buying the concession and in arranging an agreement in Bogotá. The report did say that the Panama project would cost less, provide a shorter canal, and require less transit time.

Senator John Morgan of Alabama, chairman of the Senate Committee on Interoceanic Canals, was morally and intellectually "sold" on the Nicaragua route. He introduced a bill calling for construction of the Nicaraguan canal. On January 21, 1899, by a 48 to 6 vote, it passed the Senate. At this juncture, party politics of the most petty sort intervened. William P. Hepburn, a Republican member of the House of Representatives, desired to have his name attached to the enacting canal bill. He was one of the inner circle in the Republican-controlled House and chairman of the House Canal Committee. His Republican colleagues deferred to him and buried the "rival" Morgan bill in committee.

Hepburn believed in the Nicaraguan route no less than Morgan, but the year 1899 dragged on while he delayed in getting his bill reported out. In despair Senator Morgan persuaded the Senate to attach the canal provision to the Rivers and Harbors Appropriations Bill, but the Republicans controlled both houses and the party machine functioned perfectly in conference to strike the Alabama Democrat's amendment.[6]

By this time there were powerful elements within the Republican Party set to "kill" the Nicaragua route in favor of the Panama one. At this juncture they acquired the backstage assistance of an extraordinary man—Philippe Bunau-Varilla, a talented French engineer who had worked with de Lesseps in the abortive effort to build a Panama canal. M. Bunau-Varilla was interested financially in the French company known as the New French Canal Company. This company wanted to take ever the property and diggings of the original Bonaparte-Wyse concession.[7] He may have been partly motivated by economic considerations, but he also was driven by a profound intellectual and professional conviction that the Panama route was best. He hoped that the great North American republic would provide the backing necessary to complete the undertaking of Ferdinand de Lesseps and would vindicate at least partially his admired friend and leader.

M. Bunau-Varilla came to the United States and, at the insistence of a friend, sought an interview with Myron T. Herrick, a powerful Republican politician in Cleveland, Ohio. Herrick was impressed by the manifest ability and burning sincerity of his visitor and secured for him an interview with U.S. Senator Marcus A. Hanna, chairman of the Republican National Committee. Through Hanna the Frenchman was able to get ready listeners among Republican senators, even those serving on Morgan's Committee on Interoceanic Canals. Hanna's influence in swinging doubtful Republicans toward the Panama route can scarcely be doubted.[8]

Of more debatable effect was the activity of William Nelson Cromwell, a New York lawyer. He belonged to a combination of American financial interests which had formulated a scheme to take over the French Canal company's concessions from Colombia. According to Thayer, John Hay's biographer, Cromwell donated $60,000 to the Republican National Committee for use in the campaign of 1900. The obvious implication is that the donation purchased a party abandonment of the Nicaraguan canal in favor of the Panama one. Of course Cromwell must have exerted his best efforts lobbying in the McKinley administration and in Congress. Nevertheless, it is difficult to accept without further evidence the hypothesis that a great political party sold itself for $60,000. It seems more logical to regard the Cromwell incident as just one of a series of factors which all operated together to influence the position of the party in power. Cromwell's donation may have had some effect, but it should not be overly stressed.

The Walker Commission's report probably had a much greater practical significance. Its members had cooperated with what they considered an established policy, to build the canal in Nicaragua.[9] Yet all but two of them were more favorably impressed by the technological advantages which many navy engineers had seen previously in the Panama route. Theodore Roosevelt seems to have made up his mind definitely in favor of Panama after perusing the Walker report. As a former assistant secretary of the navy he was no doubt impressed by the findings of navy engineers. President McKinley had had his doubts even before appointing the Walker Board. John Bigelow was a trusted advisor and he certainly would have been influenced by Hanna. He had also had conversations with both army and navy engineers. Some years later Hanna stated in a speech in the Senate that McKinley really had been undecided, "Just before the Philadelphia convention (referring to the Republican National Convention of 1900) President McKinley said to me 'It will not be wise to do as we have done in our platforms heretofore, to announce ourselves in favor of a Nicaraguan canal, because I appointed a Commission to investigate the subject of all the routes'."[10]

On June 20, 1900, the Republican National Convention in Philadelphia adopted a plank favoring construction of an isthmian canal. The 1896 platform had specifically called for the Nicaragua Canal. The Hanna machine was working in well oiled perfection and no dissidents arose to argue the question of the canal route.

The Democratic National Convention convened two weeks after the Republican sessions. The Democratic party, no less than the Republican, was committed to a transisthmian waterway. The anti-imperalism of William Jennings Bryan did not include attacking the expansion of overseas commerce of which canal building would be a part. Moreover the Spanish War had awakened the United States to the advantages of sea power and the importance of an isthmian canal. People everywhere recalled the famous voyage of the U.S.S. *Oregon* around Cape Horn. This commercially minded and patriotic nation would make short work of any political interference blocking the construction of a canal.

The Democratic Party's most distinguished advocate of canal

building, Senator Morgan, knew well the influences in the opposing
party which were working to scuttle the Nicaragua route. He had denounced their machinations before the Democratic caucus of the Senate.
His prestige and influence were enough to insure a Democratic stand
for Nicaragua when the National Convention met on Independence
Day at Kansas City. Except for this difference in platform wording
and its implication of a different choice of route, the canal was not an
issue between the parties in the 1900 campaign, but it now seems clear
that this election settled the fate of the Nicaraguan canal.

If the Democrats had won, it can scarcely be doubted that the
new Bryan Administration would have chosen the Nicaragua route.
The fanatical devotion of Morgan to the Nicaragua route, the prestige
which he wielded in Congress within the Republican ranks as well as
within his own party, and the wording of the Kansas City platform
would have guaranteed such a result. Where would Bunau-Varilla have
found Democratic counterparts to Herrick and Hanna? When the
Frenchman later visited Morgan in an effort to temper his hostility
to the Panama route, the Senator, in his indignation almost struck his
visitor and referred to Panama as "a rotten project."[11] Cromwell had
given $60,000 to the Republican Party so he would have had less
chance than Bunau-Varilla to influence Democratic leadership.

The attitude of the "solid South" would have been another factor
influencing a Democratic regime in Washington. In fact, the South
had a "dollars and cents" reason for preferring Nicaragua to Panama.
The average sailing time between the gulf ports and the Pacific coast
by way of Nicaragua would be two days shorter than by way of Panama.[12] If the administration had been Democratic, the Panama route
would have gotten little more than a perfunctory hearing. As it was,
even the Republican administration was able to establish the southern
route only after protracted and bitter debate.

Senator Morgan appreciated the practical importance of getting
immediate legislation to *commit* the United States government to the
Nicaragua route before the Panama idea could make further headway.
When Congress convened in December, 1900, for the short session he
made every effort to get the Hepburn Bill on the calendar for consideration.[13] The House had passed the Hepburn Bill in place of Morgan's
Senate bill on May 2, 1900. In the Senate, Morgan had then graciously
stepped aside and had tried to push the Hepburn Bill through. But
President McKinley and Hanna had applied the party brakes and the

bill did not get to a vote before the June adjournment. The true greatness of John T. Morgan is demonstrated in the grace with which he overlooked Hepburn's greed for headlines and in the work which he did to secure the adoption of his rival's bill. He now renewed the effort.

Morgan knew that the powers in the administration were holding out on the Nicaragua route without yet openly disavowing it.[14] Furthermore, he well knew that the public knew nothing of this reserved attitude and considered the Nicaragua route the official one. In a letter to Senator Allison, Morgan accused the Republican Steering Committee of delaying a vote on the Hepburn Bill and requested a definite statement on the Republican Party's attitude. He offered to resign his courtesy position as chairman of the Committee on Interoceanic Canals because he felt that the situation there had become intolerable.

Senator Allison diplomatically replied that the Republican senators considered it advisable to postpone discussion of the canal measure until the British government had passed upon the Senate's amendments to the first Hay-Pauncefote Treaty. This explanation was plausible enough, and Morgan retained the chairmanship although he still doubted the motives of some of his Republican colleagues. When the "lame duck" session adjourned there could be no hope of action until the reopening of Congress in December, 1901. Before the new session President McKinley was assassinated and Roosevelt became president.

The new chief executive replaced doubt and hesitation with conviction and action. The best evidence indicates that Theodore Roosevelt had made up his mind in favor of the Panama route before his accession to the presidency. The Walker Commission presented its report soon after he entered the White House. The technical advantages it attributed to the Panama route probably confirmed the impressions which he already had from navy sources. By this time Henry Cabot Lodge had joined Hanna in the ranks of the advocates of the Panama route. The two senators were often at the White House.

In the meantime Representative Hepburn presented to the House another and more specific measure appropriating $180,000,000 for the construction of a Nicaragua canal. It passed the House on January 9, 1902, by the tremendous vote of 308 to 2. In the Senate, Morgan went gleefully to work to speed it through that body and on to the White House. Roosevelt and Hanna were now faced with the necessity of an openly decisive action if they hoped to substitute the Panama route for the Nicaragua one. The president chose Senator Spooner of Wisconsin to be the instrument of his action, and Senator Hanna persuaded the Senate to delay action when a further report[15] of the Walker Commission publicized the technical advantages of the Panama route.

At the president's instigation, Spooner introduced in the upper House a radical amendment to the Hepburn Bill. It authorized the president to purchase the French company's rights in Panama and to acquire a "canal zone" six miles wide from Colombia. To assuage the Nicaragua route advocates the measure provided that should these things not be accomplished within a reasonable time, treaties were to be negotiated with Nicaragua and Costa Rica for a zone and for the construction of a canal along the historic San Juan and Lake Nicaragua route.[16]

The stage was now set for the first of the series of epic struggles which were to be waged openly on the floors of Congress before the issue of site would be settled. Although Spooner's name headed the controversial bill, the leader of the Panama advocates was Mark Hanna.

Cromwell conferred with Hanna and Spooner the day before the new bill was introduced in the Senate, but it hardly seems likely that he could have made any substantial contribution to drafting the amendment in that short time. He was close to Hanna, of course, and undoubtedly he gave covert assistance wherever he could.[17]

Senator Morgan naturally led the opposition. In his almost fanatical zeal the whole Panama question was a thing of evil. The Spooner Amendment was referred to his Canal Committee and there the preliminary skirmish was staged. Hanna proved to be a superb floor general in every exigency. He was an adroit parliamentarian and his prestige within his own party was obvious. In the face of Morgan's opposition he got the committee to interrogate each member of the Walker Commission and brought out the fact that all of them but two had really favored the Panama route for technical reasons and had only "gone along with the tide" in signing the original report favoring Nicaragua.[18]

Morgan's personal influence was great enough to carry his fellow committeemen. By a vote of 7 to 4 the original Hepburn Bill was reported out over the Spooner Amendment. Then Hanna and three others drafted a minority report favoring the amendment, and the issue was carried to the Senate floor. In the spectacular debate which followed, every conceivable method of molding opinion was belabored for the benefit both of Congress and the general public.[19] M. Bunau-Varilla arrived in the country from France to add his talents to the great propaganda campaign.

John Bigelow introduced Bunau-Varilla to Charles A. Dana, publisher of the *New York Sun*. Dana was persuaded to put the editorial support of the *Sun* behind the Panama route. This newspaper was very influential and began to play up the potential danger to a Nicaraguan canal from the active volcanoes along that route.[20] Bunau-Varilla also published a pamphlet based upon the engineering reports of the Isthmian Canal Commission and Senator Hanna saw to it that all of his colleagues received copies. The propaganda barrage also turned the general public toward Panama and the members of Congress began to hear from their constituents back home. The majority of newspapers seems to have resisted the pressure to go overboard in favor of Panama, but the pro-Panama articles were the more sensational and the more effective. The country was also flooded with brochures by the Bunau-Varilla forces.

Nature contributed a decisive hand to the debate when Mt. Pelee on the island of Martinique erupted with tragic results. The loss of life and property damage was appalling and every newspaper reader in the United States was informed of the potent dangers of volcanoes and earthquakes. The unfortunate choice of scenic, but smokingly volcanic Mt. Momotombo as the view shown on Nicaraguan postage stamps convincingly branded that country in North American popular opinion as an unhappy land of volcanos daily erupting death and destruction.

Senator Morgan and his cohorts found themselves almost powerless to combat propaganda so skillfully and colorfully disseminated. When each senator received a block of Nicaraguan postage stamps bearing the smoking image of Momotombo, the battle was lost. Senators Hanna and Spooner were effective in their logical, eloquent arguments while Senator Morgan was, at times, too emotional. The full weight of the White House was behind the Spooner Amendment. The well oiled Republican machine functioned well. On the crucial vote on June 19, 1902, the Senate, by a vote of 42 to 34, accepted the minority report and passed the Spooner Amendment to the Hepburn Bill.[21] The basic issue was really decided in the Senate, because the Republican Steering Committee was much more firmly entrenched in the House so virtually no opposition was even attempted there.[22]

As Professor Gerstle Mack so aptly notes, the laborious passage

of the Spooner Amendment was one of the most notorious and successful examples of lobbying on record—a combination of Hanna and
Spooner orating in the Senate; Cromwell exerting what influence he
could through the close alliance of the Republican Party with the
finance and big business interests; Roosevelt quietly lobbying from the
White House; and Bunau-Varilla, a real genius of intrigue, cajoling,
pamphleteering, inspiring editorials, and even using Nicaraguan postage stamps as testimonials for his cause, the Panama route.[23]

At the time the finality of the Spooner Amendment was not appreciated. Even Senator Morgan voted for the bill on the final roll call.
He believed that clear title to the French concession would not be
obtained and that eventually the United States would have to turn
again to Nicaragua. The final draft of the Spooner Amendment provided that this should be done, if necessary. For this reason Morgan
was able to bring himself to vote for it and to advise his supporters
over in the House to do the same. He felt that the Spooner Amendment
would be, in the final analysis, an act which would indirectly lead to
the Nicaragua canal.

Events were to prove Morgan wrong, but the bitterness of his
losing fight can not obscure the truly great role which he played in
the prolonged effort to bring an interoceanic canal into being. When
the smoke of battle cleared, his opponent, Senator Spooner, paid
tribute to this Alabama Democrat whose forceful brilliance almost
defeated the entrenched power of a popular Republican administration
in a heavily Republican Congress. "Upon whatever route an isthmian
canal shall be constructed," Spooner said, "the Senator from Alabama
will forever stand in the memory of the people as the father of the
isthmian canal; for . . . unappalled by obstacles and adverse influences,
with lofty patriotism and unfaltering purpose, he has, with rare skill,
tireless energy, and splendid advocacy, fought for an isthmian canal."[24]

While the debates over the Spooner Amendment were proceeding,
the Hay-Pauncefote Treaty also had been clearing its final hurdles and
was ratified on February 22, 1902. The United States was now rid
of its British "partnership" and committed to its own canal project
in Panama. The next step for the Roosevelt administration was the
purchase of the French concession and the acquisition by treaty of a
canal zone from Colombia. The first matter was settled easily enough
by an offer and acceptance of $40,000,000 by the holders of the New
French Canal Company, the successor to the old de Lesseps company.
This agreement was contingent upon the favorable execution of a

treaty for the canal zone.[25] The attempt to make such a pact with Colombia ran into unexpected difficulty.

The Colombian minister in Washington, Señor Tomás Herrán, saw broader implications in the canal project than did his home government. The politicians in Bogotá seemed to be primarily interested in getting the best possible financial bargain for the transfer of the isthmian rights. They appeared to be ready to deadlock negotiations endlessly to attain that end. Herrán sensed that Roosevelt and many other Yanquis were impatient with such tactics. He was keenly conscious of the potential threat of the alternative Nicaragua route and was convinced that Colombia must hasten the conclusion of its bargain with the restive North Americans or lose the opportunity forever. In the light of these considerations he took the chance of exceeding his instructions. On January 22, 1903, he signed a treaty with Secretary of State John Hay which provided for a ninety-nine–year lease of a strip of territory six miles wide, for an initial payment of $10,000,000 and an annual rental of $250,000.[26] Herrán signed this agreement under a virtual ultimatum from Hay despite the fact that his instructions were to hold out for an annuity of $600,000.

Senator Morgan and the other Nicaragua route enthusiasts would not allow this move to clinch the Panama route without one last bitter struggle to prevent it. A filibuster led by Morgan lasted until the short session expired on March 4, 1903. President Roosevelt responded by calling a special session of the Senate to consider the Hay-Herrán Treaty. The Alabama Democrat opened the debate on March 9 by discussing the purposes of the Spooner Amendment, bearing in mind that it carried the alternative authorization for Nicaragua should the Colombian negotiations fail. He offered no less than thirty-five amendments and exceptions to the treaty, saying, "I have prepared a substitute for this treaty, which I believe is a full, liberal, and almost a too indulgent or slack compliance with that law [the Spooner Law]."[27]

Theodore Roosevelt watched the Senate debate with great concern, and as it became protracted he wrote to Hay, "I am now sweating blood in the effort to get the treaties confirmed . . . The Democrats are doing their best to get into shape to vote solidly against . . ."[28]

It was considered certain by both sides that adoption of the Morgan amendments would cause Colombia to reject the treaty. The administration exerted every pressure to defeat them. Although the treaty itself had to have a two-thirds majority, the amendments could be put in by a majority vote. The Democrats remained firmly with

Morgan but the Republican majority steam-rollered the opposition and defeated the amendments by an average vote of 46 to 24. Further opposition then collapsed and the treaty was approved in its original text.[29] But now Bogatá dealt a seemingly devastating blow to the efforts of those who had worked for the Panama route.

The Colombian Senate, convinced that the United States could be jockeyed into better financial terms and heedless of the warnings of Minister Herrán, voted 24 to 3 to reject the treaty. Efforts to obtain reconsideration or amendments were impeded by procrastination. When the Colombian Senate adjourned on October 31, 1903, the Hay-Herrán Treaty was dead.[30] It seemed to many that the Panama Canal had expired as well.

6

Roosevelt and the Revolution in Panama

The disgust and chagrin of Mr. Roosevelt and his associates over the triumph of the obstructionists in Bogotá was boundless. The inner circles in the administration were determined that the United States should build the canal through Panama and considered how this might be done without Colombia's consent. Time could not be spared to allow a weak South American republic to dally with the United States for financial advantage. The Republican Party had won the election of 1900 on the issue of imperialism and it was felt that the mood of the North American people would support almost any action to insure the immediate construction of the isthmian canal. Moreover the job of selling the route had been handled well and the public wanted the Panama canal. The impasse was broken by the Panama Revolution of 1903.

For a long time there had been secessionist sentiment on the isthmus of Panama.[1] The country had always been administered with great difficulty from Bogotá because an impenetrable jungle blocked all overland communication and the trip by sea to the isthmus required a week. Many revolutions against Colombian authority had occurred during the preceding half century, and at any rate the isthmus had always enjoyed considerable autonomy. When it became known in Panama that Colombia had rejected the Hay-Herrán Treaty, secession talk was heard on every side. A group of influential newspaper publishers and businessmen organized a conspiracy.[2] This group included the general commanding the Colombian forces on the isthmus. Meetings were actually attended by the North American consul in Panama City and the local superintendent of the Panama Railroad, who of course was a citizen of the United States. The leader of the group was Dr. Manuel Amador. He came to the United States where he met Phillippe Bunau-Varilla on September 24, 1903. Bunau-Varilla then took charge. The story has been told in a number of other books[3] of how the conspiracy proceeded, both in the United States and upon the isthmus; of how encouragement and aid came from high places; of how President Roosevelt himself declared, without too much concern that his remarks might be quoted, "I should be delighted if Panama were an independent state; or *if it made itself so at this moment* [my italics] . . ."[4]

When the uprising occurred, by a happy "coincidence" United States naval units and marines had just arrived at both the Atlantic and Pacific sides of the isthmus. The U.S. consul in Panama was told and advised Washington of the very *hour* in which the revolution was scheduled to begin! When the Colombian government attempted to send forces to deal with the revolt, naval units first blocked, then hampered and delayed their disembarkation at Colón, and U.S. marines were landed under orders to prevent any Colombian troops from approaching within fifty miles of Panama City. Washington justified these actions by citing the Bidlack-Mallorino Treaty of 1846 whereby the United States claimed the right to protect North American property (the Panama Railroad) against local disturbances on the isthmus.

Mr. Roosevelt had considered invoking the 1846 treaty before the Panama Revolution occurred. He and Hay corresponded in September about the feasibility of occupying the entire isthmus and finishing the canal without any further diplomacy with anybody. But such an act of naked imperialism seemed risky with the presidential election of 1904 so close. The device of inspiring a revolt on the isthmus had much more finesse. The fact that a strong revolutionary spirit already existed in Panama was a happy coincidence indeed.

As far as the North American people were concerned, the isthmian revolution was a *fait accompli* before its significance became apparent even to the press. Among papers and periodicals only the *American Monthly Review of Reviews* had scented a revolution in Panama.[5] The fact that this magazine was edited by Dr. Albert Shaw, the friend to whom Roosevelt wrote about the delight with which he would view an uprising, made this circumstance all the more suspect. Most people assumed that the revolution was a natural isthmian reaction to the likelihood that Panama had lost the canal and that it would now go through Nicaragua.[6]

The timing was perfect. Coming as it did on November 3, 1903, the news of the revolution was submerged in the U.S. press by the returns from nationwide, state, and local elections that day. The New York newspapers were so concerned over the return of Tammany Hall to power that they gave the Panama disturbance only small and passing notices.[7] Within a few days the elections were over and the significance of what had happened began to dawn. The sequence of events was too startling. Roosevelt recognized the new republic only three days after the revolution. That seemed like indecent haste to many, but when Philippe Bunau-Varilla came to Washington carrying an honorary Panamanian citizenship from the new republic and an appointment as Minister Plenipotentiary to the United States from the new President Amador, there was real astonishment. When Bunau-Varilla and Secretary Hay negotiated a treaty for the Canal zone within another five days the storm broke and the Roosevelt administration faced a tremendous hue and cry.

The *New York World*, the leading Democratic newspaper in the nation, launched the attack. On November 9 it published a cartoon showing Theodore Roosevelt, armed with pistol, sabre, and shovel coming down a gangplank onto the Panama isthmus from what resembled a naval vessel labeled U.S.S. *G.O.P.* and saying "De-Light-Ed!" In Washington, Bunau-Varilla and Hay continued working and the new treaty was signed on November 18, 1903, only fifteen days after the revolution. The whole story behind the uprising on the isthmus and the hasty actions of the United States to guarantee the success of the venture now seemed abundantly clear to the opponents of the Roosevelt administration.

On November 23 and 24 Senator John Morgan made two long speeches of denunciation in the Senate. They fill more than thirty pages of the *Congressional Record*. He charged Roosevelt with violating the Spooner Amendment by not proceeding with Nicaragua after Colombia's rejection of the Hay-Herrán Treaty and declared that the president had performed a "caesarian operation" to take a republic of Panama "alive from the womb" of Colombia, and mocked Hay for "negotiating" a canal treaty with Bunau-Varilla "in a single session of possibly two hours."[8]

When the regular session of the Fifty-eighth Congress convened on December 7, 1903, the president submitted the Hay–Bunau-Varilla Treaty to the Senate for ratification.[9] By this convention the new Republic of Panama leased to the United States in perpetuity "the use, occupation and control" of a canal zone ten miles wide within which "the United States would possess and exercise" all the rights, power, and authority which a sovereign power might have "to the entire exclusion of the exercise by the Republic of Panama of any such sovereign rights, power, or authority." The consideration was to be the same as that promised in the Hay–Herrán Treaty—$10,000,000 initially and a yearly rental of $250,000 to begin in 1912. In addition the United States had a unilateral right to requisition further territory as the canal operation might require it, and the unilateral right to intervene and supersede the Panamanian authorities in control of water, sewage, and public health programs of Colón and Panama City. The United States also had a right to intervene in Panama to restore or preserve order whenever it might deem it necessary for the security of the canal.[10] To those North Americans who felt squeamish about "imperialism" this treaty seemed to exceed anything ever done by the European powers in Asia and Africa. Even the Panamanians were shocked. President Amador himself hurried to Washington only to find that his "honorary" Panamanian minister had settled everything in record time. There was little that the isthmian republic could do but ratify the treaty, which it did on December 2.[11]

The Democratic party, outraged anti-imperialists, and devotees of classical international relations upset by the Hay–Bunau-Varilla "negotiations" rallied to the side of Senator Morgan. The *New York World* led the newspaper assault. The "criminal aggression" against little Colombia was condemned as much in this country as in the rest of the world. A wave of "Yanquiphobia" swept Latin America and there were few approving voices in Europe outside of Britain.

Southern Democrats, particularly, injected intense feelings into the bitter controversy. They had believed that the Nicaragua canal would be a great advantage to the South. A letter to Senator Morgan illustrates the violent language which came from this sector: ". . . the high handed and treacherous action of the CREATURE now occupying the Presidency in adopting the Panama route . . ."[12]

The debate filled three hundred pages of the *Congressional Record* before it was over. The most sensational stories were bandied about in the press. The *New York World* charged that a syndicate of stock gamblers had formed around Bunau-Varilla and had manipulated the shares of the Panama Canal Company to make themselves a $4,000,000 profit. This sum was in addition to the $40,000,000 which the United States government paid the company for its rights, property, and equipment on the isthmus. No one has ever verified the truth or falseness of this report but the *World* did acknowledge years later that its source of information was an employee in the office of William N. Cromwell.[13]

The fight often threatened to transcend party lines, and Mr. Roosevelt wrote to his son on December 15, 1903:

> I have had a most interesting time about Panama and Colombia. My experiences in all these matters give me an idea of the fearful times Lincoln must have had in dealing with the great crises he had to face. When I see how panic struck the Senators, business men, and everybody else become from my little flurry of trouble, and the wild clamor they all raise for foolish or cowardly action I get an idea of what he had to stand for . . . . Why, even in this Panama business the [New York] Evening Post and this entire fool Mugwump crowd have fairly suffered from hysterics, and a goodly number of Senators even of my own party have shown about as much backbone as so many angle worms . . .[14]

The keenest observation was made by the saddened Colombian minister, Dr. Herrán who lingered on in Washington even though his government had recalled him. He wrote his estimate of the situation on several occasions:

> . . . The debates will be long and heated, but there is no doubt that the treaty will be finally approved; since the opposition does not propose to reject that one sided treaty but rather to discredit Roosevelt as much as possible in order to deprive him of the presidential nomination to which he is aspiring . . .

> . . . some of the most vehement men in the opposition have declared that in the end they will approve the treaty, because they desire to assure the construction of the canal, but they want to put in evidence the fact that Roosevelt is responsible for the iniquities committed in the Isthmus, and that his re-election for the next term would be a threat to the country. They are not thinking of repairing the damages but simply of placing the blame on Roosevelt . . .[15]

Every conceivable issue was dragged into the debate. Ironically, Senator Morgan even introduced an amendment calling for the outright annexation of Panama. When one considers the violence of the opposition and the fact that a two-thirds majority was necessary to ratify it, it is somewhat surprising that the treaty was accepted. The very extreme nature of the attacks on the treaty probably aided its ultimate acceptance because the moderates retreated when the abuse reached extreme proportions. Many senators, after hearing from their constituencies, realized that the country was largely behind the president and that the general public admired rather than condemned Roosevelt's bold and forward methods. Even though popular election of U.S. senators was not yet practiced many of them were extremely sensitive to public opinion especially since the election of 1904 was drawing near.

Most Republican senators became convinced that, as a matter of party policy, they should support the president. The presence of colorful Democrats such as Morgan, Garmack, and Gorman as leaders of the opposition tended to make the issue a party matter. Senators Hanna, Spooner, Depew, and Lodge worked night and day to hold the Republican forces in line. Senator Hanna became ill and died in the midst of the debate, on February 16, 1904, but by then the tide of opinion was running in favor of the treaty. The country was simply in no mood to see the canal, now within the grasp of the United States, lost because of personal antipathies to the president or opposition to the methods which he had employed.

The Democratic position wavered when the legislatures of Louisiana and Mississippi passed resolutions calling on their senators to support the treaty.[16] Now even Senator Morgan freely admitted that he was for *any* canal, even a Panama canal, in preference to no canal at all. The Republican Steering Committee pressed the issue to a vote on February 23 and the treaty was ratified without any amendments by a count of 66 to 14.[17] The long "battle of the routes" was over, but its repercussions were to last for many years. Senator Morgan actually took a great interest in the Panama Canal after its construction, but he continued to denounce the method by which it was achieved. The election of 1904 serves as the final demonstration that the will of the people had crystallized in favor of the treaty despite the sound and fury. It might be supposed that the Democratic party would have made an issue of President Roosevelt's conduct, but the plank in their 1904 platform on imperialism makes no mention of the Caribbean. From what they had to say about the isthmian canal an uninformed person might suppose that they had always battled for the Panama route: "The Democracy when entrusted with power will construct the Panama Canal speedily, honestly, and economically, thereby giving to our people what Democrats have always contended for—a great interoceanic canal, furnishing shorter and cheaper lines of transportation, and broader and less trammeled trade relations with the other peoples of the world." The Republicans naturally pointed out that:

> The possession of a route for an isthmian canal, so long the dream of American statesmanship, is now an accomplished fact. The great work of connecting the Pacific and Atlantic by a canal is at last begun, and it is due to the Republican Party.

> Our foreign policy under his [Roosevelt's] administration has not only been able, vigorous, and dignified, but in the highest degree successful . . .

> His prompt and vigorous action in Panama, which we commend in the highest terms, not only secured to us the canal route, but avoided foreign complications which might have been of a very serious character.

During Roosevelt's second administration the work of digging the canal went forward. It was a very politically conscious administration and everybody who had any appreciable measure of influence in Washington wanted a "Cook's Tour" to the isthmus, so that they could poke about, give suggestions, and generally make a nuisance of themselves.[18] Not the least among these offenders was the colorful TR himself. His first trip to the isthmus resulted in a flag-waving carnival which brought most productive work on the canal itself to a stop during his grand tour. He spoke in campaign style from the rear platform of his special train. His audience of several hundred contained virtually every North American on the isthmus. Despite a typical downpour of rain, they cheered the famous Roosevelt smile and listened with rapt attention to his salute to them:

> You are doing the biggest thing of the kind that has ever been done here, and I wanted to see how you are doing it. . . . As I have seen you at work, seen what you have done and are doing, noted the spirit with which you are approaching the task, I have felt just exactly as I should feel if I saw the picked men of my country

engaged in some great war. I am weighing my words when I say that you, here, who do your work will stand exactly as the soldiers of a few, and only a few, of the most famous armies in all the nations stand in history. This is one of the great works of the world. It is greater work than you, yourselves, at the moment realize. ... You men here, in the future, each man of you, will have the right to feel, if he has done his duty—and a little more than his duty right up to the handle—in the work here on the isthmus, that he has made his country his debtor, that he has done more than his full share in adding renown to the nation under whose flag this canal is being built.[19]

During his stay on the isthmus Mr. Roosevelt did have impressed upon him the absurd situation of the operation being directed by the Isthmian Canal Commission, most of whose seven members stayed in Washington, D.C. When he returned to Washington he contrived diplomatically to get the commissioners to resign and then simply failed to reappoint their successors, leaving the chief engineer, Mr. Stevens on the isthmus, as the sole remaining commissioner and therefore the undisputed single authority. When things were running smoothly the president then "packed" the commission with five army and navy officers and two civilians. This was the so-called "Shonts Commission," named after Theodore Shonts, a railroad executive who was the first civilian chairman of the initial Canal Commission. The military majority, who of course took orders unquestioningly, assured harmonious action.[20]

During the weeks of planning for the president's visit the sort of toadying for favor which surrounds every North American chief executive brought about the suspension of work on the canal so that all efforts could be channeled into completing the Hotel Tivoli in Ancon in order to provide suitable accommodations for the president of the United States. In Washington as appropriations were voted for the various phases of canal construction, all sorts of political favors were traded to insure the industries in each state their share of canal contracts. It is believed that the great civilian engineer, John Stevens, resigned because of the constant harrassment of self-appointed Congressional inspectors, although he never gave any public reason for leaving. His successor, Colonel George W. Goethals, was an army officer who managed to handle both the public relations and the construction aspects of his job quite well, and under him the canal was completed.

Roosevelt's secretary of war, William Howard Taft, was very closely involved with the canal and made a number of trips to the isthmus. When he became the Republican nominee for president in 1908 it seemed that the canal policies and the role of the Roosevelt administration in the Caribbean would continue smoothly if he were elected. The party platforms in 1908 were not particularly partisan on the subject of the canal. The Democrats simply declared that they believed the canal would prove of great value to the country and that they favored its speedy completion. The Republicans were very proud:

> The American Government, in Republican hands . . . has begun the construction of the Panama Canal.

> Time has justified the selection of the Panama route for the great isthmian canal, and events have shown the wisdom of securing authority over the zone through which it is to be built. The work is now progressing with a rapidity far beyond expectation, and already the realization of the hopes of centuries has come within the vision of the near future.

In contrast to the mild dismissal of Panama in their platform was the action of Democratic leaders during the campaign in attempting to smear nominee Taft with some of the "scandal" connected with the French canal company's sale of its assets to the United States. On October 3, 1908, the *New York World* published a story that Cromwell and Bunau-Varilla had purchased the stock and bonds of the defunct de Lesseps company for about $36,500,000 and had formed a syndicate which resold it to the United States government at $40,000,000 to make a profit of $3,500,000. Charles P. Taft, brother of the presidential candidate was declared to have been a member of the syndicate, along with other "insiders" in Washington and New York. Cromwell issued an immediate denial that such a syndicate had ever existed, ". . . no member of the Taft family . . . ever had the remotest connection with Panama. . . . The names of Caesar or Napoleon might as well have been used . . ."[21]

The *World* combed the United States and France to trace distribution of the $40,000,000 and prove their case. They kept the matter before the public by demanding a congressional investigation and issuing five more articles which were reprinted in other newspapers in various cities. They also accused Douglas Robinson, President Roosevelt's cousin, of being connected with the syndicate. The Democratic floor leader of the House of Representatives, Henry T. Rainey of Illinois, announced that he would demand a full congressional inquiry as soon as Congress convened in December. On the eve of the election the *Indianapolis News* carried a flaming editorial asking, "Who got the Forty Million?" There was a clear effect in the Indiana voting. Taft slipped through to get the state's electoral vote but most of the top candidates on the Democratic state ticket were elected.

Mr. Taft had been Roosevelt's hand-picked successor. T.R. had personally managed the campaign. He felt a deep sense of personal outrage. He declared that the editorials and articles were both scandalous and infamous, and that the money had been paid to the French government for further distribution to the company's shareholders. *The World* then said, in effect, that Mr. Roosevelt was not telling the truth and again demanded a congressional investigation.

The election had resulted in a substantial victory for Taft; T.R. felt sure of himself. On December 15, 1908, he sent a special message to Congress declaring that he had instructed the attorney general, Charles J. Bonaparte, to institute criminal libel proceedings against the *World* and the *News*:

> It is idle to say that the known character of Mr. Pulitzer [publisher of the *World*] and his newspapers are such that the statements in that paper will be believed by nobody; unfortunately thousands of persons . . . believe . . . even . . . a newspaper published by Mr. Pulitzer. . . . The wickedness of the slanders is surpassed only by their fatuity . . . In form they are in part libels upon . . . Mr. Taft and Mr. Robinson. . . . But they are in fact wholly, and in form partly, a libel upon the United States Government. . . . It should not be left to a private citizen to sue Mr. Pulitzer for libel. He should be prosecuted by the governmental authorities.[22]

The matter went to the grand jury in the District of Colombia, and on February 17, 1909, indictments were returned against Pulitzer, his news editors on the *World*, the Press Publishing Company, and Delavan Smith and C. R. Williams, owners of the *Indianapolis News*. The government failed in proceedings to bring Smith and Williams to Washington for trial and a federal judge in Indianapolis discharged them.[23] Then the attorney general dropped the District of Columbia proceedings altogether and the indictments were dismissed. As Mr. Taft was being sworn in on March 4, 1909 in Washington, the Federal Grand Jury for the Southern District of New York indicted the Press Publishing Company and news editor Caleb von Hamm for circulating the "libelous" papers on "Federal reservations," specifically the grounds of the military academy at West Point and the New York City post office. When the case came to trial the defense moved for dismissal on the ground that the charges were violations of state law and that the federal court therefore did not have jurisdiction. The trial judge granted this motion. The government appealed the ruling to the United States Supreme Court. The high tribunal unanimously affirmed the dismissal on January 3, 1911.[24]

This affair was an ill-advised proceeding and when the legalistics are eliminated it is clear that the real issue was the historical precedent which reaffirmed the principle of freedom of the press. Taft, Robinson, and Cromwell had had a remedy available to them in the civil law of libel. But the federal government's entrance into the case and its adoption of criminal proceedings smacked of persecution and Old World autocracy. The *New York World* of course gloated over its victory:

> . . . the effort to revive the spirit of the alien and sedition laws, to establish the doctrine of lèse majesté has come to an inglorious end. . . . The decision of the Supreme Court . . . while safeguarding the liberty of the press . . . yet leaves unanswered the question: "Who got the money!" . . .[25]

One rumor has a way of leading to others. Those who had opposed the Panama route were loathe to accept it. There were whispered attacks upon the men and the methods used on the construction project. Grotesque rumors about obstacles to building progress were spread in 1908 and 1909. One story told of the discovery of an underground lake beneath Gatun Dam which would render that vital project an engineering impossibility.[26] This was obviously untrue.

President-elect Taft visited the Canal Zone in January and February, 1909. On his way back to Washington he decided to speak out in the heart of the Democratic solid South in an effort to stop this whispering campaign. In a speech delivered at Meriden, Mississippi, he said, "I don't care whether you are Democrats or Republicans, you want the work done . . . you are not men to go back on the Army engineers or believe every idle story that comes from the mouth of some politician who is seeking to make himself prominent or give himself the advantage of a little unfounded sensational statement."[27]

The South, as has been noted, had been intensely devoted to the Nicaraguan route, but that was now a battle lost. President Taft was couching his appeal in the appropriate terms. There is no better proof to be found than in the words of the South's great statesman who fought so well in the losing fight. Senator John Morgan wrote:

> . . . You know that our Southern States are still buried under the ashes of the great civil war, and that an isthmian canal is the best, if not the only hope of lifting them above this debris, through the energies of production and through commercial intercourse with the Pacific Ocean.
>
> The selection of a route is a secondary consideration provided the conditions are equally favorable to all concerned.[28]

It was perhaps most fitting, after the intensity of the partisan battles, that each of the major U.S. political parties had had a turn at power during the building the Panama Canal. The great project, which was conceived and begun under a Republican administration, was completed and opened to the commerce of the world under a Democratic administration in 1914.

7

The Rainey Committee and the Thomson-Urrutia Convention

During the Taft administration the United States turned its attention once again to Nicaragua. This interest was partly due to its canal potentialities, but mainly due to the dollar diplomacy which has come to be particularly identified with Taft's Caribbean policies.[1] The Nicaraguan dictator, José Santos Zelaya, had ambitions to unite all of Central America under his domination. He resented the influence of the United States in the area and he was hostile to North American interests which had put heavy investments into Nicaragua. He was suspected by Taft and his secretary of state, Philander Knox, of harboring a scheme to give a canal concession to the Germans as a counterpoise to our project in Panama. The execution of two U.S. citizens who were part of a force of rebels operating against Zelaya was Taft's pretext for landing the marines in Nicaragua. One of the insurgent leaders, Adolfo Díaz, was then recognized as president by the United States.

Thus began an occupation of Nicaragua by U.S. forces which lasted almost without interruption until 1933. During that time, the United States "supervised" Nicaraguan elections and maintained "constitutional" governments in power. During this period North American investors in the country received stabilized returns from their investments. Toward the end of the Taft administration Secretary Knox negotiated a treaty which was to pay Nicaragua $3,000,000 for the canal rights so that any possibility of legal German penetration would be frustrated. The United States was to acquire not only exclusive canal rights but also ninety-nine–year leases on bases at the Atlantic and Pacific terminals.[2] This treaty was still before the Senate when the swing of the political pendulum brought the Democrats back with Woodrow Wilson.

The Democratic platform in 1912 had been silent on the Taft-Knox imperial incursions in the Caribbean but President Wilson had indicated his personal disapproval of dollar diplomacy in a speech at Mobile,[3] and it was expected that a new approach to Central American problems might be made. Secretary of State Bryan did come forth with a new idea—that private investments be replaced with direct inter-governmental loans. Wilson saw that such a notion would not endear North Americans any more to Latin Americans than the familiar "flag following the dollar." It would mean only that the flag walked in side by side with the dollar. Consequently the Wilson administration continued the Taft program of military occupation to guarantee private investment. Knox's unratified canal treaty was passed as the Bryan-Chamorro Treaty in 1916.[4] In return for $3,000,000 the United States received perpetual rights to the Nicaragua canal route. The United States still holds these rights but the $3,000,000 soon went down the drain of Nicaraguan financial instability. Dollar diplomacy was mitigated by removing North American bankers from the near absolute control of Nicaragua's finances which they had held for several years. A new Joint High Financial Commission was given supervisory authority over the republic's fiscal affairs. Its members were experts appointed by the Nicaraguan government and approved by the United States. Most of them were U.S. citizens but they represented the political authority of both countries rather than the interests of private investors. The plan worked fairly well as long as U.S. troops were stationed in Nicaragua but when they were withdrawn in 1925 the country almost immediately lapsed back into financial and political chaos.

Panama was also in the news, not only because of the opening of the canal and the Panama Canal Exposition at San Francisco but because the war of words was resumed over Roosevelt's taking of the isthmus. This struggle began as soon as the Democrats won control of the House of Representatives in the midterm elections of 1910. Thus Henry T. Rainey found himself in a position to push the congressional investigation of the Roosevelt administration's "misdeeds" which he had promised at the time of the *New York World's* sensational charges during the campaign of 1908. Theodore Roosevelt himself set the stage for the ensuing furor when he appeared at the University of

California for the Charter Day Address, on March 23, 1911, and made the following statement:

> The Panama Canal I naturally take special interest in because I started it. There are plenty of other things I started merely because the time had come that whoever was in power would have started them. But the Panama Canal would not have been started if I had not taken hold of it, because if I had followed the traditional or conservative method I should have submitted an admirable state paper occupying a couple of hundred pages detailing all of the facts to Congress and asking Congress' consideration of it.
>
> In that case there would have been a number of excellent speeches made on the subject in Congress; the debate would be proceeding at this moment with great spirit and the beginning of work on the canal would be fifty years in the future. Fortunately the crisis came at a period when I could act unhampered. Accordingly I took the isthmus, started the canal, and then left Congress not to debate the canal, but to debate me.
>
> In portions of the public press the debate still goes on as to whether or not I acted properly in taking the canal. But while the debate goes on the canal does too, and they are welcome to debate me as long as they wish, provided that we can go on with the canal.[5]

This statement was seized upon by all of Roosevelt's opponents as a "confession" that his administration had staged the Panamanian Revolution of 1903. Quite naturally the Colombian minister in Washington joined the hue and cry and declared that Roosevelt's "confession" of misdeeds proved his country's just claim for "satisfaction."[6] On April 6, 1911, Congressman Rainey introduced his long threatened resolution calling for an investigation.[7] It was referred to the House Committee on Foreign Affairs and the Democratic-controlled committee began its hearings. The party press was in full support and declared that the "shabby and shady" procedures would now be exposed in full.

The key witness was Henry N. Hall, a staff correspondent of the *New York World*. He had been involved in several "fact-finding" trips abroad at the time the *World* was preparing its defense in the libel cases in 1909. Congressman Rainey, acting as a sort of "prosecutor" made a speech at a public hearing of the committee on January 26, 1912 asserting:

Representatives of this government made possible the revolution on the isthmus. I will . . . show that the declaration of (Panama) independence was prepared . . . in the office of Cromwell. I will show you that our State Department was cognizant of the fact that a revolution was to occur on the third day of November, 1903. . . . My contention is that the part we played for months prior to the revolution . . . is a stain upon the history of this government.[8]

Cromwell must have been flattered by such extravagent denunciation. He shared with Theodore Roosevelt the doubtful honor of being branded as an international freebooter. Roosevelt, of course, inspired the more colorful epithets. One writer, for example, described the ex-president as one who hurried "with Tarquin's ravishing strides to make irrevocable Colombia's dismemberment."[9] Rainey declared that Cromwell was "the most dangerous man the country has produced since Aaron Burr," and a *New York World* reporter was quoted as describing the barrister as a virtual demi-god of "subtle force."[10] Rainey repeated the old charge that the plank in the 1900 Republican platform, which merely called for an "isthmian" rather than a "Nicaraguan" canal, had been bought and paid for by Cromwell's $60,000 campaign contribution. The story of the Franco-American "syndicate" and the alleged $3,500,000 profit was hashed over. The source of this story was probably one of Mr. Cromwell's press agents, Jonas Whitley, whose name recurs throughout the testimony. There is reason to believe that he was a *World* agent planted in Cromwell's office. To this day no evidence has ever been made public to prove or disprove the allegations about this syndicate with any objective finality.

The committee poured over state department papers and navy archives and examined scores of witnesses. The bulky collection of testimony and documentary evidence which it brought together[11] serves as a source of quasi-official character to substantiate a point of view aptly stated by Gerstle Mack: ". . . the people of the United States have every reason to rejoice in the Panama Canal as it exists today, but they have less cause to pride themselves upon the method of its acquisition."[12]

The Rainey Report became a justification for the Democratic party policy which claimed that Colombia had a legitimate grievance against the United States. When President Wilson took office, his party gained full control of all branches of the federal government, and an immediate effort was made to reconcile United States–Colombian relations. On June 10, 1913, Thaddeus A. Thomson was sent to Bogotá as the new minister. His instructions from Secretary of State Bryan were to seek a favorable adjustment of the dispute.[13]

The Taft administration had made one rather half-hearted attempt to mollify Colombia when it negotiated a tri-partite treaty, which included Panama. Panama was to turn over to Colombia the first ten of its canal annuities and Colombia was to have free transit of the waterway for its troops, munitions, and warships. This pact[14] was ratified by the United States Senate on February 24, 1909, but it was received with indignation in Bogotá. The Colombian Senate howled it down and there was so much feeling against the Colombian president, Rafael Reyes, for committing his administration to such a national insult that he resigned in order to forestall a revolution.

Mr. Thomson and Colombian Foreign Minister Urrutia brought forth a very different kind of an agreement. It contained an unprecedented act of contrition for a great power such as the United States, as may be seen from the following language of the first article:

> The Government of the United States of America, desirous of putting an end to all the controversies and differences with the Republic of Colombia arising from the events which originated the present situation on the Isthmus of Panama, in its own name and in the name of the people of the United States expresses sincere regret for anything which may have occurred to interrupt or to alter the relations of cordial friendship which for so long a time existed between the two nations. The Government of Colombia, in its own name and in the name of the Colombian people, accepts this declaration, in the full assurance that thus will disappear every obstacle to the reestablishment of a complete hamony between the two countries.

In addition to this apology the United States agreed to pay to Colombia the sum of $25,000,000 for the release of all claims.[15]

Ex-President Theodore Roosevelt was enraged at this reflection upon his administration. He denounced the convention as a "blackmail treaty" in a magazine article in 1915 while the Senate debated ratification.[16] The Republican members of the Senate rallied to his view. Despite Mr. Roosevelt's Bull Moose defection of 1912 and its bitter aftermath, TR had been a Republican president back in 1903. A repudiation of his acts as such would amount to condemnation of the Republican past as well.

The debate in the Senate was echoed about the country in numerous books, newspapers, and magazine articles. One of the most merciless attacks upon Roosevelt was made by an erstwhile firm supporter of his in the Progressive Bull Moose movement of 1912, Joseph G. Freehoff. Freehoff, still a registered member of the Progressive Party wrote: "Our government took the Canal Zone from Colombia at the point of a bayonet. It was unwilling to pay the price determined by due process of law. Our title is therefore stolen."[17]

The Colombian Congress approved the treaty on June 9, 1914. The prolonged hassle in the Senate in Washington embarrassed the Wilson administration throughout Latin America. The Democrats controlled the Senate but they did not have anything near the two-thirds majority necessary to ratify the treaty. The Republicans presented a solid phalanx of opposition. Against the backdrop of the tangled web of North American relations with Mexico, Nicaragua, and Haiti during this administration the Latin American anti-*gringo* zealots had a perfect talking point. *Imperialismo Yanqui* was the same whether Republicans or Democrats held power in Washington.[18] President Wilson assured Betancourt, Colombian minister in Washington, that he was doing all in his power to actuate the treaty. He did exert every influence, for seven years, without success.[19] Roosevelt was the spokesman for the Republican minority: "The proposed treaty is a crime against the United States which, if justified, would convict the United States of infamy. It is a menace to the future well being of our people . . . The payment can only be justified on the ground that this nation has played the part of a thief, or of a receiver of stolen goods."[20]

One of the interesting sidelights of this struggle is the apparent viewpoint of many, perhaps most, of the members of Roosevelt's Progressive Party. Freehoff agreed with the noted writer Mark Twain who said, "Whenever as a rule I meet Roosevelt the statesman and politician I find him destitute of morals and not respectworthy. It is plain that where his political self and party self are concerned he has nothing resembling a conscience."[21]

Had the Progressives had representation in the Senate in proportion to the vote which they polled in 1912, or even in the midterm elections of 1914, they might have been able to combine with the Democratic majority to give the treaty its two-thirds vote. But unfortunately much of the Progressive vote had been wasted in those elections because of poor organization at the grass roots. By 1916 many of the Progressives were ready to move into the Democratic Party and there is no question but that they contributed to Wilson's re-election in an important way.[22] Roosevelt on the other hand found that the common ground which he shared with the Republican leadership on the Thomson-Urrutia fight helped to ease his re-entry into the party.

Roosevelt's attack upon the treaty had one very ironic sidelight. Just about this time the former president was being very outspoken in his condemnation of the methods employed by the central European powers, particularly Germany in the alleged "rape of Belgium." The German General von Bernhardi and the Austrian Baron von Hengelmuller did not neglect this opportunity to try to counter Roosevelt's pro-Allied efforts in this country. They used his magazine article to draw analogies between the invasion of Belgium and the U.S. seizure of Panama on the principle that the "interests of the American people are higher and greater than abstract principles of international law." They declared that the same fundamental viewpoints motivated the German action in Belgium. Roosevelt had a quick answer to this line, but showed his discomfiture: "To talk of Colombia as a responsible power to be dealt with as we would deal with Holland or Belgium or Switzerland or Denmark is a mere absurdity. The analogy is with a group of Sicilian or Calabrian bandits: with Villa and Carranza at this moment. You could no more make an agreement with the Colombian rulers than you could nail currant jelly to a wall . . ."[23]

The *New York World* chortled over this exchange and threw its editorial barbs in the direction of its old enemy: "The hair shirt thus presented to Colonel Roosevelt seems to us to be a very snug fit, and we trust that he is having a "bully time" wearing it!"

The deepening crisis which finally involved the United States in the First World War gradually overshadowed discussion of the Thomson-Urrutia Treaty. In 1916 the Foreign Relations Committee recommended that the apology clause be altered to make the expression of regret for past misdeeds a mutual acknowledgement by both Colombia and the United States, but Colombia made it clear that she would not accept such an alteration.

In January, 1919 Theodore Roosevelt died suddenly and unexpectedly at Oyster Bay, and the great voice most capable of continuing the protest against Colombian indemnification was stilled. President Wilson had moved soon after the armistice to resurrect the treaty and get it passed. Many hoped that this might be done now with Roosevelt dead. The Republicans organized the Senate after the mid-term elections of 1918 and they still refused to ratify the treaty with the original language of apology.

The Republican leadership was now influenced by an entirely new consideration. The Thomson-Urrutia Treaty suddenly acquired value in the eyes of North American business interests. During World War I, certain U.S. oil interests had obtained important concessions in nearby Venezuela and there were hopes that Colombia might also have productive fields. The elections of 1920 returned the Republican Party to power in all branches of the government. People like Fall, Doheny, and Sinclair had great influence with the new Harding administration. It was imperative for their interests that a new climate of opinion exist toward the Yanquis in northern South America. Amity with the Bogotá government became their cherished aim.[24]

On July 29, 1919, the Senate Committee on Foreign Affairs, under Republican control, had reported the treaty out favorably with the "sincere regret" clause deleted as a sop to the memory of TR. It now became the job of the Harding Administration to convince Colombia that the $25,000,000 indemnity was sufficient balm. The situation in Bogotá was touchy for a time and United States oil men nervously put on more pressure as the Colombians threatened to expropriate oil fields to public ownership. But diplomacy finally succeeded. Colombian officials found the $25,000,000 attractive in the light of post-war economic difficulties which plagued South America. The indemnity was more important after all, they reasoned, than the flattering, but unsubstantial apology. And the whole world would know that the *gringos* were admitting their guilt by the mere act of paying an indemnity. Indemnities are not paid for innocence.

On December 24, 1921, Colombia agreed to the revision of the treaty striking out the words of apology, and the treaty was proclaimed in effect on March 1, 1922.[25] So ended more than seven years of partisan bickering, and the debate over the Panama Revolution thereafter belonged to the pages of history alone.

During Wilson's administration the isthmian canal was the cause of one other controversy which had some partisan overtones. This was the matter of tolls to be levied for use of the waterway. The party platforms of 1912 had taken note of this question. The Democrats said:

> We favor the exemption from tolls of Amercan ships engaged in coastwise trade passing through the Panama Canal.

We also favor legislation forbidding the use of the Panama
Canal by ships owned or controlled by railroad carriers engaged
in transportation competitive with the canal.

The Progressive Party used stronger language:

The Panama Canal, built and paid for by the American people,
must be used primarily for their benefit.

We demand that the canal shall be so operated as to break
the transportation monopoly now held and misused by the transcontinental railroads by maintaining sea competition with them;
that ships directly or indirectly owned or controlled by American
railroad corporations shall not be permitted to use the canal, and
that American ships engaged in coastwise trade shall pay no tolls.

The Progressive Party will favor legislation having for its
aim the development of friendship and commerce between the
United States and Latin American nations.

In 1912 as the canal approached completion, Congress had passed
a law containing a schedule of tolls for vessels using the canal. This
law had specifically provided that U.S. vessels engaged in coastwise
or intercoastal trade should be exempt from charges.[26] The British insisted that this provision was contrary to U.S. commitments under the
Hay-Pauncefote Treaty and that by that convention the canal was to
be open to "British and American vessels upon terms of equal treatment."[27] The treaty had also said that "all nations" would be charged
the same rates.

The outgoing Taft Administration had turned aside the British
protest with the reply that the question was as yet academic because
the canal was not open to traffic. The issue thus carried into the elections in 1912 and President Wilson felt bound to a degree by the
Democratic platform. His position was also affected by the strong
Progressive platform since he intended to try to win support from that
party. Finally there was a powerful Irish-American element within the
Democratic Party. Headed by Senator O'Gorman of New York, this
element was determined to see that England got nowhere in pressing
its claim.

Former Secretary of State Elihu Root and Joseph H. Choate, who
had helped negotiate the Hay-Pauncefote Treaty, represented a responsible Republican viewpoint. They felt that the United States had given
its word in the terms of the treaty, and Mr. Root further declared that

it should not have acquired rights upon the isthmus by acting upon one theory, and "having got them, hold them on the contrary theory." These two gentlemen met with President-elect Wilson in New York on January 24, 1913, and convinced him that their position was right. He hesitated to act on this position after taking office because of the political considerations already discussed. A year went by before he finally acted on it. He was probably influenced to do so by reports which he got from Walter Hines Page, his ambassador in London: ". . . and everywhere—in circles most friendly to us, and the best informed,—I receive commiseration because of the dishonorable attitude of our Government about the Panama Canal tolls. This, I confess, is hard to meet. We made a bargain—a solemn compact—and we have broken it. Whether it were a good bargain or a bad one, a silly one or a wise one, that's far from the point."[28] The President announced that he favored repeal of the tolls exemption in a message to Congress on March 5, 1914:

> . . . [it] constitutes a mistaken economic policy from every point of view, and is, moreover, in plain contravention of the treaty with Great Britain. . . . The large thing to do is the only thing we can afford to do, a voluntary withdrawal from a position everywhere questioned and misunderstood. We ought to reverse our action without raising the question whether we were right or wrong. . . . Whatever may be our own differences of opinion concerning this much debated measure, its meaning is not debated outside the United States. We . . . are . . . too big, too powerful, too self-respecting a nation to interpret with too strained or refined a reading the words of our own promises just because we have power enough to give us leave to read them as we please . . ."[29]

The anti-British Hearst newspapers led the assault on the president's position which the Irish-American elements in the Democratic Party also assailed. Wilson was embarrassed by the contrast between the strong Republican support of his stand and the opposition of a large segment of his own party. The president was also chagrined when railroad interests supported his stand. Their purposes were purely selfish because they wanted their waterborne competitors to have to bear the added expense of the tolls. Much of the Progressive position on the tolls question had been due to the animosity toward railroads that was always a cornerstone of "reform" movements in the early years of the twentieth century. In England Ambassador Page and the president's advisor, Colonel Edward M. House, counseled the British not to press the matter and to try to restrain their press in order not to give ammunition to the Anglophobes in the United States.

Nevertheless, Wilson was lampooned in the U.S. jingoistic press of the United States as an Ichabod Crane type of "professor" assiduously courting Britannia and licking the boots of Papa John Bull.[30]

Because the administration used the patronage whip, party lines held sufficiently to put the repealer over in the House. In the Senate there was Republican help to offset the defection of O'Gorman and others. On June 11, 1914, in a turbulent session that was enlivened by some very passionate oratory the upper chamber passed the bill 50 to 35.[31] Thus an act of national dishonor, which the *New York Nation* said would have been a greater disgrace than a naval defeat in the waters off Panama, was averted. The Senate did add a proviso that the act was not to be construed as a waiver or relinquishment of any right:

> . . . to discriminate in favor of its vessels by exempting the vessels of the United States or its citizens from the payment of tolls for passage through said canal, or as in any way waiving, impairing, or affecting any right of the United States . . . with respect to the sovereignty over or the ownership, control, and management of said canal and the regulations of the conditions or charges of traffic through the same.

This proviso was ignored by the administration, which was happy that the substance of its recommendation, the immediate repeal of the existing exemption, had been passed. Since the opening of the canal, North American ships have paid tolls on the same basis as all others transiting the waterway.[32]

8

A Yanqui Monument
in Latin America

The isthmian canal has been a reality now for more than half a century. The Canal Zone around it has become an island of Yanqui life in the Latin American hemisphere.[1] Its relationship to the continental United States is as well defined and vital, in the opinion of its resident "zonians," as that of Alaska or Hawaii. The Zone has all the aspect of a landscaped suburb in southern California. Its white and cream stucco houses, trim green lawns, and tree-shaded and well kept roadways give it a modern aspect which contrasts sharply with the old, thick-walled buildings and narrow streets of Panama City or Colón in the neighboring republic. Generations of North Americans have grown up in this transplanted civilization. It is not at all unusual to find U.S. citizens who were born in Panama, have lived all of their lives there, and yet are unable to speak or understand Spanish. They have their bridge clubs, their lodge meetings, their high school plays, their interest in stateside politics and sports, and are as thoroughly Yanqui as any citizen of Columbus, Ohio or Phoenix, Arizona. The enclave which they have created is a proper source of pride for them and their country, but it is also a continuing problem for the United States.

The people of the Republic of Panama are proud and patriotic too. There are many among them who regard the canal as a mixed blessing. Their sense of national pride is galled by the memory of the Frenchman, Bunau-Varilla, who negotiated the treaty which allowed the Yanquis to carve the Canal Zone out of their country. They feel that they are not getting the share of the economic return from the canal which is theirs by virtue of proprietary ownership. They have long been distressed by the North American exercise of sovereign power within the Canal Zone. They sometimes say that Bunau-Varilla sold their birthright for a "mess of pottage." This feeling has always been hard for citizens of the United States to grasp, for they have been exhilarated by the accomplishment of building the canal. They have had some twinges of conscience about their acquisition of the Canal Zone, but these were quickly submerged in the surge of "manifest destiny" nationalism which emphasized the great value of the canal to America and to the world. The Yanquis, however, have failed to understand that another people might also be guided by national pride, and guided in an entirely different direction. It is little wonder that Panama was always a prize exhibit in the portfolios of those who damned the *imperialismo Yanqui* during the years of the Roosevelt corollaries, the "big stick," and dollar diplomacy.

The return of the Democratic party to power in 1933 served to accelerate a change in Latin American policy which had made a slow beginning under President Herbert Hoover. The "big stick" and dollar diplomacy gave way to the Good Neighbor Policy and the Doctrine of Absolute Non-Intervention. No state in the western hemisphere has had more reason to be thankful for this change than Panama. The United States demonstrated its good faith the very year the protocol of Absolute Non-Intervention was signed at Buenos Aires.[2] This demonstration came in the Hull-Alfaro Treaty of 1936.

By this convention the United States agreed to very substantial modifications of the Hay–Bunau-Varilla Treaty by relinquishing its unilateral right to expropriate further Panamanian territory and to "preserve order" within the republic. It also increased the annual rental payments to Panama for the Zone.[3] The treaty was greeted with acclaim in Panama and local editorials hailed Franklin D. Roosevelt as recognizing the republic's rise to manhood among the nations just as another Roosevelt had "assisted at the birth" of the nation. Speaking of these concessions the *Christian Century* said, "The new treaty, added to the payment made Colombia [by the Thomson-Urrutia Convention], goes about as far as legal devices can to heal the last wounds inflicted by the elder Roosevelt's impetuous method of clearing the way for the building of the isthmian canal."[4]

But there were to be many more concessions. In 1948 the United States withdrew its forces from bases outside the Canal Zone which had been granted to it during World War II. The grant had been "for not more than one year after hostilities shall cease." The United States asked for an extension, and when the Panamanian National Assembly refused to grant it, the North Americans left even though the move meant the abandonment of millions of dollars worth of installations to the jungle.[5]

The Republican administration of President Eisenhower proved to be just as eager to cooperate as Democrats Roosevelt and Truman. On January 25, 1955, a new Panama-United States Treaty of Mutual Understanding and Cooperation became effective. Known as the Chapin-Fabrega Treaty, it allowed Panama to impose income taxes upon its citizens who worked for the United States but had previously been out of reach of Panamanian jurisdiction because they resided within the Canal Zone. It also allowed Panama to levy import duties on goods landed within the Zone but destined for consignees within the republic.[6] In 1960 the Panamanian flag was hoisted beside U.S. national colors at Balboa Heights.

This twenty-year record of concessions was imposing, but it did not satisfy Panamanian nationalism. The action of Egyptian President Gamul Nasser in successfully expelling Britain and seizing and operating the Suez Canal fired some zealots and even the moderates on the isthmus with the idea that Panama should do the same.

In 1958 when Dr. Milton Eisenhower, the president's brother, made a fact-finding, good will tour of the isthmus as an official representative of the United States, he was presented with a new series of demands: better enforcement of the 1955 treaty; cessation of all Canal Zone economic activities not directly pertaining to the maintenance and defense of the canal, such as operation of a dairy; equal wages for Panamanian workers doing the same jobs as Americans; an equal share for Panama of the canal's gross revenues; flying the Panamanian flag over the Canal Zone at least side by side with the Stars and Stripes; and adopting Spanish as the official language within the Canal Zone. The U.S. envoy was greeted by demonstrating students carrying signs saying "Go home Milton," "The Canal is Ours!" and "Fifty Percent Canal."[7] When Dr. Eisenhower left the Presidencia after a conference with Panamanian President Ernesto de la Guardia, Jr., he told reporters wearily that he had been talking with the Panamanian leader about plans for development of everything from highways to schools. What was unsaid was obvious—the United States was being asked to pay the major portion of the expenses for these developments.

Much attention has been given to Latin American opinions and demands, and to the antics of demonstrating mobs. Scant attention has been given to the reaction of public opinion in the United States. Times have obviously changed since Theodore Roosevelt's day when U.S. public opinion would have been the all-important consideration for the people in government in Washington. But, if any practical view is to be taken of this situation, there must come a time to appraise North American public opinion. There are points beyond which no U.S. administration can go, Republican or Democratic. The matter of the flag, has been enough to set off a considerable uproar in Congress and the press (see chapter 10). The hoisting of a flag other than that of the United States has never been asked in other concession areas where North Americans have far less than the perpetuity grants they hold in Panama—the naval bases at Argentia, Newfoundland, and Bermuda, for example.

Communism and the racial question are two of the thorniest issues in public life today, and they both have their ramifications on the isthmus. The Communist following is numerically small in Panama, not more than 1,000 persons probably, but its capacity for mischief is endless. It has charged the United States with several offenses. One of course is "Yanqui Imperialism" and its "exploitation" of the country through the canal. Another is the different wage level which has prevailed for U.S. citizens as opposed to all others. The fact that legislation has now provided for the same scales makes no difference. The Communists say that the United States has done this only for show and that Panamanians will simply be kept in lower payroll grades. They also assail the economic domination of the country by "Wall Street bankers and the United Fruit Company," and the cultural penetration of North American movies, reading material, and business activity which relegates Spanish to a secondary language.[8]

In the Canal Zone the Communists infiltrated a union, the United Public Workers, to such a degree that it was expelled from the C.I.O. in 1950. A new C.I.O. affiliate, Local 900 of the Government and Civic Employees Organizing Committee was organized. In spite of the decision of the Canal Zone Government to recognize it as the bargaining agent, it never achieved the membership of the old union. There are also some craft unions affiliated with the A.F. of L. The A.F. of L.– C.I.O. unions are strongly anti-Communist, but it is problematical whether they have as persuasive an influence among the unskilled workers as the Communist agitators who work tirelessly in their midst. These unskilled workers are mostly Negroes or of mixed ancestry, and they have provided a fertile field for Communist agitation.

The racial question has come to a head since the Supreme Court decisions in the United States caused non-white people everywhere to reexamine their place in social, economic, and political life. In the Canal Zone segregation had been a "way of life" since the beginning. The system was as deeply entrenched as it was in the southern United States. The contrast with the Republic of Panama was tremendous, for in the Republic there was never a "color line" except in certain social circles. This made the resentment all the more marked. The problem which continues to torture political affairs in the United States with no sign of final solution has equal importance in the Canal Zone. The Yanquis who work in the Zone are steadfastly opposed to change. Their form of "massive resistance" might be a walkout which would paralyze the canal. It is not easy to get North Americans to go to tropical lands, and there would be no local sources of technical personnel. However sincerely any U.S. administration might wish to change this situation it would have to move by slow stages. It would have to balance the demands of the equal-rights advocates both at home and in Panama against the realities. It is almost impossible to find words to explain the complexity of the problem to Panamanians. They see only the bigotry and the intolerance.

There have been some steps forward. Legislation now provides that all employees get the same pay for the same work. But the two payrolls, the "National" or "United States," and the "Local" (which in reality has meant non-Caucasian in the past), continued to exist despite the Panamanians' request that a "local" be appointed to the Canal Zone Board of Appeals, which had the final say over grades of employment and wage scales. They contended that they could thus have a representative who could expose the misuse of salary scales and employment classifications to mask racial discrimination. The problem also had other ramifications in that theatres, clubhouses, restaurants, swimming pools, commissaries, and other public facilities in the Zone were operated on a segregated basis by the simple device of limiting patrons to the "National" or "Local" rolls, as the case may be. It was only to be a question of time before this problem would take its place alongside the matter of civil rights in the United States itself.

The difficulties in U.S. relations with Panama have at times caused Washington to turn its attention once again in the direction of another country which boasts a feasible canal route over the isthmus. The

Democratic Party, to a certain extent, has always kept the Nicaragua canal "in its blood," a tribute perhaps to the thoroughness with which Senator John T. Morgan once committed it to that route. Secretary of State William Jennings Bryan negotiated a treaty giving us Nicaragua canal rights in 1914. In 1938–39 the administration of Franklin D. Roosevelt was giving serious consideration to building a second canal because the growth of modern aviation seemed to make an alternative route to Panama strategically necessary to offset possible immobilization of the existing waterway by air attack.[9] In the Truman administration a law was passed directing the War Department to make a comprehensive study, "to determine whether a canal or canals at other locations, including consideration of any new means of transporting ships across land, may be more useful to meet the future needs of interoceanic commerce or national defense than can the present canal with improvements."[10]

A commission was appointed and considered several routes and types of canals. Panama, Nicaragua, the Tehauhtepec route in Mexico, and the Atrato River valley in Colombia were surveyed. Nicaraguan authorities were excited by the prospects and Panamanians were worried that the United States might turn its main attention to a "rival" canal. The Commission's report recommended transforming the Panama Canal into a sea-level route. Because there is an eighteen-foot differential in tidal range on the Atlantic and Pacific coasts of Panama this recommendation was ridiculed in some technical quarters. The project would have cost three billion dollars and was never approved by the Truman administration.[11] Today the increased emphasis upon naval power again raises the question of the desirability of a second canal in order to facilitate passage between the oceans and to have an alternate route.[12] The voyages of the atomic submarine, *Nautilus* opened up a vista of an entirely different kind of navy—one that would emphasize the submarine. The old complaint that the existing Panama Canal was inadequate to handle the super-carriers and other huge ships is not as important strategically as it was only a short time ago. The biggest of the contemplated submarines can transit the canal with ease.

It can readily be seen that this matter is intimately tied up with the issue of U.S. national defense, the possibility of the submarine and the Polaris missile as an answer to the intercontinental ballistic missile, and the whole future role and character of the navy. In the event of war the United States Navy would have to operate around the perimeter of the Eurasian heartland. The need for the interoceanic canal in national defense is as obvious to military men today as it was in the days of the U.S.S. *Oregon*. The need for the alternative canal across Nicaragua or elsewhere may be just as imperative. As the *Nautilus* and her atomic sisters spread their nets under the seas, the isthmian waterways could assume even greater importance. The ultimate in mobility is a necessary goal if the United States Navy is to be a trump card for the Western powers.

The Republic of Panama has one of the world's largest merchant marine fleets. A large proportion of these ships are owned and operated by citizens of the United States; many of them never enter Panamanian waters; many of them do not have Spanish-speaking persons in their entire crew. In 1954 there were 1,735,000 tons of dry cargo vessels and 2,288,000 tons of tankers under the isthmian flag, and the figure was growing at the rate of a half-million tons annually.[13] The reason for this strange situation is directly traceable to political considerations in the United States. In 1916 the Wilson administration secured the passage of a measure popularly called the "Seaman's Bill" which was intended to bring about better working conditions, higher wages, shorter hours, higher standards of safety, and better living conditions aboard ship for seamen on vessels flying the U.S. flag. The various maritime unions had long worked for this goal and achieved it under an administration that was notably friendly to labor. The result was that shipping companies registered their ships with governments which were not so susceptible to pressure from organized labor. This is how the "Panamanian" merchant marine started and the World War II era saw it grow tremendously.

During the period of United States non-belligerency, when the isolationist America First movement was powerful, "neutrality laws" which excluded United States ships from all war zones were in effect. There were immense profits to be gained by carrying war materials. The Roosevelt administration saw that the neutrality laws were really helpful to the Axis by denying facilities to carry aid to the Allies. The United States government, therefore secretly encouraged ship owners to switch from the U.S. flag to that of Panama. The merchant tonnage of that nation climbed from 300,000 tons in 1939 to more than 2,000,-000 tons by 1950. Favorable laws and low taxes kept most of the ships under Panamanian registry after the war ended.[14]

The Korean War and its aftermath again stimulated the growth of Panamanian shipping. For some time ships flying other than U.S. flags traded with Red China without interference from the Seventh Fleet in the Formosa Straits. It will be recalled that Senator Joseph McCarthy was very critical of the British in this connection. What most of the North American people did not know was that U.S. shipping companies were doing the same thing under the flags of Panama and other countries, that many U.S. corporations were involved in this lucrative trade, and that many sailors on United States Navy ships in the Seventh fleet had to sit helplessly watching as vessels manned by their own countrymen moved past into the forbidden Red ports. One shipping company which tried to do this under the U.S. flag was denounced by Senator Joseph McCarthy and subjected to much vilification in the press. The British people, informed by their press, failed to grasp the vagaries of U.S. politics behind this inconsistency and were understandably indignant when Senator McCarthy pointed an accusing finger at them.

The United States government has been anxious to bring these wandering flotillas back under some semblance of supervision and has worked with the government of Panama to that end. The two countries have agreed that nautical inspectors representing the isthmian republic should be permitted to board and check vessels of Panamanian registry while they transit Canal Zone waters. The inspectors observe health and safety standards, living conditions of crews, and examine cargoes, shipping manifests, licenses, and certificates held by officers and crews.[15]

Mention has been made of the (North) "Americanization" of the isthmus. This has been a pet worry of many who loathe the thought of any loss of the historic Spanish culture. This element, sometimes called the cult of "Hispanidad," has had much to concern it. The influence of the North American enclave in the Canal Zone has spilled over into Panama with obvious effect. A few years ago an enterprising *Time* magazine reporter summed it up in this interesting way:

For Panama's modern-minded younger generation life can be very nais [sic] indeed. As a starter, senoritas may pay a visit to what they call a biutiparlor for a champu and a maniquiur. In a franker bid for a picop some apply lipstick from a vanitiqueis right out on the street. Depending on how much of a bigchot she attracts a lucky girl will eat jot dogs and aiscrim, go to the muvis, drink jai bols at a cocteil parti, or even go for a dip in the boy friend's suiminpul.

To the puzzlement of parents, many a daughter comes home bubbling about the terrific nocaut at the fights or the jonrons which piled up the escor at the beisbol game. But if her deit was real quiut, she might say very little about how they spent the evening-parqueando in his car . . .

Other (language) beacheads ranging from elegant eating (at a dinerdans) to economic blockade (boicot), include chingongo (chewing gum), guachinan (watchman), daim (dame), bichi-comer (beachcomber), blofear (bluff), quidnapear (kidnapper), and pul (pull).[16]

This trend is likely to be accelerated by the growing use of the Pan American Highway which is now completed as far south as Panama. Virtually all observers expect a heavy tourist traffic to develop between the Canal Zone and the United States.[17] The North American tourist is notoriously unable to get along with any language but English. His pocketbook is equally notoriously full in the eyes of merchants and innkeepers along his route. The cult of Hispanidad will probably have more problems if the Canal Zone continues to be controlled unilaterally by the United States.

The Panama Canal Zone occupies a unique place in the scheme of North American government and politics. The area is entirely a United States government reservation, as much so as are the grounds of the Military Academy at West Point. Except for a few functions such as the courts, under the adminstration of the Department of Justice, the most important activities in the Zone have been under the supervision of the Department of Defense for a long time.[18] There is no private ownership of land. All housing is provided by the government and allotted only to government employees, military personnel, and a few individuals such as bank employees and clergymen who are permitted to carry on activities within the Zone. All places of amusement, recreation, commissaries, restaurants, and clubhouses are operated by the U.S. government, even a dairy farm. In short, the Canal Zone is a thoroughly communal enterprise operated by the most capitalistic nation in the world.[19]

The system of law in the Canal Zone is basically the same as that in the United States, with some Latin American antecedents.[20] Many of the laws of the United States apply in the Canal Zone. Some specifically do not. This question is fully discussed in the next chapter, but it should be noted here that Panamanians have at times been bewildered by the gyrations of North American law. The Prohibition era caused much confusion. Panamanians were allowed to transport alcoholic beverages across the Canal Zone provided they were under seal and certified by the republic's authorities.[21] The Tivoli Hotel at Ancon, in the Canal Zone, was of course "dry." But what puzzled Panamanians was that the Washington Hotel, owned and operated by the United States government at Cristobal, had a flourishing bar. It was not generally realized that the Washington Hotel was just over the Canal Zone boundary in Panamanian territory. Prohibition was a bonanza for cafes and bars in Panama which were crowded with North American tourists. There was great indignation in Panama when the repeal of Prohibition brought beer back to the Canal Zone clubhouses and hard liquors to the military and naval officers clubs.

The administration in Washington has some important political patronage to distribute in the Canal Zone: lucrative jobs such as United States district judges, the United States district attorney and his staff and the federal marshals and magistrates. There are thousands of employees on civil service rolls. There are unions affiliated with the A.F. of L.–C.I.O. For years they maintained a lobby in Washington, influential enough to keep Zone employees exempt from the federal income tax. The leaders of the Canal Zone unions have been at variance with the national leadership of the A.F. of L.–C.I.O.[22] on the question of racial segregation and in this respect resemble certain labor elements in the southern United States.

There have been as many as 50,000 U.S. citizens residing in the Zone, although this figure has been greatly reduced since the 1940's. Like their fellow citizens in other United States overseas territories and in the District of Columbia, they do not have the right to vote in national elections. (There are no elective offices in the Zone). But they do have the means to exert some political influence.

Many Canal Zone voters maintain absentee polling rights in the various states and are thus enabled to exert some political influence back home. There is keen interest in political news from the States, and these items are always given due attention in the English language dailies which are published in Panama. Furthermore, the Democratic party recognized the Canal Zone's importance to the extent of inviting it to send delegates to the National Convention and giving them a seat on the National Committee. In 1932 the Canal Zone delegation joined the forces supporting Franklin D. Roosevelt at the Democratic National Convention in Chicago. Every vote was vital in that convention because a two-thirds vote was then required for nomination.

In 1914 when the Canal was formally opened, medals were struck for all U.S. citizens who worked in the Zone out of the scrap of the old French equipment. These were called Roosevelt Medals and were given for two years of continuous service during the construction period. Those who had six years of continuous service prior to April, 1915 were organized into the Society of the Chagres.

These medal holders and Chagres Society members tended to stay together after they returned to the United States to live. Little colonies of these people were established in many places, but particularly in California and Florida. Although the Society members and the medal holders were those who had actually worked on the isthmus during construction days they tended to form a nucleus for organized activity on the part of all ex-Panama Canal and Panama Railroad employees.

In a nation where people love to "join" they have constituted yet another fraternal order of a sort, which has a background much more unique than most such associations. They consider that they symbolize one of the great triumphs of North American genius in the twentieth century. This circumstance has greatly sharpened the "esprit de corps" which makes them a powerful political lobby when they move as a group to extend their influence for or against some issue. The evidence of their widespread influence has been apparent in Washington every time a modification of the canal treaties or of the exercise of U.S. authority upon the isthmus has been proposed.

9

The Yanqui Legal System in the Canal Zone

The system of democracy spread by British colonialism proved to be a powerful influence upon many nations and peoples who were not themselves of Anglo-Saxon origin. Long after these former colonies became nations politically independent from Britain, many of them retained elements of the British legal system such as the common law, parliamentary democracy, and the English court system as permanent features of government. Basic English traditions were also adopted in non–Anglo-Saxon lands through historic relationships with the United States. Both the Republic of the Philippines and the Republic of Panama, despite their Hispanic colonial traditions, adopted basically North American systems of government. In Panama this was largely due to U.S. presence on the isthmus.

The Yanqui influence can be seen in the governmental structure of the isthmian republic which has a strong executive, an independent judiciary, and a distinct legislative branch, a "separation of powers" which is not typical of Latin America. North American political techniques are noticeably part of Panamanian life. Aside from this impact upon Panama itself, the United States has complete jurisdiction over the Canal Zone. The influence of Yanqui politics on the isthmus is strongest in the Canal Zone which has functioned for all practical purposes as if it were an integral part of the United States. Thousands of U.S. citizens essentially live as though they are living in their own country, and they are as much a part of North American political trends as their fellow citizens in the States.

Every political event, every governmental operation, every national election in the United States itself has a very noticeable effect upon the Canal Zone and its inhabitants. The constant movement of people back and forth across the Zone borders, in and out of the territorial jurisdiction of the Canal Zone government; the repeated interaction of Panamanian business and commercial interests with Canal Zone residents and institutions; and the essential daily collaboration between public authorities of both the republic and the Zone have resulted in a clear extension of many features of the political system of the United States into Panamanian life.

The fact that this Anglo-American system has become so firmly implanted demonstrates very graphically that the potential influence of Yanqui political mores is of a strong and virulent nature. No one is more aware of this than the Hispanic Panamanians who despair at the encroachment of the Yanqui and his ways on Hispanic cultural traditions. Such a clash of cultures portents little but trouble for future United States–Panamanian relations at every level.

When the Panama Canal Zone came under U.S. jurisdiction in 1903, a Spanish-American legal system had been governing inhabitants and activities there for four hundred years. It was a mixture of the famous Roman codes and of ancient Iberian laws derived from native customs, all modified as the years passed to meet the conditions of the New World.

It was immediately evident that the coming of thousands of skilled and unskilled workers to take jobs related to canal building operations would pose a severe problem in judicial practice and in the method of administration of government and law. Most of these newcomers were English-speaking, whether they were Caucasians from the continental United States or West Indian Negroes from British possessions such as Bermuda or the Bahamas.[1] The system of jurisprudence under which all had lived, and their ancestors before them for generations, was based upon the English common law. On the other hand there were already thousands of Spanish-speaking Panamanians who would continue to live and work within the boundaries of the Canal Zone. A clash of differing legal systems and traditions seemed certain to be a problem.

The Hay–Bunau-Varilla Treaty,[2] by which the United States had acquired jurisdiction of the Canal Zone, allowed the occupying authority to assert full control over this and all other issues likely to arise within the ten mile-wide strip. Article II of the Treaty granted to the United States "in perpetuity" the "use, occupation, and control" of the area. By Article III, the Republic of Panama granted to the United

States "all the rights, power, and authority within the Zone . . . which the United States would possess if it were the sovereign of the territory . . . to the entire exclusion of the exercise by the Republic of Panama of any such sovereign rights, power, or authority."

The Spooner Act,[3] approved on June 28, 1902, had authorized the president to acquire the Canal Zone, and had provided for the appointment of an Isthmian Canal Commission of seven members. When the Hay–Bunau-Varilla Treaty was formally proclaimed in effect on February 26, 1904, the United States became the sole occupying power in the Zone. The president interpreted the Spooner Act as the authorization for him to establish a temporary government for the territory which Panamanian authority and jurisdiction had now vacated.[4]

On February 29, 1904, President Theodore Roosevelt appointed the first Isthmian Canal Commission which was confirmed by the Senate on March third. Rear Admiral John G. Walker was chairman of the Commission; Judge Charles E. Magoon of Lincoln, Nebraska, was appointed general counsel;[5] and Major General George W. Davis was designated the first governor of the Canal Zone. The other members of the Commission were William B. Parsons of New York, William H. Burr of New York, Benjamin M. Harrod of Louisiana, Carl E. Grunsky of California, and Frank T. Hecker of Michigan. President Roosevelt instructed this Commission as follows:

> Make all needful rules for government of the Zone and for the correct administration of the military, civil, and judicial affairs of its possessions until the close of the LVIII session of Congress. . . .
>
> The inhabitants of the Canal Zone are entitled to security in their persons, property, and religion, and in all their private rights and relations. . . . The municipal laws of the Canal Zone are to be administered by the ordinary tribunals substantially as they were before the change. Police magistrates and justices of the peace and other officers discharging duties usually devolving upon these officers of the law will be continued in office if they are suitable persons. The Governor of the Canal Zone, subject to the approval of the Commission, is authorized to appoint temporarily a Judge for the Canal Zone who shall have the authority equivalent to that usually exercised in Latin American countries by a judge of the first instance, but the Isthmian Canal Commission shall fix his salary and may legislate respecting his powers and authority, increasing or diminishing them in their discretion,

and also making provision for additional or appellate judges should the public interest require.

The laws of the land with which the inhabitants are familiar and which were in force on February 26, 1904, will continue in force in the Canal Zone and other places on the Isthmus over which the United States has jurisdiction until altered or annulled by the Commission, but there are certain great principles of government which have been made the basis of our existence as a nation which we deem essential to the rule of law and the maintenance of order and which shall have force in said zone. The principles referred to may be generally stated as follows:

'That no person should be deprived of life, liberty, or property without due process of law; that property shall not be taken for public use without just compensation; that in all criminal prosecutions the accused shall enjoy the right of a speedy and public trial, to be informed of the nature and cause of the accusation, to be confronted with the witnesses against him, to have compulsory process for obtaining witnesses in his favor, and to have the assistance of counsel for his defense; that excessive bail shall not be required nor excessive fines imposed, nor cruel or unusual punishment inflicted; that no person shall be put twice in jeopardy for the same offense, or be compelled in any criminal case to be a witness against himself; that the right to be secure against unreasonable searches and seizures shall not be violated; that neither slavery nor involuntary servitude shall exist except as a punishment for crime; that no bill of attainder or ex post facto law shall be passed; that no law shall be passed abridging the freedom of speech or of the press, or of the rights of the people to peacefully assemble and petition the Government for a redress of grievances; that no law shall be made respecting the establishment of religion or prohibiting the free exercise thereof.' . . .

The Commission may legislate on all rightful subjects of legislation not inconsistent with the laws and treaties of the United States so far as they apply to the said Zone. . . . Such legislative power shall also include the power to raise and appropriate revenues . . . all laws, rules, and regulations of a governmental character enacted by the Commission are to be submitted to the Secretary of War for approval. Gambling is prohibited in the Canal strip.[6]

It was also provided that when the Commission should be functioning as a legislative body a quorum would be four of the seven members. All laws, rules, and regulations were to be set forth and published under a caption that they were enacted by the Isthmian Canal Commission "By authority of the President of the United States."[7]

It can be seen from the foregoing that the United States, while agreeable to accepting the existing laws of Panama as a base for its administration, was reserving the power to modify that foundation as time went along. Its own "great principles of government" would certainly be imposed whenever and wherever such substitutions might be necessary or desirable according to North American ideals of a "rule of law." This could only mean the gradual building of a legal system differing in many respects from the Hispanic-American jurisprudence which had prevailed upon the isthmus beforehand.[8] It is interesting to note that these very first instructions of the president made a change in the old law by its prohibition of gambling. Not only were games of chance lawful throughout Latin America, but lotteries were often operated by governments. Panama was no exception.

In most respects the president's instructions had the effect of establishing an Anglo-American style Bill of Rights in the Canal Zone. However, it did not give the right to trial by jury. Moreover the Isthmian Canal Commission received powers, such as deportation of undesirables, not exercised by any executive or judicial bodies under the U.S. flag, except in areas under martial law.

The North American intention to center the source of government and law for the Canal Zone in Washington was nailed down by the Act of Congress of April 28, 1904, which was entitled "Act to provide for the temporary government of the Canal Zone at Panama."[9] It had the effect of ratifying all that the president had already done under the authority of the Spooner Act by stating that ". . . all the military, civil, and judicial powers as well as the power to make all rules and regulations necessary for the government of the Canal Zone and all the rights, powers, and authority granted by the terms of such treaty (Hay–Bunau–Varilla) shall be vested in such person or persons and shall be exercised in such manner as the president shall direct. . . ."

On May 19, 1904, Governor Davis issued a proclamation to the people of the Canal Zone as he took over his office. Herein he called attention to the president's instructions to the Isthmian Canal Commission, and proceeded to list again the "great principles of government" and explain their new applicability to the Canal Zone. The governor also reiterated that the basic Panamanian law in effect on February 26, 1904, would still be valid with the understood qualification, "where it did not clash violently with the 'great principles' so steadfastly put forth by the president and the governor." It is intriguing to consider the only possible meaning of all this—that at least for a time the two great systems of law in the modern world, the Roman codes and the English common law, would be fused upon the American Isthmus. It therefore seems appropriate to trace briefly the history of isthmian jurisprudence before 1904.

The law of Panama was the law of Colombia, under that nation's Constitution of 1887.[10] The isthmus had a legal tradition of its own, however, dating back to the early colonial period when Panama was an "audiencia" of the Spanish Crown. Panama had been one of the earliest settlements of the Spaniards upon the American mainland.

In 1503 Spain had established the "Casa de Contratación" at Seville to regulate colonial trade and to devise methods and rules for governing her rapidly growing empire. In 1524 Charles V established the Council of the Indies, which governed the colonies subject to the King's veto. Spain's colonial laws were collected and digested in 1680 in a collection known as the *Recopilación de las leyes de las Indias.* It was provided that the laws of Castile were to prevail in cases not covered by the *Recopilación.*[11] The law of Castile was taken largely from the codes of Rome, but in some instances derived from ancient Iberian tribal customs. Castilian law was codified in 1505 in a compilation known as the *Leyes del Toro.* The *Recopilación* comprised nine books arranged in 218 titles and 6447 laws. Later editions were published in 1756, 1774, and 1791. It was provided that where Castilian law was extended to the new world it had to be by specific decree of the Council of the Indies. Consequently not every Castilian ordinance was so extended. The Council also made some regulations for America which had no application in Spain. To a degree, therefore, the Latin American colonies developed their own forms of law.[12]

Most Latin American states codified their law after the wars of independence separated them from Spain. Many of them used the Code Napoléon as a model for their civil codes. This represented no drastic change, because the old Justinian Code, so influential in Spanish law, was practically restated in the Napoleonic Code.

Panama was a part of the new Republic of Gran Colombia for nine years after independence was achieved in 1821. Gran Colombia's first code of civil procedure was dated May 13, 1825, and stated the order by which former Spanish colonial laws would now have application. Article 188 of the new republic's constitution, proclaimed at Cucuta in 1821, had ordained that the law of the old regime should remain effective, except where it was in conflict with the new constitution or statutes which might be passed by the Colombian Congress. Royal decrees and ordinances down to March 18, 1808, the *Recopilación de las Indias* and the *Leyes del Toro*, were to be given force and effect in that order of priority.[13]

The mining laws of Spain as they had applied to the old Viceroyalty of Peru were made applicable in Gran Colombia by a decree of Simon Bolívar on October 24, 1829. The Spanish commercial and maritime codes declared in 1737 by Philip V were also adopted and remained the law of Colombia long after they were replaced in Spain itself by a new commercial code.[14]

Gran Colombia disintegrated in 1830 when Venezuela and Ecuador separated from it. The remainder, including the Isthmus of Panama, was known for a time as New Granada. The autonomy of the provinces within this republic developed to such an extent that Panama was given a special status as a federal sovereign state in 1855 by a constitutional amendment.[15] When seven other provinces attained this status, the country was called the Granadine Confederation.[16]

Panama now had its own legislative assembly. In 1869 a judicial code was adopted which specifically repealed, without exception, all Spanish laws still in force.[17] That same year a mining law was adopted and in 1870 a commercial and a military code were passed.[18] Dr. Justo Arosemena, one of Latin America's greatest legal minds, edited an Administrative Code and Compilation of Sundry Laws in 1870.[19]

With a new constitution adopted in 1886–87, the Granadine Confederation again became unitary republic named Colombia. It was now also necessary to unify the national law, and to supersede the quasi-independent codes which had been adopted by the several states, which now became departments. The new law codes of Colombia were promulgated in 1887, and these were the laws inherited by the Republic of Panama when it separated from Colombia. They were now to remain in effect within the Canal Zone until superseded or modified by the North American administration. It is interesting to note that some of the Colombian codes had been reenactments of the laws of the Federal State of Panama, so excellently formulated that the reunified republic had accepted them for the whole nation in 1887.[20]

On May 9, 1904, an Executive Order of President Roosevelt

directed the Isthmian Canal Commission to exercise its power under the supervision of the Secretary of War, and repeated the promise that the system of government within the Canal Zone would continue under "the laws of the land with which the inhabitants are familiar."[21] The Civil Code of the Republic of Panama was translated into English and published by the Isthmian Canal Commission in 1905 in order to facilitate its use by the authorities and by the public.[22]

The machinery of a new government, and of a new judicial and law enforcement system soon came into being. At first there was a Canal Zone Supreme Court, whose three justices sat separately as judges in the three circuit courts. There were five municipal courts. There was no appeal beyond the Canal Zone Supreme Court to any court in the United States. The circuit courts had jurisdiction over civil actions where the amount involved exceeded $100 or could not be estimated, over matters concerning real estate, taxation, admiralty, probate, trusts, divorces, and annulments. Criminal jurisdiction covered cases where conviction would bring a fine exceeding $25 or thirty days in jail, or both. The municipal courts sat in each town and had jurisdiction in civil cases up to $300, and criminal cognizance in matters where conviction could draw a fine up to $100 and thirty days in jail, or both. They also had jurisdiction over actions involving possession or title to realty regardless of value, and sat as examining magistrates in criminal actions. The municipal judges and their constables served for four years and were appointed by the governor. The Circuit-Supreme Court jurists were also initially appointed by the governor, but were later named by the president. There was a federal prosecuting attorney who had three deputies. The chief of the Canal Zone police served as coroner of the zone and as marshal to the Supreme Court of the Canal Zone. Appeals lay from the municipal courts to the curcuit court of the town's judicial district.[23]

The Canal Zone police were organized as a civilian body separate from the military police. Personnel were recruited largely from former enlisted men of the United States armed forces, a procedure of staffing which largely continues to the present time. The Zone police have acquired a reputation for proficiency and efficiency over the years. Servicemen from World War II days will readily testify to that. When certain unscrupulous taxi drivers used the cover of the blackout to "roll" and rob their fares they were always careful to do so outside the Canal Zone and the jurisdiction of the ever-vigilant Zone police. This is not to say that there has not been complete amity and cooperation between the Zone police and their counterparts in the Republic of Panama. The two agencies have operated in complete harmony since May 9, 1909 when the chief of police of Panama issued an order emulated a few days later by the chief of the Canal Zone police.[24] However, for many years good feeling did *not* characterize the relationship between the Panamanian police and U.S. troops. Soldiers and sailors on liberty in the Republic frequently were involved in disorders in the bistros and in the *distrito de luz roja* in both Panama City and Colon.[25] But these situations did not usually involve the Canal Zone police force or prejudice their relations with the neighboring law enforcement units.

It will be recalled that the president's original instructions to the Isthmian Canal Commission empowered it to act "until the close of the LVIII Session of Congress." On March 4, 1905, the Fifty-eighth Congress ended its term without providing legislation for the government of the Canal Zone, and failed to make permanent the "temporary" authority which it had confirmed in the president by the Act of April 28, 1904. Thereafter the Isthmian Canal Commission ceased to exercise legislative functions except in the field of municipal ordinances and the president continued to govern the Zone by executive order.[26] All formal municipalities in the Zone were abolished November 17, 1906, and their various officials discharged. Ordinances which had been enacted by municipal councils under the old Panamanian practice were now promulgated by the Commission, subject to the approval of the secretary of war.[27] On January 8, 1908, all authority within the zone was vested in the chairman of the Commission, with the other members simply attesting to his actions. Laws were now simply made or changed by his fiat, with no more formality than a confirming order by the president of the United States.

On January 27, 1914, President Wilson issued an Executive Order placing the formal stamp of approval on a "permanent administration" for the Zone. The Isthmian Canal Commission was ordered out of existence as of April 1, 1914. The governor would rule absolutely, subject to the secretary of war and the president. The Zone government, aside from the judicial branch, was divided into six parts: (1) Maintenance Division, (2) Purchasing Division, (3) Supply Department, (4) Accounting Department, (5) Health Department, and (6) The Executive Secretary. This last division was analogous to the office of secretary of state usually found in the cabinets of the forty-eight continental states. His jurisdiction included police and prisons, fire protection, land, schools, clubhouses, the law library, post offices, customs, and excise collections. This system of government by Executive Order has continued in the Panama Canal Zone to this day.[28]

As the construction period drew to a close, certain reorganizations took place. By Act of Congress,[29] all private land titles were extinguished within the Zone and all inhabitants who did not have some connection with the operation or defense of the strip were expelled. All housing was now provided by the United States government. A new system of courts was created. When the municipalities were abolished, the municipal courts had been replaced by four district courts with roughly the same jurisdiction. Now the district courts were reduced in number to two, sitting at Balboa and at Ancon. They were upgraded, however, and assumed the former jurisdiction of the circuit courts and the Canal Zone Supreme Court, which was abolished. The right of appeal was now given to circuit courts and to the Supreme Court of the United States.[30] The Zone's district courts became very similar to the United States district courts in the continental United States.[31] This act provided for trial by jury in civil or criminal cases upon the demand of either party.

Trial by jury was one part of Anglo-American heritage which had not been extended to the Canal Zone by President Roosevelt's original instructions to the Isthmian Canal Commission. There were many who were critical of this situation, especially when the death penalty was meted out in murder cases and some of the defendants were colored British subjects from the British West Indies, Bermuda, and other places where trial by jury was a long established right. The Supreme Court of the Canal Zone held that the United States Constitution, as such, did not apply to the Canal Zone, and that civil and political rights beyond those specified in the presidential instructions could only be extended to the Zone by act of Congress.[32] The United States Supreme Court steadfastly refused to take jurisdiction of any cases from Canal Zone courts. This procedure was in harmony with Panamanian tradition, because Latin American procedure did not provide for jury trials in the Anglo-American sense.

In 1908, J. C. S. Blackburn, who was head of the Department of Civil Administration in the Canal Zone, wrote to President Roosevelt that he believed that trial by jury fell within the scope of those "great principles of government which have been made the basis of our existence as a nation and which we deem essential to the rule of law and the maintenance of order." The president, by executive order, then established trial by jury in criminal cases where the penalty might be affixed at death or life imprisonment.[33]

The process of building a body of law at variance with Latin American tradition within the Canal Zone began in September, 1905, when the supreme court of the Zone rendered its first decision with such effect. A man charged with operating a roulette wheel in defiance of Canal Zone law posed as his defense a concession granted to him by the Republic of Panama and pleaded the continuance of the laws of that nation within the Zone. The court upheld his conviction on the grounds that ". . . The United States has full control of the Canal Zone, just as though it were the actual sovereign of the territory, free from all anterior obligations or concessions of any kind, and it also has full power to legislate for the Zone. . . ."[34]

The supreme court of the Canal Zone then took judicial notice[35] of the phraseology of a Colombia statute still part of the law of Panama, but then proceeded to give a common-law interpretation to the words in determining their legal effect.[36] The case involved the doctrine of *respondeat superior*. The Panamanian law did not distinguish between negligent acts done in an employer's business from malicious ones, or those done outside the scope of employment.[37]

It was the practice of Canal Zone courts to take judicial notice of the Colombian-Panamanian laws which were in effect upon the Isthmus as of February 26, 1904.[38] But native interpretations of these laws had to be introduced in evidence. North American judges found such precedents persuasive "if not inconsistent with the common law." In the view of the United States Supreme Court, expressed years later in the case of *The Panama Railroad Company* v. *Bosse*,[39] this was proper: ". . . The President's Order continuing law then [1904] in force was merely the embodiment of the rule that a change in sovereignty does not put an end to existing private law, and no more fastened upon the Zone a specific interpretation of the former Civil Code than does a statute adopting the common law fasten upon a territory a specific doctrine of the English courts."

However, in cases involving transitory causes of action arising within the Republic of Panama where both parties were non-citizens of the United States and the Canal Zone court took jurisdiction because service was obtained upon the defendant, it was held that the applicable Panamanian law would have to be introduced in evidence before the Canal Zone court could apply it.[40]

It was not always the practice to adhere to the letter rather than the spirit of the Colombia-Panama code. For example, the Supreme Court of the Canal Zone allowed recovery in tort for mere pain and suffering in two historic cases.[41] The Panamanian law, unlike the common-law jurisdictions, had developed a rule allowing such damages. The Canal Zone Court said, ". . . physical pain being a substantial and appreciable part of the wrong done, allowed for in the customary compensation which the people of the Zone have been awarded in their native courts, was properly allowed here. . . ."[42]

The Canal Zone system thus became ever more *sui generis* as time went by, and each phase of its peculiar twin ancestry retained vitality. The administration of the criminal law in the Zone has, it is true, come to be virtually identical with that in the continental United States. But the noncriminal phases of the law remain partially grounded in Latin American tradition. An Act of Congress of August 24, 1912, stated that "All laws, orders, regulations, and ordinances adopted and promulgated in the Canal Zone by order of the President for the government and sanitation of the Canal Zone . . . are hereby ratified and confirmed as valid and binding until the Congress shall otherwise provide."[43]

After the Act of Congress of June 19, 1934, the Canal Zone might certainly be classed as a "code jurisdiction." By the language of this act, "The seven titles hereinafter set forth shall constitute the Code of Laws for the Canal Zone for all purposes, establish conclusively, and be deemed to embrace all the permanent laws relating to or applying in the Canal Zone on the date of the enactment of this Act, except general laws of the United States as relate to or apply in the Canal Zone."[44]

This code goes on to include all former acts of Congress applicable to the Canal Zone, all acts and ordinances of the Isthmian Canal Commission and executive orders of the president relating to the Canal Zone and issued prior to 1912 which were ratified and confirmed by the Act of Congress of August 24, 1912.[45] The Act of 1934 has remained substantially unchanged.[46] Canal Zone law thus continues to have significant roots in Latin American jurisprudence.

The Canal Zone Code formalizes the administration of justice within the Isthmian strip. The District Court is now one court, with divisions at Balboa and Ancon; it has jurisdiction over all criminal cases where punishment upon conviction may exceed a fine of $100 or a jail term of thirty days, or both; over all equity cases;[47] over all admiralty matters in the same manner as other United States District

Courts; over divorce and annulment, over all cases at law involving more than $500; and over any other matter wherein jurisdiction is conferred by the codes of law and procedures of the Canal Zone.[48]

The District Attorney of the Canal Zone has such assistance and clerks as the president may authorize.[49] He may proceed against a suspected criminal if a magistrate fails to hold the person for trial.[50] There is a U.S. marshal and such deputies as the president may authorize. Trial by jury is guaranteed. Those eligible for jury duty are all citizens of the United States employed by the Panama Railroad or Canal in the Zone, and residing in a government-owned residence.[51] The District Court makes its own rules, and a change of venue from one division of the district to the other can be granted either to the government or to the defendant in a criminal proceeding.[52] Shortly before the passage of the Canal Zone Code the president, by executive order, had transferred the district court, the district attorney, and the United States marshal and their staffs from the cognizance of the Department of War to that of the Department of Justice.[53]

There is now a magistrate in each Canal Zone town. Their jurisdiction is coextensive with that of the subdivision. It extends over all civil cases up to $500 in controversy and over all criminal cases wherein punishment upon conviction may be a fine up to $100 or thirty days in jail or both; also over all actions involving forcible entry and detainer of real estate. The magistrates may also hold preliminary hearings in all charges of felony and misdemeanor where punishment on conviction would class the case beyond the jurisdiction of the court, and commit or bail in bailable cases to the district court.[54] The right of appeal extends from the magistrate's court to the district court in all civil cases, and in criminal cases where imprisonment or a fine in excess of $25 would be the punishment upon conviction.[55] The code of Criminal Procedure, insofar as it affects trials before a magistrate, may be amended by the president.[56] The magistrates are appointed for four years by the governor and take their oaths before notaries public, who are also commissioned by the governor of the Canal Zone.

One of the most confused subjects within Canal Zone jurisprudence is the question of applicability of the general laws of the United States to persons and property within the Zone. This field of the law is still further complicated by the constantly resurgent issue of U.S. control and jurisdiction versus residual Panamanian sovereignty within the ten mile strip.[57]

There is no clear line of demarcation concerning the applicability of United States statutes which do not specifically contain language making them pertain to the Canal Zone. Many laws are specifically applicable in the Zone: the Federal Employers Liability Act,[58] the Bank Conservation Act,[59] the Investment Company Act,[60] and others.[61] Some specifically exclude the Canal Zone, such as the Food, Drug, and Cosmetics Act,[62] the Federal Communications Act[63] and the Nationality Act.[64]

Generally, in nearly all matters involving the security of the United States and the enforcement of its criminal codes, the Canal Zone is like any other territory under U.S. jurisdiction. The laws of the United States relating to extradition and rendition of fugitives from justice were extended to the Canal Zone by Congress in the Act of 24 August, 1912 (37 Stat. 569); the Defense Bases Act includes the strip among "the territories or possessions of the United States outside the continental United States;[65] the War Damage Corporation Act applies to the Zone;[66] the Neutrality Act of 1917 states that the term " 'United States' . . . includes the Canal Zone and all territory and waters contiguous or insular subject to the jurisdiction of the United States."[67]

In the matter of trade, commerce, taxation, fiscal regulations, tariffs, and postal laws, a court case would have to be decided in the light of many considerations which might seem extraneous to law and legal precedent.[68] Foreign policy, and the United States' particular relationship to the Republic of Panama might materially affect such a case.[69] On June 24, 1904, the president issued an executive order making the full tariff rates of the United States applicable to the Canal Zone and stipulating that they should apply even against imports into the Zone from the Republic of Panama. He also applied the domestic United States postal rate to letters within the Zone (2¢) but ordered the foreign rate (5¢) for mail addressed across the border to destinations within Panama. The young isthmian republic delivered a vigorous note of protest against these discriminations on July 27, 1904.[70] After considerable diplomatic discussion the president issued a revised order on December 3, 1904, resulting in the exception of Panama from the tariffs and providing for the use of Panamanian postage stamps within the strip which would be overprinted by the Canal Zone government.[71] The United States has always made it clear, however, that this was only an accommodation for the Republic of Panama and no concession of its viewpoints with respect to the right to exercise sovereign powers.[72] The United States holds that it possesses complete authority over commerce within, into, and out of the Zone, and that any special rights which Panama may have there are exercised only by express and formal concession.[73]

In the case of *Wilson* v. *Shaw*,[74] decided in 1907 the Supreme Court of the United States said, ". . . It is hypercritical to contend that the title of the United States is imperfect, and that the territory described does not belong to this nation because of the omission of some of the technical terms used in ordinary conveyances of real estate."

Following this case the United States Supreme Court seems to have sought to avoid the issue of sovereignty altogether. In the case of *Luckenbach Steamship Co.* v. *the United States*,[75] decided in 1920, the Court said, "the issue . . . depends upon long continued legislative and administrative construction of such statutes and without regard to whether under the treaty of cession titular sovereignty over the Zone remains in the Republic of Panama. . . ."

In the case of *Vermilya Brown Co.* v. *Connell*,[76] decided in 1948, Justice Reed, speaking for the majority, said that the power of Congress to regulate labor contracts, wages, and hours rests upon *control* of a territorial area rather than upon sovereignty:

> . . . a fortiori . . . civil controls may apply, we think, to liabilities created by statutory regulation of labor contracts, even if aliens may be involved, where the incidents regulated occur on areas under the control, though not within the territorial jurisdiction or sovereignty of the nation enacting the legislation. This power is placed specifically in Congress by virtue of the authorization for 'needful rules and regulations respecting the territory or other property belonging to the United States. (Constitution, Article IV, p. 3, cl. 2). It does not depend upon sovereignty in the political or any sense over the territory. . . . Where the purpose is to regulate labor relations in an area vital to our national life it seems reasonable to interpret its provisions to have force where the nation has sole power, rather than to limit the coverage to sovereignty. Such an interpretation is consonant with the Administrator's inclusion of the Panama Canal Zone within the meaning of 'possession'. . . .

The whole issue of sovereignty was dynamically present in the negotiations of the Eisenhower and Johnson years during which several efforts to produce a new treaty delineating the role of the United States in Panama were attempted. The U.S. position on the Canal Zone's domestic juridical structure encompasses two main points:

1. Since the attention given by the United Nations to the issue of colonialism, the United States has consistently declared that a "residual sovereignty" rests in the Republic of Panama over the entire Canal Zone.
2. In trying to place some interpretation on the wording of the Hay–Bunau-Varilla Treaty which assigns authority to the United States to exercise all power which it would "possess and exercise *if it were* sovereign" (article 3), it is sufficient for our purposes here to say that the United States does exercise sufficient *Majestas* within the Panama Canal Zone to be the only authority capable of promulgating, interpreting, and enforcing law throughout the territorial strip.

It seems quite clear that the treaty negotiated in 1967 and 1968 by the Johnson administration in the United States and the Robles administration in Panama would concede *all* aspects of sovereignty to the isthmian republic. This concession would affect the status, nature, and function of the Canal Zone's juridical system. In the meantime, so long as attempts to revise the basic treaties are abortive there will continue to be an Anglo-American structure of courts and law superimposed upon a Latin American and Roman tradition which has managed to endure in some significant aspects.

10

Eisenhower and
the Panamanian Questions

Throughout his administration President Dwight D. Eisenhower labored diligently to find a lasting settlement for the problems plaguing the United States and Panama: the exclusive North American operation of the Canal and its control over the Canal Zone.

The Chapin-Fabrega treaty revision of 1955 proved to be a temporary palliative. It obligated U.S. authorities on the isthmus to give preference in their purchases to Panamanian products meeting U.S. standards, and to pay the same wages to Panamanians as to U.S. citizens.[1] The Panamanians had also demanded the cessation of all U.S. economic activity in the Zone not directly connected with the Canal's operation, such as the dairy. In September, 1959, Foreign Minister Miguel J. Moreno, Jr. denounced the United States in the U.N. General Assembly for discrimination against Panamanian workers and declared that the equal wages clause was not being fully honored.[2] It also became clear that Panama would not be satisfied with the raised annual canal rentals of $1,930,000.

During President Eisenhower's second term, U.S.-Panamanian relations sank to their lowest ebb since the 1920's, an ironic situation in view of the president's consistent policy to soothe all of the old resentments. However, this situation was only a part of the larger problems between the United States and most of Latin America, which were aggravated by the Castro revolution in Cuba. Of all the countries of Central America and the Caribbean few are more susceptible to Castro and Communist propaganda than Panama. The nation has been infiltrated with Cuban agents of both Soviet and Chinese antecedents, well supplied with cash and finding ready allies among nationalistic anti-Yanqui zealots.[3]

In 1960 Panama's economic situation grew steadily worse, and the Panamanians charged that the United States was responsible for widespread unemployment, low pay rates, and continuing slums in workers' living areas. The United States, as the owner and operator of the Canal—the biggest isthmian "industry"—was accused of being the cruel capitalist who exploits his workers in the typical Marxian case study of the class war. In 1960 there was a strike of banana plantation workers who proceeded to set up "Soviet Village Council's," and tenant farmers openly declared that they were "Communists" because Communists "will help the poor."

Other agents, Arabs, came to the isthmian nation to supplement the work of the Communists. Although there are very few people of Arabian heritage in Panama, the United Arab Republic established a sizable mission at its legation. The minister, Mohammed et Tabei, was known to have made intimate contacts with two anti-Yanqui leaders, Aquilano Boyd and Ernesto Castillero. His arrival in Panama was accompanied by acts of Anti-Semitism. Swastikas were daubed on the property of Jewish storekeepers and Jews living both in Panama and in the Canal Zone received scurrilous letters through the mail captioned with swastikas and the legend "Jew, go home to New York!" This outburst fitted the pattern of the cold war waged upon Israel by the Arab states and the Soviet Union.

Violence against the United States erupted seriously in November, 1959, during the anniversary of Panamanian independence. Panamanian mobs attacked the U.S. Embassy and ripped down the flag. Demonstrators stoned the U.S. Information Agency building and attacked private North American business concerns. A crowd of several hundred attempted to enter the Canal Zone from Panama City with the avowed intention of planting Panama's flag in Zone territory. Canal Zone police and U.S. Army troops met them in force at Ancon and a pitched battle ensued with tear gas and small arms being used to disperse the "invaders." More than forty Panamanians were wounded but fortunately no one was killed.[4] The then president of Panama, Ernesto de la Guardia, Jr., condemned the violence of his countrymen but went on a radio broadcast to the nation and charged the United States with responsibility and provocation of the incident by rejecting Panama's complaints and demands relative to the Canal and the Canal Zone. The foreign minister, Miguel Moreno, Jr., handed an even stronger note to U.S. Ambassador Julian Harrington. It was essentially a reply to a Washington protest against the attacks upon the Embassy and the Canal Zone border.

The note "lamented" the violence but went on to accuse the United States of "unjustifiable acts" such as firing upon unarmed citizens of Panama and throwing tear gas bombs across the border into Panamanian territory. It also declared that armed forces of the United States had "mishandled" the Panamanian flag. Moreno said his government hoped that United States authorities in the future would "act . . . with greater deliberation and prudence to avoid a repetition of the occurrences that we all regret."

This unhappy incident had immediate results in Washington. Secretary of State Christian Herter informed Ambassador Ricardo M. Arias that the United States would dispatch Livingston T. Merchant, deputy under secretary of state, to Panama City to confer with Panamanian authorities. Mr. Merchant arrived in the isthmian capital on November 21, 1959, and went at once to the Presidencia for talks with President de la Guardia. Other top level conversations were held and Mr. Merchant left an impression with his conferees that Washington would certainly move to meet at least some of Panama's demands.[5] During the next year, these moves came to some fruition.

In March 1960, two commercial concessions were made, one being the purchasing of supplies in Panama for resale in the Canal Zone. Panamanian businessmen were reported as well pleased with results. U.S. purchasing agents were also instructed to stimulate production of farm commodities in Panama which would meet health and inspection standards suitable for use in the Zone. The second concession put a $50 limit on luxury goods sold in Canal Zone commissaries and military post exchanges.

In April Panama's new ambassador in Washington, Erasmo de la Guardia, was informed that the Eisenhower administration would prepare new concessions on housing and employment rights for Panamanian citizens on the rolls of both the Canal and the Railroad. Very shortly thereafter President Eisenhower signed an Executive Order raising the pay of 10,000 Panamanian Zone workers by an average of ten percent. Tensions relaxed noticeably. The U.S. Information Agency reopened and soon had almost as many visitors as before the November riots. The Panamanian-American Center for Cultural Exchanges reported an upsurge of people enrolling for a study of the English and Spanish languages.

The most momentous act of any since 1903 came on September 17, 1960, when President Eisenhower ruled that the flag of the Republic of Panama would henceforth be flown in the Canal Zone to symbolize the Isthmian Republic's "titular sovereignty" over the area. According to the presidential order, the flag of Panama would fly beside the Stars and Stripes in one place, a public plaza called Shaler's Triangle located between the Legislative Building on the Panamanian side of the border and the Tivoli Hotel, which is just over the line in the Canal Zone.[6]

On September 22, 1960, the flag raising took place, but under something less than fortuitous circumstances. President de la Guardia sounded the first sour note by refusing to attend the ceremony because no provision had been made for him to personally raise his nation's flag. James E. Patterson, a civilian employee of the U.S. army's Caribbean radio network, was stabbed by an assailant who darted from the crowd as the band was playing the "Star Spangled Banner." Fortunately his wounds were not serious and his attacker was later discovered to be a mental patient. About fifty students from the National Institute demonstrated on the fringes of the crowd carrying signs proclaiming the flag raising "a joking concession" and chanting "Yanqui go home!" On the positive side it must be noted, however, that a crowd of 5,000 spectators gave these fanatics no support whatever but watched with respectful silence as the two flags broke side by side upon this historic occasion. To complete the day upon a favorable note President de la Guardia received the recently appointed U.S. ambassador, Joseph Farland, very cordially at the Presidencia after the ceremony and the two drank a toast to friendship between the two nations.[7]

This final action by President Eisenhower probably accomplished more than anything else. It was done in the hope of settling, as the president said, "by voluntary and unilateral decision on the part of the Government of the United States," the thorny issue of Panama's residual sovereignty over the Canal Zone. Now that the United States had allowed this symbolic act of Panamanian sovereignty, there would be no doubt that the North American authority in the Canal Zone was simply that of a lessee-custodian of a part of the Republic of Panama's national territory. It is significant that no serious further outbreak against the United States plagued the Panamanian scene during the Eisenhower presidency.

Nineteen-sixty was an election year both in Panama and in the

United States. President Eisenhower's Panamanian policies provoked vociferous opposition from a Democratic quarter. On January 9, 1959, Representative Daniel J. Flood, Democrat, of Pennsylvania had made a bitter speech in the House of Representatives at Washington. He had warned that the Panama Canal Zone threatened to become "another Berlin" on our southern doorstep. He had declared that moves by Panamanian nationalists and politicians were aimed at undermining U.S. control of the Canal. His remarks received little attention from the U.S. press, but on January 13, the Panamanian National Assembly unanimously voted him the isthmian republic's "Public Enemy Number One." The Panamanian press headlined his speech for days.[8]

Flood was understandably excited by rumors that the Republican administration was about to make the flag concession. In February, 1960, he was instrumental in persuading Congress to pass a resolution declaring its opposition to flying the flag of Panama within the Canal Zone. Such a resolution would not be binding upon the president because the decision upon the issue would be purely an executive prerogative. Flood feared and believed that the Eisenhower administration intended to ignore the opinion expressed by the Democratic Congress. In June, 1960, he warned Secretary of State Herter that he might face impeachment proceedings if the Panamanian flag were officially raised in the Zone.

During his exchange with the secretary of state, Flood contended that the administration was planning to wait until Congress adjourned before going ahead with the flag plan. (Events proved that he was right about this.) He declared that this would be a "treacherous act," contrary to law and against the spirit of the Hay–Bunau-Varilla Treaty, which gave the United States the Canal Zone "in perpetuity." Secretary Herter answered, "On that point, I shall be guided by the same concern for national interest and constitutional responsibility which governs all of my activities as Secretary of State."

When Congressman Flood learned of President Eisenhower's order on September 17, 1960, he stated that, "In the years of American history impeachment of Presidents has been urged for far less than this. This action . . . is a further appalling example of American diplomatic appeasement, loss of leadership, and weakened integrity in the eyes of the World." Columnist Drew Pearson also found the spectre of partisan politics behind Eisenhower action. The president's announcement came just as the Republican nominee for president, Vice President Richard

M. Nixon, began the intensive phase of his campaign in mid-September. Pearson commented in his nationally syndicated column under the heading "Concession to Nixon":

> Shrewd timing was behind the White House announcement that the Panamanian flag would be permitted to fly over the Panama Canal Zone, thus acknowledging Panama's technical right of sovereignty.

> The U.S. Army and many congressmen have long opposed this. They feared it would be an entering wedge by which Panamanian politicians might later pull a Nasser and demand the canal. The flag dispute has continued between the United States and Panama for over 50 years, and the reason President Eisenhower chose last week to make his announcement was because of Vice President Nixon.

> On November 3, which is Panama's "Fourth of July", a new Panamanian demonstration was planned against the United States similar to last year's riot in which the flag was spat upon and torn to pieces.

> Nixon strategists were worried over the idea of anti-American riots in Panama just five days before the American people went to the polls November 8 to choose between Kennedy and Nixon. It was feared that these riots would recall our other serious troubles in Latin America.

> So, after waiting until Congress was out of town, the White House announced this major concession to Panama regarding sovereignty over the Canal Zone.

Representative Flood's angry blasts at President Eisenhower and Secretary Herter were undoubtedly based upon sincere convictions. Yet he did not seem to have been so critical of a former Democratic president whose expression of views about the Panama Canal during these years were considerably more advanced than anything Mr. Eisenhower seems to have ever dreamed of doing or advocating. In 1945 at the Potsdam Conference, President Truman had shocked almost everybody having any interest in the matter by proposing that the Panama Canal be internationalized along with other waterways of world commerce. The proposal did not get anywhere because Premier Joseph Stalin had no intention of internationalizing waterways then controlled by Russia or its satellites, notably the Danube River where the Soviets were already blowing asunder an International Danubian Commission which had had jurisdiction for nearly a hundred years.[9]

Mr. Truman's proposal would have been anathema to Panamanians as well as to all those concerned about the U.S. position on the isthmus. This view would certainly have been reflected in a majority of the members of Congress. The leaders of the armed services undoubtedly would have taken a strong stand against this proposal. Yet, former President Truman apparently did not subsequently change his views. On November 30, 1958, he appeared on Edward R. Murrow's television show "Small World", along with former British Prime Minister Clement Atlee. The following interchange occurred between Murrow, Atlee, and Truman:

> Murrow "Lord Atlee seems to believe that some of the trouble spots, including Formosa, ought to be internationalized. How do you feel about that, Mr. President? I seem to remember that as far back as 1945 as Potsdam that you suggested certain areas should be internationalized, including, I believe, the Suez Canal."

> Truman "Yes, I did. And the Rhine-Danube Canal, the Kiel Canal, and the Panama Canal. All those waterways, and the Bosporous too, ought to be internationally controlled, and then there wouldn't be any trouble over them."

> Atlee "Yes, I remember very well your putting that forward at Potsdam, and I agreed with you entirely."

> Truman "You certainly did, and we tried our best to get some action on it, but the Russians wouldn't agree to it."

When the outcome of the Suez crisis placed Nasser in successful control and operation of the Suez Canal that episode became the rallying example for Panama's extreme nationalists. They were quick to quote Mr. Truman's words placing the Panama and Suez Canals in the same category, although conveniently ignoring the fact that his proposal for *internationalization* was quite the *antithesis* of both what Nasser accomplished in Egypt and what they urged for Panama.[10] There can be little doubt that Mr. Truman's remarks did more to cause trouble for the United States in Panama than any of Mr. Eisenhower's efforts to eliminate the causes of trouble by making concessions. It appeared to some that Mr. Flood and other Democratic opponents of President Eisenhower's policy were content to overlook Mr. Truman's stand on the matter. But many people, regardless of party affiliation, agreed with Congressman Flood whose influence will have to be taken into account before any new treaty arrangement is concluded.

The Democratic Congress elected in 1956 revived the issue of an "alternative route" to the Panama Canal, a subject which has seemed to attract their party since the days of Senator Morgan. In November, 1957, Congress appointed a group of experts to investigate the future of transisthmian waterways with a particular injunction to look into "alternate locations in the isthmus." Representative Daniel Flood, who was known as a "latter day Morgan," introduced a bill calling for the construction and operation of an interoceanic canal across Nicaragua, essentially the route recommended during the Grant Administration. Before this report was given, President Kennedy took office. Although Mr. Kennedy was politically indebted to the Democratic Party of Pennsylvania in which Congressman Flood was influential, it is difficult to ascertain whether he ever really influenced the new president to any extent on the subject of Panama. In any event the issue was fairly quiet during the Kennedy administration. Mr. Flood remained completely convinced that the Eisenhower administration had initiated an entirely improper course in U.S. dealings with Panama. He became bitterly critical of Democratic President Lyndon Johnson who followed Eisenhower's example with respect to U.S.-Panamanian relations.

During the Eisenhower administration, the nationalized Mexican oil industry, Petroleos Mexicanos, announced that it was studying the feasibility of constructing another deepwater canal across the Isthmus of Tehuantepec, another historic route. This waterway would be quite divorced from questions such as Panamanian sovereignty, U.S. control, and internationalization which constantly plague the operation of the present canal. It would be an enterprise of the Mexican government, across Mexican territory, unconcerned with the status of any other power or state. During the 1960's nothing was done about the idea, but as long as the ultimate fate of the Panama route remains in doubt, Tehuantepec is an ever-present shadow over the future.

The presidential election of 1960 in the Republic of Panama appeared to result in improved relations with the United States. The administration of former president Ernesto de la Guardia, Jr. had been basically friendly to Washington, but weak at times in the face of ultranationalistic drives against the old bogey of *Imperialismo Yan-qui*. Its attitude toward the United States seemed tempered by the reaction of the anti-Yanqui zealots, as was demonstrated during the riots of November 1959.

In 1960 there were three principal candidates for the Isthmian presidency. The candidate for the National Patriotic Coalition (de la Guardia's supporters) was Ricardo Arias. Several members of his famous family had been Panamanian presidents and statesmen of great stature. For the Opposition National Union the candidate was Roberto Chiari, a wealthy sugar planter and dairy farmer, and the son of a former Panamanian president. Victor F. Goytia ran on the Popular Alliance ticket. A distinguished lawyer, diplomat, and statesman, he was supported by many leftist elements.

The voting was conducted in the excited atmosphere typical of Panamanian elections, but with remarkably little violence. People stitched the names of their favorite candidates on their shirts, and automobile caravans moved about flying rival party banners. But about the only untoward incident occurred in Panama City where hoodlums invaded five precinct polling places and seized the ballots and record tallies to prevent their delivery to the National Election Jury. This body makes the official count, and in 1960 it took them thirteen days to complete the tally. There can be little doubt that the election was handled with scrupulous honesty, because the administration candidate lost by a substantial plurality, despite widely circulated rumors that technicalities would be used by the Election Jury to throw out opposition votes.

The figures were announced officially on May 21, 1960. Chairi received 100,152 votes, Arias 86,192, and Goytia 55,613. The Panamanian election was a splendid example of peaceful democratic procedures working smoothly and effectively in Latin America despite all manner of political turbulence in neighboring republics during the same election year. The people of Panama had every reason to be very proud of this performance, but unfortunately it was not destined to be the pattern of future isthmian elections.[11]

Both Panama and the United States moved into 1961 with a turnover to new administrations which had ousted the incumbent political parties. After it took office in October 1960 the Chiari administration, controlled local Communists much more firmly than had its predecessor. Yanquis from the Canal Zone were once more buying in Panamanian shops and seeking recreation and entertainment in Panama

City and Colón. Denunciation of Castro in Panamanian newspapers and public forums was more outspoken than in most other Caribbean countries, and the Chiari government followed other hemispheric states in breaking diplomatic relations with Cuba.

The tragically short administration of John F. Kennedy was pre-occupied with international areas other than Panama. At the time of Kennedy's death in November, 1963, former President Eisenhower's were the most positive actions taken toward solving the canal issues, despite the Democratic opposition in Congress led by Representative Flood. Most observers were convinced that no single action of the past twenty-five years had had as much of an effect as President Eisen-hower's decision to fly the flag of Panama inside the Canal Zone. This action was a palliative to wounded Panamanian national pride and to the feeling that Panama had been deprived of a part of its sovereign birthright. Nevertheless, some Panamanians still advocated a Nasser-like takeover of the Canal. They sought a more definitive recognition of Panamanian sovereignty over *all* of its national territory. During the Kennedy administration, the two crises in Cuba so preoccupied the diplomats of the Western Hemisphere that headlines dealing with the Bay of Pigs, Punta del Este, and the missile confrontation relegated Panama and the Canal to secondary consideration.

President Kennedy was personally involved in only one signifi-cant meeting with Panamanian President Roberto Chiari. In June, 1962, when President Chiari spent a week in Washington, D.C., the two presidents conferred for many hours about isthmian matters. However no discernible results emerged from their conversations which in any way affected the status quo which Panama was so eager to change.

President Kennedy is remembered in Panama as the creator of the Peace Corps.[12] This agency has achieved some remarkable results in many parts of Latin America and has given a new and favorable image to *el gringo*. The young men and women who came to Panama with the Peace Corps deliberately stayed aloof from most other United States personnel on the isthmus, whether diplomatic, military, or civil service "Zonian." They dedicated themselves to social and economic improvement and almost always worked directly through official Pan-amanian agencies. They mingled freely with and were accepted by the Panamanians. The wild rioting of 1964 left this group of North Amer-icans and their work virtually untouched.

Another Kennedy innovation was the Alliance for Progress.[13]

Considerable sums of money, proportionate to the republic's total economy, were dispensed in Panama mainly through the Agency for International Development (AID). The United States financed the bridge which replaced the old Thatcher Ferry at the Pacific end of the Canal and finally brought the Pan American Highway to Panama City. But the United States rejected the Panamanian suggestion that this structure be called the "Bridge of the Americas." This rejection and the probability that much of the material benefit of *Alianza Para Progresso* (the Alliance for Progress) as well as other funds ultimately went to the oligarchy instead of the needy masses undoubtedly blunted both the practical and psychological effects of economic assistance.

The replacement of Ambassador Joseph S. Farland in August, 1963, was an event of clear psychological disadvantage to the United States. Mr. Farland was not a "career diplomat" in the classic sense, and had been a more or less political appointee of the Republican Eisenhower administration. The new Democratic regime in Washington did not find him *simpático* even though the Panamanians did. During his years on the isthmus, Mr. Farland achieved a reputation for being a true friend of Panama and its people. This did not endear him to "Zonians," or to the military, and when he was thought to be opposed to *Alianza Para Progreso*, that supposition ended whatever slight chance there might have been of Washington retaining him as ambassador to Panama.[14]

Actually he was critical of the *Alianza* for failing to recognize the great social welfare needs of Panama, and his apprehension that its programs would be more helpful to the great families than to those who needed it most was perceptive. Nevertheless, his resignation, which was tendered as a matter of form with the change of administration in Washington, was accepted. When he arrived home he was not even given the usual debriefing which almost always accompanies an ambassador's terminating a mission. His successor had not been appointed when President Kennedy was assassinated. Thus the events of January, 1964, caught the United States without an ambassador in Panama City.[15]

11

President Johnson
Fails to End
the Panama Problem

The first major international crisis that President Lyndon Johnson had to handle exploded in Panama where such a vital problem was to be least anticipated. In January, 1964, rioting, caused by resentment over U.S. control of the Canal Zone, broke out quite unexpectedly. The immediate cause of the riots was undetected and the scope which it ultimately attained was unforeseen. Before the fighting was over, almost 700 people were killed or injured. U.S. property sustained more than $2,000,000 in damages and relations between the United States and Panama deteriorated considerably.[1] The new U.S. president faced a flaming revival of old issues only a little more than a month after the assassination of John Kennedy.

On January 9, 1964, about two hundred Panamanians marched into the Canal Zone from Panama City. They were conducting a demonstration to protest the refusal of Balboa High School to fly the Panamanian flag beside the U.S. flag.[2]

The Panamanians were making an undeniably valid point. Robert J. Fleming, Jr., governor of the Canal Zone, had ordered the Panamanian flag to be flown alongside the United States flag at all civilian locations in the Canal Zone. In the event any facilities such as the Balboa High School would not do this, no flag at all was to be flown. These orders resulted from the agreement which the United States had made with Panama during the Eisenhower administration.[3]

A large group of U.S. citizens—men, women, and children—were gathered on the school lawn near the flagpole. About thirty students of the Balboa High School staged a sit-down strike around the flagpole and refused to move. When the crowd began to sing the "Star Spangled Banner," Captain Gaddis Wall, district chief of the Canal Zone police, fearing violence, asked the Panamanians to leave. When they refused to go, the police officers backed them away with riot sticks and during the scuffle the Panamanian flag became torn. A full-scale battle ensued with Panamanians throwing stones into the police lines. More demonstrators arrived and began to break street lights and attack passing automobiles. As the mob moved past Gorgas Hospital, some threw stones at its windows. Canal Zone police were ordered not to make any arrests as long as the mob kept moving toward the Panama City boundary. Canal Zone officials requested the Panamanian government to send the Panamanian National Guard to the scene to help restore order. Such support was never sent despite calls made by the United States Embassy in Panama City. On the contrary, the Panamanian president, Roberto F. Chiari, instructed the National Guard not to interfere or try to control the crowds.[4] This action was accepted by the rioters as a presidential blessing to burn, wreck, and shoot at will in the "Yanqui occupied" Zone.

In the meantime other mobs in Panama City began to attack U.S. citizens in the streets and to set fire to their cars. Invasions of the Canal Zone at many points caused still more property destruction and attacks upon U.S. citizens. In several hours the demonstrations spread from Panama City on the Pacific to Colón on the Atlantic side of the isthmus, and Cristobal in the Canal Zone. Molotov cocktails, machetes, guns, and other dangerous weapons were widely employed by the mobs, which ran wild.

The acting governor of the Canal Zone, David S. Parker, then called for help from General Andrew P. O'Meara, Commander of the U.S. Southern Command in the Canal Zone. General O'Meara ordered the Pacific area of the Canal Zone cleared of all unauthorized personnel and alerted authorities on the Atlantic side. When the rioting spread from Colón to Cristobal, the Atlantic side was also cleared. The U.S. troops used only tear gas despite sniper fire being directed toward them near the Hotel Tivoli in the Canal Zone town of Ancon. Because the Panamanian National Guard continued to withhold its help, General O'Meara finally approved the use of thirty-caliber rifles by trained army marksmen.[5]

The mobs continued to riot throughout the night and into the next day. By this time, five North Americans had been killed in the Canal Zone—four soldiers and one civilian. Many others had been injured and heavy property damage was reported. Panama Canal offices and buildings, the Ancon railroad station, the Cristobal YMCA, the Masonic Temple, a number of churches and many other buildings were destroyed or severely damaged. Hundreds of automobiles were gutted by fire. Even the convent of the Maryknoll sisters was attacked and the nuns were forced to flee for their lives. During all of these bitter hours, Panamanian radio and television stations as well as newspapers beat out a steady stream of anti-Yanqui abuse which obviously further incited Panamanians into broader actions.

About noon on January 10, 1964, President Chiari, now thoroughly alarmed at a situation which seemed completely out of hand, informed General O'Meara that the National Guard would take action against the rioters. General O'Meara then issued a cease-fire order, but it soon became apparent that the Panamanian Guard was still doing nothing. During the night of January 10, sniping and other attacks threatened U.S. troops, who were under orders not to return the fire. On January 12, U.S. troops used tear gas to reduce the rioting on the Pacific side, but on the Atlantic side the Panamanians increased their attacks until General O'Meara decided that his soldiers had no option but to return sniper fire. Finally on January 13, the Panamanian National Guard moved to restore order in Panama City and in Colón. At 8:00 A.M. on Thursday, January 16, General O'Meara withdrew military control of the Canal Zone and turned it back to civilian authority under Governor Fleming. There had been an entire week of bitter turmoil without precedent in the history of the Canal Zone.[6]

President Roberto F. Chiari had ordered the Panamanian ambassador to leave Washington and had "suspended" relations between his country and the United States, charging aggression against the people of Panama. The Republic of Panama then appealed to the United Nations and to the Organization of American States, charging unprovoked aggression against Panama by the United States.

Although the break in diplomatic relations had appeared to be at first a very serious move, the Panamanian government soon announced that it would resume relations with the United States after a "cooling off period."[7] Through the mediation of Costa Rica, which was named to handle Panamanian affairs in Washington during the break, an agreement was reached by Edwin Martin, a special envoy appointed by President Johnson, and Panamanian Foreign Minister Galileo Solis to negotiate differences through the Peace Committee of the Organization of American States. On January 15, the OAS had stated that "formal discussions will be initiated thirty days after diplomatic relations are re-established by representatives who will have sufficient powers to discuss without limitations all existing matters of any nature which may affect the relations between the United States and Panama."[8] The Martin-Solis talks began the next day.

On February 4, 1964, the Council of the Organization of American States, acting as the "Consultative Organ," in accordance with the Rio Charter Treaty of 1947, voted to declare that U.S. troops had used a "disproportionate amount of firepower" to quell the disturbances. The OAS refused, however, to find that the United States had committed an "aggression" against Panama. (The United States, Panama, and Bolivia abstained from these votes.)

During the aftermath of the January rioting, the Panamanian Bar Association requested the International Commission of Jurists in Geneva, a privately supported organization with consultative status at the United Nations, to make an impartial inquiry. These jurists were sent by the International Commission to look into the Panamanian affair. They reported that the force used by the United States was justified in order to protect lives and property against mob action.[9] They exonerated the Canal Zone administration and the United States Army except in the area of possible measures which might have been taken to prevent the flag incident from growing to such proportions. The Commission's inquiry declared that Panamanian authorities actually adopted means "to incite and misinform the Panamanian public without any action by the Panamanian authorities to curtail or moderate such activities."[10] On June 10, 1964, State Department Press Officer Richard I. Phillips declared in Washington, "We welcome this detailed study by an impartial body giving an objective account of the unfortunate events of January."

The report also exonerated the United States of the charge that it violated the universal Declaration of Human Rights of the United Nations, a charge which the International Commission of Jurists had specifically been asked to investigate by the National Bar Association of Panama. The report concluded with the hope that the work of the International Commission of Jurists would contribute to the growth of understanding, cooperation, and amnesty between the two countries and their peoples in order that they might move forward in the furtherance of mutual vital interests. The findings of this Commission constituted the only action taken by a United Nations body regarding this affair.

The simple fact that both Panama and the United States were scheduled to have presidential elections in 1964 complicated the situation immensely. U.S. public opinion, aroused by the riots in the Canal Zone, reacted strongly against any U.S. compromise which would "appease" the Panamanian radicals. Representative Daniel Flood said that flying both flags was the original mistake. Representative August B. Johanson of Michigan, Republican, denouncing any appeasement of Panama, recalled that in 1960 the House of Representatives had passed a resolution prohibiting the use of U.S. funds for flying Panama's flag in the Zone.

There was even disagreement over the exact meaning of the communiqué issued in both English and Spanish by the OAS Peace Committee.[11] The Panamanians translated it as saying that the United States agreed to "negotiate" a new Canal treaty as soon as peace was reestablished. The United States interpreted it as an agreement to "discuss" Panama's grievances. A prolonged debate over this misunderstanding delayed arrival of the new Panamanian ambassador in Washington until May, 1964. This actual resumption of regular relations indicated that the Panamanian version was finally accepted.

When Marco Robles[12] was elected to the Panamanian presidency, tension between the U.S. and Panama was still escalating. For several months, any further talks concerning new treaties between the two countries had been languishing because of President Johnson's reluctance to be accused of giving in to the demands of a Panamanian street mob and prejudicing the peacemaking efforts of the United States. Flag incidents had continued. On March 27, 1964, Panamanians were pleased that the U.S. flag in the Canal Zone was flown at half-staff beside Panama's flag in commemoration of former President José Pezet. Yet in April when General Douglas MacArthur died, the Panamanians refused to permit their flag to be lowered in honor of him, saying that the flag of the republic would never be kept at half-staff in tribute to a United States Army officer.[13] President Roberto Chiari further demanded that the Panamanian flag in the Canal Zone which was lowered in honor of General MacArthur be raised.

Both Panama and the United States strongly suspected that Communist agents of the Castro government had been playing a large part in Panamanian troubles.[14] Three well-known Communist leaders had been observed taking active parts in the January riots: Floyd Britton;

Thelma King, a member of the Panamanian Assembly, who knew Castro and frequently visited Cuba; and Victor Avila, a student leader at the University of Panama who was known to have been trained in Cuba. President Robles commented that "In every country of Latin America we are suffering from the pressure of international Communism either directly from the Iron Curtain countries of Europe or through the island of Cuba—I want to tell the Communists here and abroad that they don't have the opportunity to achieve their objectives in this country—during my administration there will be no opportunity for extremist groups to try to block the development of our country." Robles further declared that he had two basic objectives. First he hoped to negotiate a new Canal treaty which would be "fair and just from the viewpoints of both countries." Second he wanted to stimulate to the maximum "all possibilities for the economic and social development of Panama."

In January, 1965, on the first anniversary of the bloody 1964 riots, demonstrators again attempted a march on the Canal Zone. About one hundred students and labor organization members started to move toward the zone boundary across the street from the Legislative Palace. President Robles ordered the Panamanian National Guard to break up the movement. A few moments after six grenades of tear gas were hurled into the crowd, the whole area was cleared and traffic returned to normal.

Earlier, 1500 marchers had paraded to the grave of the student Ascino Arosemena, who was the first of twenty-one Panamanians and four North Americans to die in the 1964 rioting. The marchers carried many anti-U.S. banners and chanted slogans. As usual, well-known Communists were prominent in the procession. But far more Panamanians attended ceremonies at a private cemetery on the outskirts of Panama City where the other Panamanian victims of the 1964 riots were buried. The government sponsored this observance which was broadcast over the national radio networks.

Later, in November, 1965, President Robles called upon the National Guard to disperse about 2,000 students gathered outside the Legislative Palace. The students, organized mainly by a leftist student organization to demonstrate for a strong line in negotiations with the United States over the Panama Canal Zone, were defying a ban against demonstrations issued by the municipal administration and approved by the national government. Because the National Guard acted promptly, using tear gas and clubs to disperse the crowd, the affair amounted to very little. President Robles also firmly rejected demands that the National Guard be removed from the Canal Zone boundary where they had been stationed to prevent demonstrators from entering the Canal Zone. Fifteen intersections leading into the United States area were policed in this manner with very effective results.[15]

From time to time, President Robles also ordered the arrest of certain Communist leaders when their plans to disrupt negotiations with United States appeared to be serious. In February, 1965, twelve Communist leaders were jailed under this policy.

The Communist party continued to be outlawed in Panama but about 500 hard core members, using other party designations, were active in political affairs. About 300 people believed to have been trained in Cuba lived in Panama. Another 5,000 Panamanians, many of them high school and university students, worked closely with Communist leaders. The Communists charged that President Robles was too cooperative with the United States and they were ever watchful for opportunities to cause trouble in the Canal Zone.

In 1966 President Robles had to deal with outbursts in both Colón and Panama City when a student leader, Juan Pojaro, was murdered and a presidential partisan was charged with the slaying. There was not the slightest evidence that any agent of the Security Investigation Department had killed Pajaro, as the left wing indictment declared. After he had been found with a crushed skull on a roadside near Colón, groups of youths and adults in Panama City and Colón overturned garbage cans, turned in false fire alarms, threw fire bombs, and hurled bricks at cars. Again Robles acted with firmness, speaking to the nation in a radio broadcast in which he charged that the outbreak was a Communist plot to destroy democracy in Panama. He promptly ordered the National Guard to disperse the mobs.[16]

These incidents on the isthmus caused President Johnson to explain the U.S. position:[17]

> The United States tries to live by the policy of the good neighbor and expects others to do the same. The United States cannot allow the security of the Panama Canal to be imperiled. . . . We have a recognized obligation to operate the Canal efficiently and securely and we intend to honor that obligation in the interests of all who depend upon it. Many serious differences exist in the relations between the United States and Panama but these can be solved if they are approached with an open mind and open heart.

Mr. Johnson said that he was certain that the claims of Panama are "based on a deeply felt sense of the honest and fair needs of Panama" and not on malice or hatred of the United States. He contended that "It is our obligation as allies and partners to review these claims and meet them, when meeting them is just and possible. . . . We are prepared to review every issue that now divides us and every issue which the Panamanian government wishes to raise."

Time and the strong anti-Communist policy of President Robles did much to assuage U.S. fears that some damage might result from concessions to Panama. In the fall of 1965, Presidents Johnson and Robles jointly announced an agreement to renegotiate the old canal treaties and to write a new one recognizing Panama's sovereignty. The present Zone was to be gradually integrated with the rest of Panama until such time as a new canal would be built. The United States expressed its intention to build a new sea level canal and to grant Panama full sovereignty over the present canal and Canal Zone at such time as the new waterway would be open to traffic.[18]

The Panama Canal with its six locks will soon be obsolete if it is actually not so already. More than 300 of the world's leading ships are too big to pass through it. President Johnson asked for surveys of four possible routes for a new sea level canal. Two of these routes are in Panama, one is in Colombia, and one runs through Nicaragua. These new surveys will take several years and actual construction of a new canal should take from fifteen to twenty years more.

Mr. Johnson's announcement of the U.S. intention to grant Panama full sovereignty over the Canal Zone as soon as a new canal began operation was termed "transcendental" by President Robles. But there were doubts among some of Robles' countrymen who recognized that Panama's economy depends on continued operation of the Canal. The possibility of a waterway through Colombia or Nicaragua was not one Panamanian business interests could accept calmly.[19]

Naturally, the "Zonians," or transplanted North Americans who have lived on the isthmus for so many years and have made the Zone a kind of United States surburbia, were antagonistic to a new treaty. The attitude of James Jenkins, a young man who led the flag raising act in front of Balboa High School and set off bloody clashes between soldiers and Panamanian mobs[20] in January, 1964, is typical.

Jenkins, whose father was employed as a locomotive operator at the Canal locks, had lived in the Canal Zone for 15 years. He said that he thought rioting would have occurred sooner or later anyway. He was critical of the Canal Zone police for not meeting the Panamanians head on and preventing them from entering the Canal Zone. He undoubtedly expressed the views of thousands of Zonians: "I personally don't like the Panamanian flag flying at an American school."

The gap between the two cultures on the Isthmus grows deeper all the time. Most United States personnel stay close to the Canal Zone. Free passage back and forth across Fourth of July Avenue has become a thing of the past. Signs warning Yanquis that they are not welcome have appeared in Panamanian bars, restaurants, theaters, and hotels. Because the Canal Zone is self-sufficient, most "Zonians" appear not to care that the gulf thus widens. They bridle with anger at every new report of efforts at diplomatic negotiations which "threatens" their enclave. All too often they appear to be defensive and superpatriotic in their attitudes, bearing an unfortunate resemblance to the colonial imperialists of old which have long been the standard targets of Communist agitation.

President Johnson's announcement included a promise that ultimately the United States would dig a new interoceanic canal in Central America. Panamanians were disturbed when he indicated that four locations were to be evaluated and that only two were in Panama. The four[21] under consideration were (1) the site of the present canal, (2) the Atrato River Valley in Northwestern Colombia, (3) The San Juan River Valley in Nicaragua which the McKinley administration had favored because of the Walker Commission's recommendations, and (4) the Sasardi-Morti, Panama, route.

However, an entirely new possibility concerning the new canal was suggested. A sea level canal could be built at a comparatively moderate cost if nuclear explosives rather than conventional methods were used for the excavation. Engineers favor a route through the sparsely populated Darien province south of the present canal in Panama and the cost is estimated at one billion dollars. This is a rather modest cost for such a tremendous feat. The main engineering problem would be the safe use of atomic energy so as not to endanger people and property. U.S. engineers have proposed that nuclear devices be buried deep in the earth and detonated in a line across the isthmus to open the bed of the canal. Dr. Glen T. Seaborg, chairman of the U.S. Atomic Energy Commission, declared early in 1965 that he could deliver reasonably safe atomic devices for the project if the AEC were given a five-year period to research all aspects of the question.

The canal carved out by this procedure would be 1,000 feet wide and sixty feet deep. Over a two- to three-year period approximately 300 nuclear devices would be exploded. Several would be linked in single shots and the total number of detonations would range between fourteen and twenty-one. Of these, thirteen would release approximately ten megatons of explosive force. Engineers estimate a total of 166.4 megatons needed to carve out the canal. This is about 8,320 times more powerful than the Hiroshima bomb. This nuclear device would be set so that the craters would have the most desirable depth and shape, with a maximum center depth of about 250 feet for the range diameter. Holes to depths of from 550 to 2100 feet would be drilled across the isthmus.

In addition to the problem created by the small population actually living in the region (about 30,000 Indians) there is a complication in the field of international law. The Nuclear Test Ban Treaty prohibits releasing into the atmosphere any radioactive materials which might cross the borders of another country. It is likely that a number of tests would have to be made to determine whether blasts from the canal would hold any potential for atomic poisoning of the atmosphere. It also seems likely that the Soviet Union, Britain, and any other signatories of the Nuclear Test Ban Treaty might be asked to agree to a waiver of the ban for this purpose so obviously beneficial to mankind. It can be seen how problematical such an approach to the Soviet Union might be. It is hard to conceive that the Soviets would give their consent without demanding some *quid pro quo* that the United States either could or would not be ready to grant.[22] On August 8, 1967, President Johnson sent Congress the third annual report of the Atlantic-Pacific Interoceanic Canal Study Commission which has been evaluating technical data to determine the feasibility of a new waterway.

The Commission's data collected on the four proposed routes indicated that nuclear explosives might feasibly be employed in the excavation of sites in the Darien region of Panama or in the Atrato River Basin in northwestern Colombia. The report also indicated that nuclear explosives could not be used either to reconstruct the present canal or to excavate the San Juan–Lake Nicaragua route.

In a message to Congress, President Johnson said that increased traffic would necessitate building the waterway sooner than anticipated and asked Congress to approve a two and one half year extension of the Commission's existence as well as $17.5 billion to enable it to continue its study of feasible routes for a new canal.

According to an Associated Press dispatch of November 8, 1970, the Commission's report to President Nixon stated that nuclear excavation would not be feasible largely because of the political problems engendered by the nuclear test ban treaty and that using "conventional explosives" to dig a canal would cost an estimated three billion dollars. The Commission also indicated its preference for a Panamian canal route because the estimated cost of non-nuclear excavation in Nicaragua and Colombia would be prohibitive.

The construction of a new sea level canal would be enormously advantageous to world commerce, but Panama would suffer from almost certain economic disaster if the site of the new canal were outside its boundaries. Panama offers the best and most economical sea level route between the two oceans. Furthermore, the possibility of earthquakes—controversial in Theodore Roosevelt's time—is much less in Panama than in either of the alternative nations.

As potentially disrupting as earthquakes, however, would be the threat of Panamanian mob outbreaks against U.S. activity in the Canal Zone. A thorough analysis of this factor might lead Washington to seek outside of Panama for an alternate route, despite costs. Colombia offers such a route for a sea level canal capable of carrying almost any conceivable volume of shipping. The Lake Nicaragua route in the San Juan region offers an equally attractive possibility. Since 1964 the United States has conducted negotiations with Colombia and Nicaragua, as well as the talks concerning treaty revision with Panama.

Experts agree that by 1980 interoceanic traffic would exceed the present canal's capacity. Ships will then be required to wait in line for passage, at great expense to ship owners and to consumers. At the present time the canal's systems of locks 1,000 feet long and 110 feet wide prevent its use by modern U.S. aircraft carriers, super tankers, and the larger passenger liners. A new canal without locks would also have the advantage of a smaller working force, about one tenth of the number of men required to operate the present intricate system.[23]

Soon after President Robles was elected in 1964, he appointed Fernando Eleta foreign minister of Panama. Señor Eleta publicly supported the Morti route in southeastern Panama and expressed the fear, shared by many of his countrymen, that Panama would suffer dire economic consequences should the canal be built elsewhere. Cynical opponents of the Robles administration pointed out that Eleta's family allegedly owns a large tract of undeveloped land in the Morti area and that they would receive tremendous sums to compensate for any acreage given up for a canal project.

President Robles tied his hope for a new canal route in Panama to the Panamanian ambition to end U.S. control of the present Canal Zone.[24] A sea level canal would be simpler to operate and harder to sabotage. It would require only hundreds rather than thousands of men to maintain and operate it. The United States would have no need to maintain large military and civilian establishments, or to control a zone on the isthmus. This is an appealing argument to Panamanian nationalists who have continuously contended that Panama ought to exploit its economical geographical position without U.S. control, intervention, or influence; for instance, Panamanians would like to charge higher tolls on ships' transitting. These tolls would bolster Panama's economy. Panamanians even talk of borrowing money from a great power other than the United States, even Russia, so that Panama itself could build a new canal. Obviously this is an attempted counterfoil to the possibility of the United States building a canal elsewhere.

The Soviet Union would have a much greater potentiality for mischief if it aided Panama to build a canal than it did when it gave Nasser the Aswan Dam and supported Egypt's restricted use of the Suez Canal.

Unfortunately the entire matter was beclouded once more by the imminence of presidential elections in both Panama and the United States. In Washington, all the old protests against surrendering of sovereignty over the Canal Zone were being renewed. In the Republic of Panama, political foes of President Robles, particularly the ultranationalists and the Communists, opposed any of the agreements made by his administration. The Canal was one of the main issues of the Panamanian election.[25] Former President Arnulfo Arias vowed to attack any new treaty no matter what it contained. Arias considered any kind of U.S. influence in Panama to be Yanqui colonialism, whether found in the present Canal Zone or in the operation of a future canal zone. Yet some informed "insiders" believed that, if elected, Arias would push ratification of the treaties.

In April, 1967, at the Inter-American Conference in Punta del Este, Uruguay, Presidents Robles and Johnson had agreed to negotiate a new Panama Canal treaty as quickly as possible. President Johnson said that only two matters were still unresolved, (1) the question of revenues and (2) the application of procedures of justice in the question of how to treat certain lands. He then declared, "We will meet again in the next few months to wrap it up."

On June 26, 1967, the two governments announced that they had reached an agreement on draft treaties. The terms of the Robles-

Johnson agreements have never been announced formally. The explanation given was that such treaties had to be signed and submitted for ratification according to the constitutional procedures of each signatory before an official text could be released. However, the time-honored Washington device of the "informed source" was quoted in various press, radio, and television stories so that the complete version of the terms of the proposed treaties was soon known. Apparently the Johnson administration believed that, if fully informed, the U.S. public would support an effort to end Panamanian problems in view of the crises which had occurred since 1964. The president, however, did not realize the political power of those who were opposed to any concessions to Panama.

According to the terms of the tentative agreement made public in June, 1967, the United States was to surrender all vestiges of sovereignty over the Panama Canal Zone. Panama would share in the administration and operation of the Canal, as well as in any sea level canal that might be built on its soil in the future. The present canal would become the property of a "United States–Panamanian Authority" to be created jointly by the two governments and the Canal Zone would be considered an integral part of Panama.

Actually, three treaties were involved in the negotiations between the United States and Panama. One concerned the present canal, another dealt with the sea level canal, and the third covered the defense of the canal and its neutrality. The new treaties were to end the Hay–Bunau-Varilla agreement, the central political issue in Panamanian politics which led to the riots of January, 1964.

Under the new agreement, Panama was to receive a much higher share of the canal tolls although the exact percentage was not made public. Presumedly President Johnson was referring to this point at Punta del Este. The present canal was to continue to be opened at all times to vessels of all nations. The United States also agreed to provide increased economic aid to the Republic of Panama.

Not only were the new treaties an issue in the Panamanian elections but congressional anger exploded in Washington, D.C.[26] Representative Daniel J. Flood of Pennsylvania declared on the floor of the House of Representatives, "I am so mad about this, coming on top of the Mideast situation, that I could spit." Mr. Flood urged his colleagues to exert every effort to block ratification, saying that "the Panama Canal is the jugular vein of hemispheric defense." He said that to relinquish United States sovereignty would speed Soviet Russia toward its goal of controlling most of the vital waterways of the world. The day that the United States abandons its "indispensable authority" over the Zone, he said, "Panama will cease to be a free and independent country and will go down the Communist drain." Representative Robert Taft, Jr., Republican of Ohio, said it was "particularly unfortunate . . . that such a step should be proposed at this time when the Middle East crisis has raised complicating factors about international access to waterways . . ." Mr. Taft added that the treaty was announced just as Soviet Premier Alexei Kosygin arrived in Cuba, "the center of Communist subversive activity in this Hemisphere."

Kosygin's visit to Havana seemed to many people to be proof of the continuing danger of Communist subversion throughout Latin America. The obviously strategic nature of the Panama Canal made it a prime target for subversion in their minds. Senator Norris Cotton, Republican of New Hampshire, said that surrender of sovereignty "could pose a grave threat to U.S. security." He added, "Until a new canal is constructed, the Panama Canal is the lone link for our naval forces and other shipping between east and west coasts." Representative Archer Nelsen, Republican of Minnesota, urged that the United States retain its jurisdiction of the Canal. He declared, "Forfeiting control of the Panama Canal with Castro offshore stirring hemispheric revolution is like planting a land mine underneath our own house." Senator Strom Thurmond, Republican of South Carolina, emphasized "the property that now would be abandoned is federal property as sure as any national park or military reservation." He also declared that if U.S. national interest truly demanded a divestiture of its authority in the Zone—and emphasized that it does not—then the U.S. taxpayer "ought to recover something on his investment." But of course under these treaties Panama was to receive funds, not *pay* them. Representative Edna Kelly, Republican of New York, also joined in attacking the treaties. Representative Lenore K. Sullivan, Democrat of Missouri, made a long and very vitriolic speech. Mrs. Sullivan said, "Remember what has happened to the Suez Canal. Remember what happened to Cuba. It is not news to anyone that Communists are active in Panama!"

Mrs. Sullivan was Chairman of the Panama Canal Subcommittee of the House Merchant Marine and Fisheries Committee. She was the presumed leader of a bloc reportedly numbering more than 120 congressmen who sought to prevent Senate ratification of the three new treaties covering the Panama Canal. Mrs. Sullivan submitted a resolution urging the House to declare that the proposed transfer of control of the Canal to a joint U.S.-Panamanian commission "is not in the national interest of the United States—the canal is a vital element in our defense and must be free of interference by local nationalistic pressures."

In the House, the Foreign Affairs Committee held closed hearings on the proposed new treaties and Mrs. Sullivan was one of the first witnesses. She declared, "Panama's government has never been interested in the people. All they care about is how fast they can get their hands on how much money." She declared that backers of the new agreement expected the maritime industry to launch a campaign to block ratification but she doubted that the opponents of the treaties would get any help from the ship-owners. "When the canal tolls are raised, they'll just pass the increase along to shippers and the shippers will pass the cost on to you and me."

Under the new agreement, Panama could get as much as $22,-000,000 a year in tolls compared to the current payment of $1,930,000 a year by the U.S. She asserted, "Panama's oligarchy will swallow up all the money. The Panamanian people will get nothing.

"Our negotiators gave up more than they needed to satisfy the Panamanians, and nothing they could do would really satisfy the Panamanians unless we gave them the Canal and everything, lock, stock, and barrel."

It was a cardinal error, she declared, to give up United States sovereignty over the Canal Zone. "That zone is just like a foreign embassy in Washington," said Mrs. Sullivan. "The host country has no authority there. I'd have been willing to drop the offensive words 'in perpetuity' from the 1903 agreement, but I'd have insisted on 99 years, or some number of years of U.S. sovereignty." She continued, "Sovereignty allowed the U.S. to keep troops in the zone where they could defend the Canal properly. Even though United States troops might remain in Panama under another treaty, there is nothing to stop the Panamanians from renouncing the new treaty and demanding that our troops leave."

In Panama, Major General Robert J. Fleming, Jr., governor of the Panama Canal Zone for more than four years and a key figure in negotiations with Panama over the new treaties, was a moderate voice heard in the controversy: "I knew it was going to be a tough job and I wasn't going to win any popularity contests. I don't know how I got selected for the job. I didn't want it. After all, I am a soldier. There were things I wanted to do in the military service but I called a senior officer for advice and he counseled me to 'do as you are told.' And I came. My reputation was established and the way I operate is well known. So the people who sent me down here knew what they were getting."

In its issue of August 3, 1966, the *Panama Star and Herald* published a news story which quoted General Fleming as saying that he was appointed governor of the Canal Zone for the purpose of scuttling U.S. control. All of this was an assault upon the general which coincided with a nationwide campaign in the United States against the various threats of a reputedly right wing organization, the Liberty Lobby, to launch an emergency mailing which would call the treaties "a sellout of U.S. sovereignty and an act that will expose the Canal to communist take-over. Fidel Castro's ships are using the Canal Zone to carry supplies to North Viet Nam. The State Department admits this but does nothing to stop it even though these supplies will be used to kill American soldiers." Representative Daniel Flood referred to this point and remarked that the United States had the authority to halt this traffic under Article II of the 1903 Treaty, providing for the "construction, maintenance, operation, sanitation, and protection" of the Panama Canal. Under this provision, five months before Pearl Harbor, all transit of the Panama Canal was denied Japanese ships on security grounds and he cited that precedent.

Mrs. Edith K. Roosevelt, a syndicated columnist whose views on the subject would have met with the approval of President Theodore Roosevelt, also launched an attack on General Fleming. She declared in one of her colunms that General Fleming was the real instigator of President Johnson's promise to end American sovereignty in the Canal Zone. She identified Governor Fleming as one "who knows how to please the new Left" in the State Department and quoted him as saying,

I have been paving the way for what is literally a sellout: I had no detailed instructions on what to do when I came. I made my own analyses, made up my own mind on what should be done, and I started out to get it done. It would be stupid of me to say that I have had no instructions but practically all of these later instructions have been confirmations of what we down here had recommended. I can say that every action the United States has taken since I have been here has been the end product of the most thorough consideration by the United States Government.

The new treaties were to have been ready for signature by the summer of 1968. But opposition developed in both countries as soon as the substance of the proposed terms became known. Congressman Flood proclaimed his anger to have reached a stage where he felt like spitting. In short order all of the traditional foes of concessions to Panama joined the firing line. These included such powerful groups as the Daughters of the American Revolution, the American Legion, and the Military Order of the World Wars. Democratic Senator Talmadge of Georgia joined Republicans Thurmond of South Carolina, Dirksen of Illinois, and Hickenlooper of Iowa in expressing either downright opposition or serious reservations. Since ratification of treaties by the United States requires a two-thirds vote of the Senate, Mr. Dirksen's stand would have been a critical factor if the proposals had come to a vote.

The proposed Joint Authority which would operate the canal was unacceptable to many Panamanians. This proposal called for five U.S. and four Panamanian members of the Authority or four U.S. members and one U.N. representative, a U.S. majority in both cases.[27] The Panamanians argued that this would, in effect, give the United States a power which it could exercise at will, and which would be broader than that held under existing treaty reservations and limitations. The separate treaty covering U.S. bases, their operation, and their extension was interpreted as giving Yanqui military forces a free hand to remain on Panamanian soil in perpetuity.

The approach of the 1968 presidential elections in both countries foredoomed any "non-political" consideration of the treaties. Panama's leading contender for the presidency, former President Arnulfo Arias, practically killed any hope for early Panamanian ratification. He denounced the treaties as the partisan work of outgoing President Robles and declared that they should "never" be approved in the form which Robles had apparently accepted. He made every effort to show that Robles, his arch political enemy, was inviting more Yanqui "exploitation."[28]

The U.S. domestic situation in 1967 and 1968 held the fascinated attention of the entire world. Race riots engulfed scores of cities, major public figures were assassinated, youth rebelled in great numbers against the "established political, moral, social, economic, and military" mores of the older generation. Most of the nation appeared so disillusioned by the Viet Nam War that President Johnson decided not to seek re-election in the face of political opposition to the Democratic party and his administration. Even Panamanian nationalists conceded that, momentarily at least, the United States could hardly be expected to give proper attention to Latin American issues generally or to Panamanian problems in particular. After the November balloting there was even more confusion as to what the attitudes of the new Republican President, Richard M. Nixon, might be.[29] He was not considered a dedicated friend of Latin America. Many remembered the tumultuously hostile receptions which he had received in 1958 when he toured certain Latin American nations as Vice President.

In Panama the election returned Arnulfo Arias to a third term in the Presidencia, a not unexpected result. The reasonably unbeclouded election procedures and the fact that the Robles administration peacefully vacated office attracted much favorable comment and attention. Unfortunately, only eleven days after taking office in October, 1968, President Arias was overthrown by a junta led by General Omar Torrijos, Commander of the Panama National Guard, who was assisted by Colonels José M. Pinella and Bolívar Urrutia. Arnulfo Arias was the victim of history repeating itself. He had suffered two previous depositions from the presidential office and the National Guard had played key roles on both of those occasions. In Panama, as in the United States, domestic turmoil had obscured the ratification of the treaties, which may remain unconfirmed indefinitely.

12

What of the 1970s?

Shortly before the Nixon administration took office in January, 1969, it was announced that Governor Nelson Rockefeller of New York would undertake a "fact-finding" tour of Latin America for the new president. In many circles this tour was regarded as a diversion designed to dominate headlines for a few months while masking U.S. neglect of Latin American relations. The preoccupation with Viet Nam, which had characterized the Johnson administration was expected to continue into the new Republican administration since President Nixon had stated his intention to devote major attention to an effort to end the Viet Nam conflict.

Throughout Latin America, Panama being one of the few exceptions, the Rockefeller party was beseiged by anti-Yanqui zealots. A student was killed in Costa Rica during a wild demonstration and hostile crowds imperiled Rockefeller and his party of twenty experts in El Salvador, Honduras, and Nicaragua. ABC news commentator Charles Murphy declared on June 16, 1969, that only in nations which were under the tight control of military dictatorship did the New York governor escape an unfriendly and even violent reception. Of course the military junta governing Panama placed the isthmian republic in Mr. Murphy's characterization.

The Rockefeller party did enjoy a relatively uneventful visit to Panama.[1] About 200 persons greeted him at Tocumen National Airport, and the motorcade passed along well guarded streets into Panama City without incident. Machine guns were placed at every vantage point along the route and plain clothes officers mingled among the sparse street crowds. Even the commander of the National Guard, General Omar Torrijos, was recognized standing in civilian dress at the airport. The foreign minister of the Republic, Nader Pitty, welcomed the visitors to Panamanian soil, and the meetings at the Presidencia were of greatest interest to observers because of the comments made after the sessions by General Torrijos. He seemed to have no compunction about acting as spokesman, despite the fact that Colonel José M. Pinella was the actual provisional president, albeit a figurehead chief executive.

General Torrijos announced that he personally had assured Mr. Rockefeller that elections would be scheduled in 1970 and that the Electoral Tribunal had already been directed to proceed with the necessary preparations.[2] The governor had declared during the Tocumen Airport reception that he hoped the regime would soon return "the blessings of Democracy" to the people of Panama. After conferring with the leaders at the Presidencia he said, "under the firm promise of your government to return to democracy I am sure that Panama will progress even more swiftly and surely in the future."

Mr. Rockefeller is reputed to have advised the junta representatives that the United States would be reluctant to negotiate a new treaty with the military regime because it might be repudiated by a future constitutional government.[3] Although ex-President Arnulfo Arias had expressed hostility toward the "Robles Treaty" during the election campaign of 1968, his brief eleven days in office indicated that he was repudiating the Robles administration rather than completely rejecting the three canal pacts. Apparently he was prepared to continue the negotiations with the hope of bringing out an acceptable draft which could go down in history as an "Arias Treaty." The overthrow of the constitutional Panamanian president dismayed U.S. diplomats who had long since prepared themselves to work with Dr. Arias, despite his criticism of Yanquis. This realistic view of Panamanian affairs too often had been absent from past Washington policy, and might well have introduced a most favorable atmosphere for further relations between the two republics. But the overthrow of Dr. Arias cancelled this projected new relationship with him and his nationalists.

After the ouster of Dr. Arias, the United States considered a pointed breach in diplomatic relations with Panama but, after some obvious hesitation, did finally decide to maintain the full staff in the mission including Ambassador Charles Wallace Adair, Jr. For Mr. Adair, who had been appointed to his post following the harsh events of the 1964 riots, the uncertainty could hardly have been a new experience. He had maintained a calm and much needed aura of diplomatic expertise in his relations with everyone from the Presidencia to the military in the Canal Zone. He brought to the Panamanian assignment the advantages of a long career in consular and diplomatic service, and experience in previous Latin American posts. His particular competence in economic and financial fields was most appropriate in view of the issues. The Panama Canal and Railroad operations had long beclouded almost every effort to establish a *modus vivendi* between Panamanian merchants and the U.S.-controlled Canal Zone. Among recent United States ambassadors he probably was second only to the esteemed Joseph Farland in gaining the respect of Panamanians. Therefore he was extremely well qualified to cope with the difficult ideological problems created by U.S. recognition of an unconstitutional government, even on a "transitional basis."

Under the circumstances, the future of Panamanian-U.S. relations would be determined to a large extent by just what sort of person President Nixon would send to replace Mr. Adair and whether he would delay sending anyone at all. Many hoped Mr. Nixon would not make a move which could be construed as conferring any U.S. approval of an unconstitutional military dictatorship. They were understandably disappointed when Mr. Nixon waited no later than July 9, 1969, to appoint Robert M. Sayre to the ambassadorship. Mr. Sayre, a career diplomat, had been U.S. ambassador to Uruguay. Criticism of the appointment was directed at the timing and very act of the appointment but not at Mr. Sayre personally.

This criticism emphasized the almost immediate resignation of Jerry L. Dodson, U.S. consul in David, the third largest city in Panama. Mr. Dodson cited U.S. support of the junta as his reason for resigning. He asserted that the United States had trained, equipped, and continued to finance General Omar Torrijos' National Guard forces which had ousted the legally elected president and Congress of Panama.[4] Dodson's resignation coincided with, and may have inspired, discussion of a subject which previously had been almost unmentioned in U.S. newspapers and periodicals: the use of bases in the Canal Zone for training military personnel from all over Latin America in anti-guerilla warfare. Washington had managed to either minimize this information or keep it out of the news altogether. Ever since the early 1960's "schools" at places like Fort Gullick, Fort Davis, Albrook Air Force Base, and Fort Clayton had trained thousands of officers and enlisted men in anti-guerilla tactics, special police methods, military communications, cartography, weaponry, intelligence procedures, and other means by which "anti-Communist" governments menaced by "Cuban style" revolutions could deal with Castro-inspired subversion. Panama had long been a prime target for Cuban infiltrators and Panamanian personnel were often enrolled at these training schools. The Nixon administration's recognition of the Torrijos regime gave the junta the opportunity to benefit from this program in the Canal Zone. The junta, as a "legitimate government," thus gained U.S. assistance which would enable it to cope with possible insurgency. This information indicates that the charges made by Jerry L. Dodson had obvious substance.

Left wing periodicals in the Central America–Caribbean area had long been fulminating against these training bases as evidence of Yanqui "Imperialism." A good example was *Thunder*, a bi-monthly magazine published by Cheddi Jagan's supporters in Georgetown, Guyana. The circulation of these sheets was small, however. A much wider audience of readers now became aware of the Canal Zone "schools" by virtue of a sensational three day series which appeared in North American papers in the spring of 1970. (See the *Philadelphia Sunday and Evening Bulletin*, March 15–17, 1970.) The authors were Nathan A. Haverstock and Richard C. Shroeder, both having had the advantage of lengthy residence in and extensive travel throughout Latin America. They wrote about these anti-insurgency training facilities in the Canal Zone under such attention-compelling headlines as "U.S. uses its Canal Zone base for impact on Latin America"; "U.S. Forces in Canal Zone turn up when Latin American crises erupt"; and "Hemisphere Watchdog–More Vietnams just over horizon, U.S. Forces in Canal Zone fear."

Standing out in these articles were such statements as "Canal Zone officials don't like to comment on the extent of U.S. involvement. Much of it is clandestine" (March 16th story). It is very likely that their comment in the March 17th article that "These activities, many of them secret, have had considerable impact on the Latin American political and military tide," was very accurate. For all of those many Panamanians who are anti-Yanqui for one reason or another the existence of these "anti-subversive" training programs in the Canal Zone is one of the worst features of the presence of the United States upon the isthmus. Not only does it symbolize the constant complaint that the small Panamanian republic is a helpless captive of colossal North American power, but it proves in many minds the alliance which Mr. Nixon's administration is alleged to maintain with repressive, tyrannical, and often unconstitutional forces in Latin America. The junta which ousted the duly elected president of Panama in 1968 and clamped an iron military dictatorship upon the country seemed to be a classic example of such forces.

On August 7, 1969, Congressman Flood commented on the isthmian situation:

> Mr. Speaker, in various addresses in and out of Congress, I have repeatedly described the Isthmus of Panama as a land of endemic revolution and endless political turmoil. In contrast, the constitutionally acquired domain of the United States known as the Canal Zone has been an "island" of stability and security. To that territory, on many occasions, Panamanian leaders have fled for a haven of refuge to escape assassination.

> The latest example of such use by Panamanian leaders was on October 11, 1968, when the duly elected President of Panama, Dr. Arnulfo Arias, with high officials of his government, after having served only 11 days, was overthrown in a military coup d'etat and sought a sanctuary in the zone territory.[5]

On October 28, 1969, another U.S. career diplomat, Donald Downs, Deputy Chief of Mission at the Panama City embassy, was expelled by the junta on the charge of "interfering in Panamanian internal affairs . . . by being publicly critical of certain conditions in Panama." In Washington several senators showed their antagonism toward the Torrijos regime by opposing further large scale military aid to Panama.[6]

Mr. Flood's appraisal of isthmian politics in his August 7th speech proved to be prescient. The fluid character of Panamanian affairs which he so accurately portrayed was not long in demonstrating that the Nixon administration's precipitate recognition of the Torrijos government was unwise. In December another and very bizarre military coup d'etat almost toppled Torrijos while he was away in Mexico on a pleasure trip.

In a swift and bloodless maneuver Colonel Ama do Sanjur, third in command of the 5,000 man National Guard led an uprising after which Colonel Ramiro Silvera became provisional president. The Torrijos family was taken into "protective custody." No one could have predicted how long this latest unconstitutional administration would control Panama's government but it may have established a new record for brevity.

On December 16, 1969, General Torrijos flew in a private plane from Mexico City to David and was greeted there by loyal elements of the National Guard led by Major Roberto Diaz Herrera, director of information. At about the same time his supporters in the capital city arrested Silvera and Sanjur and put them in the city jail. They had ruled Panama for only a few hours.

Torrijos drove from David to Panama City in a triumphal motorcade to the cheers of townspeople and farmers alike. More than 3,000 people lined the sides of the roadway over the Bridge of the Americas spanning the Pacific end of the Panama Canal to acclaim his reentry into the capital. He at once restored his junta compatriots to office and announced that Sanjur and Silvera would be tried for subversion. He ridiculed their charge that he had been "soft" on communism although Torrijos had once been a member of the pro-Communist People's Party. Furthermore his second in command, Colonel Boris Martinez, had been the acknowledged leader of the Communist youth group at the University of Panama when he was a student there.

Some observers professed to see a conciliatory gesture toward Washington in Torrijos' announcement, made soon after his return to the Presidencia, that Demetrio B. Lakas, a civilian novice to politics who had been educated in Texas, would join the previously all military junta. Señor Lakas soon replaced José M. Pinella as provisional president in the junta's administrative facade, but everyone knew of course that Torrijos continued to be the "strong man" of the regime. Lakas achieved a notoriety of a kind during the riots on U.S. college campuses in the spring of 1970 by issuing pronouncements against "long haired, bearded, and raggedly dressed persons" and declaring that foreigners of such description would be banned from entering Panama and would be summarily returned to their country of origin if they did somehow slip in (possibly by way of the Canal Zone). But far more significant was Torrijos' order of December 21, which forbade ten business, labor, and political leaders to leave the country. While Torrijos was in Mexico, these people had signed a manifesto which appeared in newspapers asking for a return to civilian, constitutional government. Their action and the general's reaction must be evaluated in light of a decree issued in October, 1969, barring all political parties from the projected 1970 voting for a "Constituent Assembly" whose first reform was scheduled to be an extension of the presidential term from four years to six.[7]

Considering these developments, the 1970 elections, which General Torrijos had promised Governor Rockefeller, would have had a predictable outcome. But as 1970 came to a close the popular elections had not been held, nor are they likely to be held very soon if the general's regime stays in power. The Nixon administration's early recognition of the junta has hardly improved the image of the United States among the untold thousands of Panamanians who detest the idea of a military dictatorship ruling the republic. By a policy of watchful waiting, the Washington government might have achieved some rapport with these Panamanians. As it is they are more hostile than ever towards the United States. These feelings are exacerbated by information, leaked to the news media, that General Torrijos had staged his successful return to power with the assistance of Nicaraguan President A. S. Somoza, also a military dictator. Somoza enjoys full diplomatic "recognition" in Washington. Panamanian feeling toward the United States is now 180 degrees opposite the feeling during World War II when thousands of North Americans stationed on the isthmus were warmed by the daily opening announcement of the Panama City radio station, "This is the Voice of Democracy!"

On October 30, 1969, President Nixon made public the substance of the Rockefeller fact-finding mission report. The governor made a strong recommendation for continued military assistance to *all* Latin American governments, including the dictatorships, as a means of combating "Communism." This was a chilling and foreboding statement for partisans of constitutional government in Panama and elsewhere. José Figueres, twice president of neighboring Costa Rica, expressed the fear that "announcement of normal relations with dictatorial governments" on the part of the United States might well encourage new military coups in Latin America.[8]

David Bronheim, former assistant coordinator of the Alliance for Progress and a member of the Rockefeller mission, was quite blunt:

> If the president is using Rockefeller as the stalking horse on military assistance policy, and if the governor's recommendations on military assistance are combined with the president's announced policy on economic assistance, the U.S. is about to embark on a course as pernicious as it is nonsensical. Duvalier and Eric Williams, Frei and Stroessner, Lleras and Onganía, Callera and Velasco—all are to be treated equally in their efforts to obtain economic and military assistance. All are threatened by communists, and all must be given the tools to resist. We will be the laughing stock of the western world. If there is anything that we

should have learned recently, it is that economic and military assistance given to a dictatorship will prove to be practically and philosophically unsound.[9]

During his visit to Panama in May, 1969, Governor Rockefeller declared that the future of relations between Panama and the United States would definitely "depend importantly" upon the successful resolution of pending issues regarding the Canal." General Torrijos remarked at the same time that Panama would soon resume its talks with the United States regarding the proposed treaties. He said that Panama had not been satisfied with the drafts negotiated in 1967 and 1968 because "they did not eliminate points of friction." He did not elaborate upon the nature of these points but it can be assumed that they would include virtually all of the traditional economic, social, and political disputes between Panama and the Canal Zone. In the meantime some very interesting new developments may have beclouded the whole question of whether *any* new canal is to be built in Panama and whether the United States will ever definitely renegotiate the status of the present canal.

In June, 1969, the president of Colombia, Carlos Lleras Restrepo, visited President Richard M. Nixon in Washington, D.C. Mr. Nixon then said that his administration was considering some basic changes of policy with respect to our relations with Latin America.[10] He expected the Rockefeller mission to provide some data upon which such policy reviews could be premised. In a move calculated to promote hemisphere understanding and good will, it was announced that the mission had been officially sanctioned by the permanent secretary of the Organization of American States.

Any review of relations between Colombia and the United States by the presidents of the two countries would have to include the possibility of a new trans-isthmian canal in Colombian territory along the Atrato River Valley line, a subject of greatest concern to Panamanians. The sparse population in that area adds to the feasibility of using atomic energy to build a sea level canal, and the endless political problems with Panama serve to force North American attention toward the possibilities of an agreement with Colombia for an alternative canal site. There was no public comment on the matter, of course, but it seems scarcely possible that the Atrato River canal could have gone without mention in the Nixon-Lleras talks.

In September, 1969, the junta had tried to resume official talks with the United States about the canal treaties. But Secretary of State Rogers had given a hedging reply only that the Washington government was taking the matter "under advisement." In a move that may have been intended to force some response from the United States the governments of Colombia and Panama then issued a joint proposal on September 27, 1969, for building a sea level canal fifty-one miles long.[11] In October the United States Atlantic-Pacific Oceanic Canal Study Commission did begin detailed hearings on this proposal. No one seriously believed Panama and Colombia to have the capability for undertaking such a project without the United States.

The Commission, created by Congress, was authorized to spend $24,000,000 on field work and feasibility analyses of the five possible routes for a new sea level canal. It is expected to report by December, 1970, and, as noted in the preceding chapter, the rumor was "leaked" from highly placed sources that it would not find nuclear excavation feasible. One of the biggest issues it will have had to consider is the possibility that intermingling the marine life of the Western Atlantic and of the Eastern Pacific in a sea level canal may produce some kind of a biological disaster.

Scientists disagree over what may result from the mixing of the oceans. There are 6,000 marine species in the Atlantic and some 4,000 in the Pacific. Professor John Briggs of the University of South Florida predicts that a sea level canal will "result in the greatest extinction of species the world has ever seen." He cites the threat of the hardier Atlantic species literally gobbling up its cousins from the milder Pacific waters.[12]

Clearly political ramifications would accompany a loss of feeding grounds supporting the Pacific fishing industry, and the intrusion of Pacific parasites into Caribbean oyster beds would create similar reactions. Many members of the United States Senate and House of Representatives became concerned over this problem, including those who had a continuing interest in Panama, notably Senator Strom Thurmond of South Carolina and Congressman Daniel Flood of Pennsylvania. These two leaders, one a Republican and one a Democrat, indicated the concern of both parties. Many pages in the *Congressional Record* during 1969 were filled with debate over this issue.[13]

John Sheffley, Executive Director of the Canal Study Commission, tried to minimize the threat of a biological catastrophe in testimony before a House Committee. He pointed out that for fifty-five years there have been limited exchanges of water and marine life between the oceans through the locks of the present canal. The salt water Tarpon is known to swim through, barnacles and other organisms clinging on the hulls of ships pass through daily, and ballast water is taken on from one ocean and dumped into the other. Sheffley had to concede however that no one could be sure of the effect of removing all barriers between the Atlantic and Pacific by opening a sea level canal.[14]

In order to find some objective answers the Commission finally decided to engage the Batelle Memorial Institute of Columbus, Ohio to study the issue. Inasmuch as there is existing scientific disagreement over the matter it is very possible that the ultimate findings of the Batelle Institute will settle nothing. Some authorities claim that no comparisons would be valid in attempting to study the potentialities of the tropical isthmian canal against the existing joining of the oceans around Cape Horn and through the Straits of Magellan because the species there have been acclimated by the colder water temperatures.

The entire controversy illustrates again how domestic political concerns in the United States can affect the isthmian canal. There are now powerful forces in Yanqui politics which will utilize any argument to vitiate new approaches to Panama and even to construction of any new canal within that nation. The threat of a "biological catastrophe" which filled page after page of the *Congressional Record* in 1969 can be a potent weapon for these forces. Their efforts cast more doubt than ever over the likelihood of an early solution to isthmian canal problems.

Even more intriguing is an idea advanced by Rear Admiral R. H. Gibbs, U.S. Navy (Retired), in the April, 1969, issue of the *United States Naval Institute Proceedings*. Admiral Gibbs proposes that the United States abandon all plans for the digging of a new canal, lock type or sea level. He says that the solution lies in the development of a super high speed railroad across the southwestern part of the United States from the Gulf of Mexico to the Pacific, a distance of 1,085 miles. He believes that changes in technology of cargo handling have made the rapid and efficient transfer of cargoes at the Gulf and Pacific terminals feasible. The railroad would be a straight-line construction cut directly through mountains and bridging streams and canyons. The admiral estimates that the movement of goods from the Atlantic to the Pacific by such a facility would save a lot of time and would eventually become a less expensive operation overall than the canal. Admiral Gibbs refers to his proposed facility as a "land canal."[15]

Such a "land canal" built across United States territory in its entirety would completely eliminate all of the political and diplomatic issues of control and sovereignty over the Canal Zone which have plagued our relations with Panama and which would certainly be reiterated in negotiating any pact for a new and different canal whether it be in Panama, Colombia, Nicaragua, or through the Isthmus of Tehauntepec in Mexico. Many would view the elimination of negotiations a result worth achieving at any cost.

The *U.S. Naval Institute Proceedings* is not an official government publication, but it is undoubtedly read in the Pentagon, the State Department, and probably the White House. The men who write for this magazine have professional standing which commands the attention of those who are concerned with strategic decisions determining national policy. As Admiral Gibbs points out, we have long range commitments in Asia and in the Pacific which will mandate an increasing volume of interoceanic cargo movement for years to come. The apparent inadequacy of the present Panama Canal has engendered pressure for some major palliative to the problem,[16] such as the "land canal."

The Republic of Panama would be faced with an economic and financial earthquake if the United States decided to build either a "land canal" or another sea canal in Colombia, Nicaragua, or Mexico. Panama, which has been the "crossroads of the world" for more than fifty years, would suddenly become just another small republic with little importance to anyone but itself, and an economically depressed area of the first magnitude. For there is no escaping the fact that the present canal is the major industry of the nation.

Until recently some observers believed that Nassar's success in operating the Suez Canal would indicate a favorable prospect for Panama, should it take over the operation of the isthmian canal. But since the Mid-East War of June, 1967, the Suez Canal has been out of commission. The cargo carriers of the world have built larger and faster ships designed to forego any need for the shorter Suez route. At present, after two years of disuse that canal lies filled with silt and sand, and damaged by sunken hulks. Clearing and restoring it would cost vast sums which Egypt does not have and world commerce has learned to operate without it. There is serious doubt that the Suez Canal will ever function again. Here, too, a political question exacerbates the issue. There is no sign that the Arab-Israeli dispute can be settled soon and as long as it rages there is no possibility of restoring the canal to service.

Thus there is no longer any guarantee that the Republic of Panama has here a priceless asset of indefinite value. Ocean shipping may find it just as feasible to bypass the Panama Canal as the Suez Canal.[17] Therefore, a U.S. commitment to the construction of a new sea level or other type of modernized waterway across Panamanian territory would obviously be in Panama's own best interest economically. Time may be running out on such an arrangement, but the turbulent politics of the isthmus continue as usual, seemingly oblivious to the threat of economic ruin which hangs over the republic if the canal becomes a relic of the past.

The "canal politics" of Washington also seem to follow the same old patterns but with far fewer serious potential consequences for the United States. The influence of the "Zonians" is ever present in Washington because they have grass roots in every one of the fifty states. There is also a Congressional group determined to strenuously resist any further concessions to Panama. Representatives Flood, Sullivan, and others are still reinforced by such powerful political forces as the American Legion. Their influence was only too well illustrated by their reaction to a report published in March 1967 by the Georgetown University Center for Strategic Studies. The report was prepared by a nine member panel formed to study the Panama Canal treaties and the issues involved. Former Ambassador Joseph S. Farland was chairman of this group, the majority of which rendered an expected report calling for an improved isthmian canal and for flexible language in the treaties. Early implementation of whatever actions the experts should finally recommend, based upon technological, engineering, and economic findings would thus be facilitated. However, the release of a minority report written by two members of the panel must have pleased people like Congressman Daniel Flood very much indeed.

These minority dissenters were Professor Donald M. Dozer, a most distinguished Latin Americanist and member of the faculty at the University of California in Santa Barbara, and Vice Admiral T. G. N. Nettle, U.S.N. (Retired). They declared that the joint statement issued by Presidents Johnson and Robles on September 24, 1965, and Mr. Johnson's remark of September 25, were unacceptable to U.S. interests. Both of these statements had indicated U.S. acceptance of an *ultimate* Panamanian sovereignty beyond dispute or limitation as a basis for treaty revisions. Dozer and Nettle urged the United States instead to ". . . terminate immediately its present negotiations with Panama . . . reassert its position of sovereign control over the Canal and the Canal Zone . . . insist upon Panamanian recognition of the full force and validity of the 1903 Treaty . . . abandon plans for the digging of a new canal, whether by nuclear or conventional methods . . ."

This proposal would require Panama not only to abrogate its present demands but also to relinquish many modifications of the original Hay–Bunau-Varilla Treaty of 1903, embraced in subsequent pacts such as the Hull-Alfaro and the Chapin-Fabrega Treaties. It is difficult to understand how a sophisticated student of Latin America such as Professor Dozer could have seriously sponsored such a proposition. Nevertheless, the language of this minority report eloquently and succinctly represents the attitude of a large and forceful segment of opinion within the political spectrum of the United States which will have to be reckoned with by any president who attempts to settle Panamanian issues.[18] These forces mustered a vote of 380 to 12 in the House of Representatives in February, 1960, to reject legislation which would have recognized Panama's right to fly its flag within the Canal Zone. President Eisenhower's executive order which opened the door for the flag display was made in the face of violent domestic opposition.

Panama, like most of Latin America, will watch President Nixon very closely during his first years in office to detect any signs of change in policy or attitude toward hemispheric and national problems and relations. The new president does not have a favorable image in Panama, although he does have the advantage, which his predecessor did not have, of personal acquaintance and friendship with individual Panamanians and Panamanian families of prominence. This relationship dates from visits he made to the Isthmus as vice president during the Eisenhower administration. Some of these Panamanian friends speak in very kind terms of President Nixon, and they represent a force favorable to future discussions, negotiations, and relations in general. Their influence was apparent in the conciliatory attitude displayed by the short lived Arias administration. But presently they are disappointed with Washington's recognition of the junta.

University students in Panama are among the most radical and leftwing oriented in the Americas.[19] During the campus disturbances which swept the United States during the spring of 1969, President Nixon made a comment about the "weakness" of Latin American universities as educational centers. He attributed this to the widespread power and influence of students in those universities and his remarks were intended to warn of a similar loss of academic strength in U.S. institutions of higher learning should a "surrender" to "student power" occur there. The president undoubtedly recalled his harrowing experience at the hands of Venezuelan students in Caracas in 1958, but however justified his remarks may have been, they were not judicious when considered in view of the effect which they would certainly have in Latin America. The University of Panama is an even hotter anti-Yanqui hotbed since the Nixon Administration took power. Cuban leader Che Guevara,[20] now dead, and Mao Tse Tung[21] are as much venerated there as the U.S. president is execrated.

This situation exemplifies probably one of the greatest difficulties facing the new Republican administration in Washington as it attempts to set its future policy toward Panama. Republicans are traditional friends of the "free enterprise system" and exponents of Capitalism. Both of these concepts are utter anathema to untold thousands throughout Latin America, including Panama. Republican presidents have tended to send business executives and industrial leaders on diplomatic missions to Latin America, and to appoint campaign contributors or people with "proper" credentials to ambassadorial posts. Even Nelson Rockefeller, *simpático*, Spanish-speaking, and clearly experienced and well versed in Latin American affairs, is "Standard Oil personified" to millions.

Paradoxically those who could do the new Washington administration the most good in Latin America are to a large extent ignored by it. These are the college professors and journalists who have devoted a lifetime to a career of studying, residing within, and writing about Latin America. They know the region and its inhabitants better than many government officials whose contacts are limited mostly to oligarchic interests who are the local representatives of some great North American manufacturer, or industry, selling its goods and services for attractive profits under the venerated "free enterprise" system. Although there are comparatively few "intellectuals" with Republican or independent backgrounds, the Nixon administration unfortunately has failed to use the services of many who are both willing and competent to give expert advice on Latin American affairs. The disposition to serve one's country in such a capacity is usually not limited by partisan considerations.

In Panama the scholarly *catedrático* is possibly the most admired of all professional men. The public servants of the republic often have a background of philosophy, letters, and the law. The revered Ricardo J. Alfaro, one of the great statesmen of the Western Hemisphere, was an authority on the Law of Nations, and in Panameño eyes the prototype of what a diplomat should be. Sumner Welles was probably the last North American representative of this ideal. Mr. Nixon's assistant secretary of state for Latin American Affairs is Mr. Charles Meyer, an affable, able, and conscientious man who speaks Spanish and has spent much time in Latin America. He has made a generally favorable impression. But in Panama, like most of the Southern Hemisphere, he has the disadvantage of being regarded as a "Sears and Roebuck" man, because it was as a representative of that company and other concerns that he travelled widely and received his experience.

Another consideration as we move into the 1970's is the preoccupation of the United States with the Viet Nam War and its own domestic crisis in the cities. How can the issues of the Panama Canal claim much attention against such competition? Obviously they can not, unless some explosive situation on the isthmus forces attention from the U.S. government. Panama is thus a potential powder keg because volatile elements within the Panamanian population are always only too ready and too happy to stir up trouble with the Yanqui. Many U.S. customs have influenced Panama and probably none has taken deeper root than the art of playing politics with almost every question before attempting to find viable solutions. "Politics as usual" in Panama means "Yanqui baiting," for the Panamanians feel secure in the knowledge that the United States will not react in any punitive fashion but may even grant concessions in order to quiet things down.

This predictable reaction may be about to change. The minority report of the Georgetown panel on "Panama: Canal Issues and Treaty Talks" may be the same kind of appeal to a unilateral decision based upon force as the "Law and Order" slogan has become to U.S. politicians who increasingly exploit the backlash vote in election campaigns. The prospect for a calm bilateral appraisal of Panameño–U.S. relations for the 1970's is therefore not very promising. Partisan politics and policies are likely to prevail for some time in both nations. In the meantime, the need for *any* transoceanic canal may subside into a matter of little relative importance—a disastrous prospect for the Republic of Panama. At such a juncture the great need is for well qualified and well intentioned statesmanship from both republics. Whatever the long range future may hold, the present canal and the Canal Zone are the problem, and Governor Rockefeller was quite right to declare that the future of relations between Panama and the United States is going to depend upon the resolution of these present issues.

In 1965, a Panamanian journalist[22] wrote the following lines which are as valid today as they were then, and they will be true as well for the tomorrows that are to come in the relations between the United States and the Republic of Panama.

It is one thing to write a treaty: it is much different to live with it. Furthermore, it is rather naive to consider treaties as merely official arrangements between governments. Actually, the best ones are often between the peoples of two countries.

Someone has to sell the terms of the agreement to the public, and the timing of such salesmanship is important.

The initiative in salesmanship must be taken by the Nixon administration if the present impasse is to be broken. The task is doubly difficult when satisfaction must be given to a politically minded majority *both* in the United States and upon the isthmus, and when the whole picture is clouded by exasperating and seemingly insoluble crises which claim so much priority all over the world, from the Middle East through Central Europe and into South East Asia. History has a way of producing men to meet the needs of their time. Mr. Nixon came into office with a well earned reputation for political astuteness. As he leads his country into the 1970's he may find answers for most of the troublesome issues which have plagued his predecessors who built and maintained the transoceanic canal; the canal which generations of men dreamed about; the dream to which many gave their experience, ability, fortunes, and even health to bring to reality.

Postscript

On Saturday, September 12, 1970 a UPI dispatch reporting an interview with General Omar Torrijos was published in papers throughout the United States. The Panamanian dictator had met with a UPI reporter in the back seat of a black, bullet-proof Cadillac limosine. From this bizarre setting, General Torrijos made several statements which appeared to destroy all hope of an early agreement between Panama and the United States. The general announced a determination to end "U.S. control of the Panama Canal Zone," and said that the United States was "obligated morally to cede all claims to the 558 square miles in the Zone." Furthermore, he "wanted no part of the three draft treaties negotiated in the Marco Robles and Lyndon Johnson administrations."

Torrijos called for "abrogation" of the Hay–Bunau-Varilla Treaty of 1903—such action had been intimated in a Robles-Johnson communique in 1965—and the execution of a new treaty simply recognizing unconditional Panamanian sovereignty over the Canal Zone. The general warned that failure to follow these suggestions would very likely result in the eruption of new waves of anti-U.S. violence on the isthmus, as severe or worse than the fatal 1964 riots. He said he would agree to the United States' assuming an obligation to maintain and defend the canal installations, but declared that complete Panamanian sovereign control would be necessary to execute his aim of total social, economic, and political integration of the Canal Zone into the Republic of Panama.

A few days before this interview the Panamanian government had seized the military training base maintained by the United States at Rio Hato in central Panama. The Washington government had sought renewal of the expired fifteen-year lease on this installation, but the request had been ignored; the United States had not even been notified of the intended takeover. A major in the Army Corps of Engineers had to perform the "honors" of formally relinquishing the 19,000 acre site with its 8,000 feet of hard surface runway to Torrijos and Provisional President Demetrio Lakas when they appeared to take over the base.

The United States Army's 193rd Infantry Brigade at once evacuated the property and moved into the Canal Zone.

These events coincided with an editorial published in the *New York Times* on Friday, September 11, 1970. This comment from one of the greatest and most influential of North American newspapers emphasizes several considerations which exacerbate the tense situation.

> Three treaties involving the future of the Panama Canal, which required three years of painstaking negotiations to produce the represented major concessions by the United States, have been formally rejected by Panama. Whatever lame explanations the Panamanians put forward, it is clear that the rejection is due much more to the domestic political needs and desires of General Omar Torrijos Herrera's Government than to the content of the treaties.
>
> The whole dreary episode raises the question of whether any Panamanian leader, in or out of uniform, will ever find it politically possible to negotiate a fair and reasonable solution of his country's long-standing grievances against the United States over the Canal Zone. . . .
>
> Unhappily the general found . . . that he . . . had to ride the tide of Panamanian Nationalism. . . . He is naive if he believes he can exact more generous terms from a Republican Administration certain to be far more susceptible than Mr. Johnson was to charges that even the 1967 treaties constituted a "sellout" of American rights and interests.*

Considering the influence of the *New York Times,* this editorial reflects what is probably an overwhelming reaction to Panamanian actions and attitudes from many shades of opinion within the United States, both in and out of government. It is apparent that the problems of domestic politics, both on the isthmus and in the United States, will continue to cast a long shadow over the future of any interoceanic canal in Central America.

---

* © 1970 by The New York Times Company. Reprinted by permission.

Appendix

"PROGNOSIS FOR THE PANAMA CANAL"*

Statement of Representative Daniel J. Flood of Pennsylvania

As a member of the subcommittee of the House Committee on Appropriations charged with the formulation of appropriation bills for the Armed Forces and as a student of Panama Canal history and interoceanic canal problems over many years, I have read with the greatest interest the article by Professor Miller.† All thoughtful members of the Congress that I know concur with his conclusion that: "Any real erosion of our position in the Canal Zone is bound to have widespread and adverse effects throughout the Caribbean, in Latin America generally, and on our global relationships." This is a realistic appraisal of the situation now facing the United States with respect to the Panama Canal, which has long been the key target for the Communistic revolutionary conquest of the Caribbean.

The sovereign status of the United States over the Canal Zone and Panama Canal is the direct result of a long-range commitment by our government for the construction, and perpetual maintenance, operation, sanitation, and protection of an Isthmus Canal by whatever route that may be considered, pursuant to the 1901 Hay-Pauncefote Treaty with Great Britain and the 1902 Spooner Act authorizing the securing of perpetual control of the Canal Zone by treaty with the sovereign of the Isthmus of Panama.

As a result of the Panama Revolution of 3 November 1903, and the diplomatic intervention of President Theodore Roosevelt, the

* Reprinted by permission from *U.S. Naval Institute Proceedings,* vol. 90, no. 6 (June 1964), pp. 113–15. Copyright © 1964 by the U.S. Naval Institute.
† Miller, August C., Jr., "Prognosis for the Panama Canal," *U.S. Naval Institute Proceedings,* vol. 90, no. 3 (March 1964), pp. 64–73.

necessary treaty was made with Panama, a successor state, rather than with Colombia, the sovereign of the Isthmus prior to the 1903 revolt. This treaty, prepared under the close supervision of Secretary of State John M. Hay, granted sovereignty *en bloc* over the Canal Zone to the United States, "in perpetuity" and most significantly to the "entire exclusion of the exercise by the Republic of Panama of any such sovereign rights, power or authority." Moreover, the United States obtained ownership of all land and property in the Canal Zone by purchase from individual owners as well as sovereignty of the entire Canal Zone and its auxiliary areas by payment of $10,000,000 as indemnity.

This control and ownership of the Canal Zone and Panama Canal was formally recognized by Colombia in the Thomson-Urrutia Treaty of 6 April 1914, proclaimed 30 March 1922. In return, Colombia received certain rights for transit of the Panama Railroad comparable to those enjoyed by the governments of the United States and Panama.

Thus the commitments of the United States, as regards the perpetual operation of the Panama Canal, are rooted not only in law but also in three important treaties. The width of the Canal Zone and the grant of sovereignty in perpetuity over it are not happenstances attributable to unauthorized clandestine maneuvering of foreign agents, as partisans have implied, but are due to the important studies made by the Isthmian Canal Commission (1899 to 1902) headed by Rear Admiral John G. Walker, one of the most distinguished officers of the Navy. In his report on 18 January 1902, he emphasized that suitable treaty arrangements must be made "if an isthmian canal is to be constructed by our government across the Isthmus of Panama," that "the grant must be not for a term of years, but *in perpetuity*, and a strip of territory from ocean to ocean of sufficient width must be placed under the control of the United States," and that "in this strip the United States must have the right to enforce police regulations, preserve order, protect property rights, and exercise such other powers as are appropriate and necessary.

History has amply justified the vision of this distinguished naval officer in laying the basis for United States treaty-granted exclusive sovereignty over the Canal Zone and Panama Canal in an area that has been the scene of endless bloody revolution and poltical instability. The Isthmus is less stable today than it was in 1903, and the challenge of the 1903 Treaty by Panama has not been met in a forthright manner by the United States. Experience has certainly shown that should the time ever come when any part of the Canal Zone or Panama Canal becomes a political pawn of Panamanian politicians, the days of U.S. control will be numbered. The inevitable result will be taken over by communist revolutionary power.

Lest the current enthusiasm for a second Isthmian Canal serve to divert due consideration from fundamentals, attention is invited to the following facts:

1. The United States has a fine canal at Panama now, but it is rapidly approaching saturation.

2. Experience has shown that it will work, that our government knows how to maintain and operate it, and how to provide for its major increase of capacity and operational efficiency without the requirement of a new treaty with Panama, all of which are paramount considerations transcending wishful thinking of promoters and idealists.

3. This modernization program, which was developed in the Panama Canal organization from meticulous studies of operations during World War II, provides for the adaptation of the existing Canal to the principles of the Terminal Lake solution. This idea has been authoritatively recognized by maritime agencies of our government and independent engineers, navigators, and lawyers as providing the best operational canal practicable of achievement, and at the least cost without involvement in treaty negotiations. The last, indeed, is a prime consideration.

4. The United States now has workable treaties for the Panama Canal granting the indispensables of undiluted sovereignty and ownership over the Canal Zone and Panama Canal and its auxiliary areas, and the protection of the summit level water supply of the Chagres River Valley.

5. The United States has suffered abrogation by ill-advised treaty amendments and nullification by Executive actions of vital parts of the 1903 Treaty through policies and practices in direct opposition to the 1923 position of Secretary of State Charles E. Hughes, who considered such reversals unthinkable.

6. The United States has had to defend its sovereignty over the Canal Zone by the use of force—an action absolutely necessary to protect the lives of our citizens and to save the Canal itself from destruction by Red-directed mobs from Panama.

7. The United States has a treaty for a canal at Nicaragua, which would require a supplementary treaty with that country to supply necessary details as well as conventions with Costa Rica, Salvador, and

possibly Honduras, but it has no treaties for a canal at any other site.

8. The United States would have to defend a new canal at any site of any type of construction in addition to the Panama Canal from "lawlessness and disorder" as was illustrated at Panama from 9 to 11 January 1964, and against aggressive warfare.

9. The use of nuclear explosions for excavation is limited by the nuclear test-ban treaty and, in any case, is still in the conjectural stage, requiring from seven to ten years of experiment and the expenditure of some 250 million dollars to develop proper devices for such excavation by nuclear explosion.

10. The expenditure of vast sums on an extravagant so-called sea-level project in the Canal Zone in the name of "security" and "national defense" will inevitably divert huge sums from other, more pressing programs for the defense of the United States, and, on the whole, will involve much greater fixed costs than the present canal as improved by the economic means of additional locks. Moreover, dogmatic assertions that a canal at sea level would only require a small number of employees, perhaps 500, to operate and maintain it are perfectly absurd. A much larger number would be required because of the related conditions involved.

11. While it is true that a sea level project at Panama has the support of the National Rivers and Harbors Congress and industrial interests and professional engineers associated with it, there has been, and still is, sharp opposition to this project on the part of many independent nuclear warfare, engineering, maritime and other ship canal experts who cannot be dismissed as uninformed, incompetent, or inexperienced.

12. If the United States does not stand firm at Panama it cannot stand anywhere else, and weakness at Panama will cause other nations having possible canal sites to be more demanding in their consideration of treaties for new canal construction.

Certain writers, whose experience hardly entitles them to speak with authority, have urged that the United States surrender its sovereignty and jurisdiction over the Panama Canal to the United Nations or some other international body. They do not reveal that such transfer has been a prime objective of Soviet policy since 1917 and is directly related to Soviet aims to secure the control of the Dardanelles. Moreover, such a transfer would not solve problems but would be an abdication of responsibilities and would bring about the complete extinction of the Monroe Doctrine designed for the protection of the Western Hemisphere. In the light of what has happened in the Caribbean since 1959 when Castro took over Cuba, any such proposal is, to say the least, naive and, in its effect, amounts to downright subversion.

The Isthmian Canal Policy of the United States, as basically evolved, has had for its objective the best canal at the best site for the transit of vessels of commerce and war on terms of equality and at low cost of construction, maintenance, operation, sanitation, and protection in the interest of tolls which interoceanic commerce can bear.

The most comprehensive, scholarly, forthright, and objective yet brief and rigorous clarification of over-all canal problems ever written is that by Captain Miles P. DuVal.* This article has become a state paper of the first importance and is must reading for all who wish to know the truth about this very confusing subject.

In planning our future interoceanic canal policy, it is imperative to stick to fundamentals. And the first of these is retention of indispensable and undiluted sovereignty of the United States over the Canal Zone and the Panama Canal, for if any part of the Zone or interest in the Canal becomes a political pawn for Panamanian politicians, the days of efficient operations of the Panama Canal, indeed, will end. Moreover, no one has ever been able to explain how the United States can adequately maintain, operate, and protect the Canal with less authority than that accorded in the 1903 Treaty.

* Miles P. DuVal, "Isthmian Canal Policy—An Evaluation," *U.S. Naval Institute Proceedings,* vol. 81, no. 3 (March 1955), pp. 263–75.

Notes

PARTY ATTITUDES PRIOR TO THE MEXICAN WAR

1. Numerous works have dealt with the isthmus in colonial times. Some of the most readable are Philip A. Means, the *Spanish Main, Focus of Envy 1492–1700*, (New York, 1935); C. L. G. Anderson, *Old Panama and Castilla del Oro*, (New York, 1911); John E. Minter, *The Chagres, River of Westward Passage* (New York, 1948); F. T. Humphries, *Indians of Panama, Their History and Culture*, (Panamá, R.P., 1944); Farnham Bishop, *Panama, Past and Present* (New York, 1913); Miles P. DuVal, *Cadiz to Cathay, The Story of the Long Struggle for a Waterway Across the American Isthmus* (Palo Alto, 1940); Gerstle Mack, *The Land Divided, A History of the Panama Canal and other Isthmian Projects* (New York, 1944); Merritt P. Allen, *Sir Henry Morgan, Buccaneer* (New York, 1931); and Willis F. Johnson, *Four Centuries of the Panama Canal* (New York, 1906).
2. Gargáz, Pierre-André, *A Project of Universal and Perpetual Peace*, ed. and trans. George S. Eddy (New York, 1922).
3. Thomas Jefferson, *Writtings Official and Private*, ed. H. S. Washington (Washington, D.C., 1884), vol. 2, pp. 325–97.
4. William S. Robertson, *The Life of Miranda* (Chapel Hill, 1929), vol. 2, p. 240 et. seq.
5. Alexander von Humboldt, *Political Essay on the Kingdom of New Spain* (London, 1822), vol. 1, pp. 10–50.
6. Jefferson, *Writtings*, vol. 2, p. 351; vol. 12. p. 68.
7. Arthur P. Whitaker, *The United States and the Independence of Latin America* (Baltimore, 1941), p. 92.
8. Ibid., p. 189.
9. DuVal, *Cadiz to Cathay*, p. 23; Reuben E. Backenhus, Harry S. Knapp, and Emory R. Johnson, *The Panama Canal* (New York, 1915), p. 11.
10. DuVal, *Cadiz to Cathay*, p. 24; Joseph B. Bishop, *The Panama Gateway* (New York, 1913, 1915), p. 32.
11. The full story of the Panama Congress of 1826 is given in Whitaker, *Independence*, pp. 564–84.
12. *The First International American Conference; the Congress at Panama and Subsequent Movements*, 4 vols. (Government Printing Office, Washington, D.C., 1890), "Historical Appendix," vol. 4, p. 143.
13. Johnson, *Four Centuries*, p. 42.

14. Backenhus et al., *Panama Canal*, p. 11; DuVal, *Cadiz to Cathay*, pp. 13–14.
15. Gordon Ireland, *Boundaries, Possessions, and Conflicts in Central and North America and the Caribbean* (Cambridge, Mass., 1941), p. 222; Bishop, *Panama Gateway*, p. 33.
16. *Senate Document #54*, 57th Congress, 1st Session, pt. 1, pp. 41–42.
17. Bishop, *Panama Gateway*, p. 34; Backenhus et al., *Panama Canal*, p. 11.
18. The Mexican state papers on the Tehuantepec project are found in Jose F. Ramirez, ed., *Memorias para servir a la Historia de la Comunicación Interoceanica por el istmo de Tehuantepec* (Mexico, D.F., 1853). A view of U.S. expansion dealing with Polk's intent to annex Yucatan may be found in John D. P. Fuller, *The Movement for the Acquisition of All Mexico 1846–1848* (Baltimore, 1936), pp. 158–59; reprint ed. (New York, 1969).

THE CLAYTON–BULWER TREATY

1. Samuel F. Bemis, *The Latin American Policy of the United States* (New York, 1943), pp. 101–2.
2. Thomas A. Bailey, *A Diplomatic History of the American People*, 6th ed. (New York, 1958), p. 226.
3. The controversy over the Mosquito Coast is handled with scholarly detail in Ireland, *Boundaries*, pp. 170–88.
4. *Diplomatic Correspondence of the United States*, ed. W. R. Manning (New York, 1925), vol. 3, pp. 324–31, 404–8.
5. *Treaties and Other International Acts of the United States of America*, ed. Hunter Miller (Washington, D. C., 1937) vol. 5, p. 115.
6. *Diplomatic Correspondence*, vol. 3, pp. 50, 55, 57, 71, 91–134, 360–69, 375–86.
7. Wheaton, J. Lane, *Commodore Vanderbilt, An Epic of the Steam Age* (New York, 1942), pp. 85–138.
8. This story is very colorfully told in Minter, *Chagres*, pp. 197–236.
9. *Panama Star and Herald* newspapers for the period 1849–1870 are available on microfilm (N. A. Kovach, Microfilms, 4801 Second Avenue, Los Angeles, California).
10. DuVal, *Cadiz to Cathay*, p. 61.
11. Norman J. Padelford, *The Panama Canal in Peace and War,* (New York, 1942), p. 7.
12. Treaty Series #122, Department of State Archives; see also *Papers Relating to the Foreign Relations of the United States*, Government Printing Office (New York, 1925), vol. 1 (1882), pp. 271–83; vol. 1 (1901), pp. 238–41; vol. 1 (1912); pp. 482–83, 556; *Senate Document #474*, 63rd Congress, 2nd Session, pp. 272–76.
13. DuVal, *Cadiz to Cathay*, p. 61.

FROM BUCHANAN TO CLEVELAND

Much of this period is very objectively discussed in Jackson Crowell, "The United States and a Central American Canal, 1869–1877," *Hispanic American Historical Review*, vol. 45, no. 2 (February, 1966), pp. 27–52.

1. Minter, *Chagres*, p. 237 ff.
2. Quoted in André Siegfried, *Suez and Panama* (London, 1940), p. 225.
3. Edward Everett to Mrs. Charles Eames, January, 1855, Edward Everett papers, Mass. Historical Society Collection, Boston, Mass.
4. A Pulitzer prize winning treatment on the 1850s which stresses the role of the party as a cohesive factor is Roy F. Nichols, *The Disruption of the American Democracy* (New York, 1948).
5. For a full account see Cyril Allen, "Felix Belly: Nicaraguan Canal Promoter," *Hispanic American Historical Review* vol. 37, no. 1 (February 1957), pp. 46–59.
6. Paul J. Scheips, "Gabriel Lafaond and Ambrose W. Thompson: Neglected Isthmian Promoters," *Hispanic American Historical Review*, vol. 36, no. 2 (May 1956), pp. 211–21.
7. Ibid., pp. 221–22.
8. DuVal, *Cadiz to Cathay*, p. 71.
9. Ibid., pp. 34–35.
10. James D. Richardson, ed., *Compilation of the Messages and Papers of the Presidents* (Washington, D.C., 1899), vol. 5, pp. 639–40.
11. Leander Chamberlain, "A Chapter of National Dishonor," *North American Review* (February 1912), p. 152.
12. George H. Sullivan and William N. Cromwell, eds., *Compilation of Executive Documents and Diplomatic Correspondence Relative to a Transisthmian Canal in Central America* (New York, 1905), vol. 2, pp. 1100–1220.
13. Paul J. Scheips, "Lincoln and the Chiriqui Colonization Project," *The Journal of Negro History*, vol. 37, (October 1952), p. 428; Ralph Korngold, *Thaddeus Stevens, A Being Darkly Wise and Rudely Great* (New York, 1955), p. 150.
14. Sullivan and Cromwell, *Executive Documents*, pp. 1240–47; Ireland, in *Boundaries*, says that the Colombian Congress rejected the treaty but does not cite his authority.
15. Quote in Siegfried, *Suez and Panama*, p. 228.
16. Richardson, *Papers of the Presidents*, vol. 7, p. 33.
17. John Bassett Moore, *Digest of International Law as Embodied in Treaties and Diplomatic Discussions* (Washington, D.C., 1906), vol. 3, p. 22.
18. "The Complete Report of the Interoceanic Canal Commission, 1872–76," *Senate Executive Document #15*, 46th Congress, 1st Session.
19. Richardson, *Papers of the Presidents*, vol. 7, pp. 585–86.
20. Moore, *Digest*, vol. 3, pp. 14–15.
21. Minter, *Chagres,* p. 308.
22. Quoted in Padelford, *Panama Canal*, p. 11.
23. Siegfried, *Suez and Panama*, p. 247.
24. DuVal, *Cadiz to Cathay*, p. 82.
25. Richardson, *Papers of the Presidents*, vol. 8, p. 11.
26. *Foreign Relations of the United States*, vol. 1 (1881), pp. 538–59; vol. 1 (1882), 302-14; vol. 1 (1883), 477–78.
27. *Senate Report #1*, 57th Congress, 1st Session, pp. 345–52.
28. Moore, *Digest*, vol. 3, pp. 197–98.

THE ABROGATION OF THE CLAYTON–BULWER TREATY

1. Padelford, *The Panama Canal*, pp. 13–14.
2. Richardson, *Papers of the Presidents*, vol. 7, p. 4888.
3. *Senate Report #1*, 57th Congress, 1st Session, p. 439.
4. President Cleveland withdrew the Nicaragua treaty on March 13, 1885, saying that he wished to "re-examine" it, but of course it was eventually retained (see n. 2). For information concerning the Maritime Canal Company of Nicaragua and its concession, see *Foreign Relations of the United States*, vol. 1 (1887), p. 115; vol. 1 (1888), pp. 100–6; vol. 1 (1897), pp. 417–19. See also *Senate Executive Document #99*, vol. 5, serial 2337, 49th Congress, 1st Session; *Congressional Record*, 51st Congress, 2nd Session, vol. 22, pt. 2, p. 1123; pt. 3, pp. 2224–34, 2970–90, 3052–70, 3073–76; pt. 4, p. 3410; "The Report of the Isthmian Canal Commission 1899–1901" and the "Supplementary Report 1902," contain summaries of the efforts to gain official U.S. financial backing and support. All of the various commission reports are embodied in *Senate Document #222*, 58th Congress, 2nd Session, pts. 1 and 2, which was published in 1904 after the battle over the routes was history. This document includes maps, photographs, illustrations, appendices, and other statistics.
5. Eugene H. Roseboom, *A History of Presidential Elections* (New York, 1957), pp. 277–84.
6. Siegfried, *Suez and Panama*, pp. 267–70.
7. The Resolution read that such European control would be "injurious to the just rights and interests of the United States and a menace to their welfare." The resolution passed the Senate, in Executive Session, but it did not pass the house. See *Senate Document #471*, 63rd Congress, 2nd Session, p. 14; Dexter Perkins, *The Monroe Doctrine, 1867–1907*, (Cambridge, Mass., 1955), p. 107.
8. Moore, *Digest*, vol. 3, pp. 203–9.
9. Julius W. Pratt, *A History of United States Foreign Policy*, (New York, 1955), pp. 332–35.
10. *Selections from the Correspondence of Theodore Roosevelt and Henry Cabot Lodge, 1884–1914*, 2 vols. (New York, 1925), vol. 1, p. 139.
11. *Abridgement of the Message of President McKinley, December, 1898, to Congress on the State of the Union* (Government Printing Office, Washington, D.C., 1899), vol. 1, p. 5.
12. Bailey, *Diplomatic History*, p. 486.
13. DuVal, *Cadiz to Cathay*, pp. 113–14.
14. W. R. Thayer, *Life and Letters of John Hay*, vol. 2 (Boston, 1915), p. 339.
15. Charles C. Hyde, "The Significance of the Hay-Pauncefote Treaty," *Harvard Law Review*, vol. 14 (1900), pp. 52–58.
16. Thayer, *John Hay*, vol. 2, p. 339.
17. Bailey, *Diplomatic History*, p. 487.
18. Thayer, *John Hay*, vol. 2, p. 229.
19. Pratt, *U.S. Foreign Policy*, p. 399.
20. Bailey, *Diplomatic History*, p. 487–88.
21. *Senate Document #474*, 63rd Congress, 2nd Session, pp. 292–94.

NICARAGUA OR PANAMA?

1. Ulysses S. Grant, "The Nicaragua Canal," *North American Review* (February 1881), pp. 107–116.
2. Siegfried, *Suez and Panama*, p. 232.
3. *Senate Executive Document* #123, 48th Congress, 1st Session, contains a report of the French operation in Panama which is typically disparaging.
4. DuVal, *Cadiz to Cathay*, p. 111.
5. *Senate Document* #54, 57th Congress, 1st Session, p. 59; *Senate Document* #222, 58th Congress, 2nd Session, p. 2843.
6. *Congressional Records*, 55th Congress, 3rd Session, p. 2843.
7. The "New French Canal Company" was organized on October 20, 1894, and received an extension of its concession to October 20, 1904, from Colombia. It raised some new capital and resumed the work left by the old de Lesseps Company. But everything was on a much more modest scale and funds were soon running low. After 1898 the New Company kept activity at a level which would barely hold the Colombian concession. See "Report of the Isthmian Canal Commission, 1899–1902," *Senate Document* #222, 58th Congress, 2nd Session, pt. 2, pp. 481–82.
8. DuVal, *Cadiz to Cathay*, pp. 149–53.
9. *Senate Report* #1, 57th Congress, 1st Session, pp. 309–10.
10. *Congressional Record*, 57th Congress, 1st Session, p. 6998.
11. Dwight C. Miner, *Fight for the Panama Route* (New York, 1940), p. 115.
12. Mack, *The Land Divided*, p. 422.
13. *Congressional Record*, 56th Congress, 2nd Session, pp. 2884–87; 2949; 3517–19.
14. He denounced covert political maneuvering, that of William N. Cromwell particularly, in a special report to the Senate. See *Senate Report* #1337, 56th Congress, 1st Session, pp. 9–10.
15. *Senate Document*, #123, 57th Congress, 1st Session, p. 10.
16. The text of the Spooner Law is found in *Statutes at Large*, 57th Congress, 1st Session, vol. 32, pt. 1, pp. 481-84.
17. Mack, *The Land Divided*, p. 43.
18. *Senate Document* #253, 57th Congress, 1st Session.
19. These debates may be found in the *Congressional Record*, 57th Congress, 1st Session, vol. 35, pts. 6 and 7.
20. *New York Sun*, May 17, 1902.
21. *Congressional Record*, 57th Congress, 1st Session, p. 7072 et. seq.
22. The vote in the House was 259 to 8.
23. Mack, *The Land Divided*, p. 435.
24. *Congressional Record*, 57th Congress, 1st Session, p. 6984.
25. *Senate Document* #123, 57th Congress, 1st Session.
26. *Senate Document* #474, 63rd Congress, 2nd Session, pp. 277–88, contains the text of the Hay-Herran Treaty.
27. Congressional Record, 58th Congress, 1st Session and Special Session of the Senate, vol. 37, pp. 1, 13.
28. Quoted in DuVal, *Cadiz to Cathay*, pp. 210–11.
29. Mack, *The Land Divided*, p. 450.

30. *Congressional Record*, 58th Congress, Special Session of the Senate, vol. 37, pp. 3, 67, 106, 140.

ROOSEVELT AND THE REVOLUTION IN PANAMA

1. The nature and background of this feeling is discussed by a distinguished Panamanian scholar, Ricardo J. Alfaro in the 50th Anniversary publication published by the Panamanian government, *Panamá, 50 Años de República* (Panamá, R.P., 1903), pp. 11–116.

2. Ernesto J. Castillero Reyes, *La Cause Imediata de la Emancipación de Panamá* (Panamá, R.P., 1933).

3. Minter, *Chagres*, pp. 328–43; W. Stoors Lee, *Strength to Move a Mountain*, pp. 29–63; DuVal, *Cadiz to Cathay*, pp. 273–340; William D. McCain, *The United States and the Republic of Panama*, (Durham, N.C., 1937), pp. 12–22; and Bunau-Varilla's own accounts, *Panama, the Creation, Destruction and Resurrection* (New York, 1914); *The Great Adventure of Panama* (New York, 1920); and *From Panama to Verdun* (Philadelphia, 1940).

4. Bishop, *Theodore Roosevelt and His Time* (New York, 1920), vol. 1, p. 279; Also *Works of Theodore Roosevelt*, Scribner's Memorial Edition, vol. 23, p. 322.

5. *American Monthly Review of Reviews* (November 1903), pp. 525–26.

6. For this typical reaction see *World's Work Magazine* (November 1903), p. 4049.

7. *New York Herald*, November 4, 1903.

8. *Congressional Record*, 58th Congress, 1st Session and Special Session of the Senate, vol. 37, pp. 426–30. See also Charles D. Ameringer, "Philippe Bunau-Varilla, New Light on the Panama Canal Treaty," *Hispanic American Historical Review*, vol. 68, no. 2 (February 1966), pp. 28–52.

9. *Senate Document* #32, 58th Congress, 2nd Session.

10. The text of the treaty is in *Senate Document* #474, 63rd Congress, 2nd Session, pp. 295–313.

11. *Documentos Fundamentales para la Historia de la Nación Panameña* (Panamá, R.P., 1953), p. 412; also *Compilación de Ciertos Tratados y Convenciones Relacionados con la Zona del Canal (1903–1950)* (Panamá, R.P., 1952), pp. 3–21.

12. Quoted in DuVal, *Cadiz to Cathay*, p. 403.

13. Ibid., p. 412.

14. Quoted in Bishop, *Theodore Roosevelt*, vol. 1, p. 280.

15. Quoted in DuVal, *Cadiz to Cathay*, pp. 407, 410.

16. Bunau-Varilla, *Panama, the Creation*, p. 413.

17. *Congressional Record*, 58th Congress, 2nd Session, p. 2260; for debates, see vol. 38, pts. 1, 2, 3.

18. Very colorfully described in Lee, *To Move a Mountain*, pp. 146–71.

19. Quoted in Minter, *Chagres*, pp. 354–55.

20. Lee, *To Move A Mountain*, pp. 110–16.

21. *New York World*, October 4, 1908.
22. Theodore Roosevelt, *Works, Presidential Addresses, and Papers*, vol. 8, p. 1997; Richardson, *Papers of the Presidents*, vol. 16, p. 7348.
23. *United States* v. *Smith*, 173 F. 227 (1909); see also *Harvard Law Review*, vol. 23 (1909), p. 309.
24. *United States* v. *The Press Publishing Company* (1911), 219 U.S. page 1; 31 Supreme Court Reports, p. 212; 55 L ed. p. 65; *Virginia Law Register*, vol. 16 (1911), p. 782; *Bench and Bar Magazine*, vol. 24, (1911), p. 43. A factual study of the cases is contained in Clyde Peirce, *The Roosevelt Panama Libel Cases*, (New York, 1959). This is probably the best narrative treatment of the historic lawsuits aside from official records.
25. *The New York World*, January 3, 1911.
26. Bishop, *Panama Gateway*, pp. 206–7.
27. Ibid.
28. DuVal, *Cadiz to Cathay*, p. 424.

THE RAINEY COMMITTEE AND THE THOMSON-URRUTIA CONVENTION

1. Dana G. Munro, "Dollar Diplomacy in Nicaragua, 1909–1913," *Hispanic American Historical Review*, vol. 38, no. 2 (May 1958), pp. 209–36.
2. Samuel F. Bemis, *Latin American Policy of the United States* (New York, 1943), p. 164.
3. Pratt, *U.S. Foreign Policy*, p. 432. The speech was delivered at the Southern Commercial Congress at Mobile, Alabama, October 27, 1913.
4. Treaty Series, #624, Department of State; *Foreign Relations of the United States*, vol. 1 (1916), p. 849; *Congressional Record*, 64th Congress, 1st Session, vol. 3, p. 2770.
5. Reported in the press nationwide, March 24, 1911.
6. E. Taylor Parks, *Colombia and the United States* (Durham, N.C., 1935), p. 437.
7. House Resolution #32. *Congressional Record*, 62nd Congress, 1st Session, vol. 1, p. 113; *Senate Document* #474, 63rd Congress, 2nd Session, p. 602.
8. Leander Chamberlain, "A Chapter of National Dishonor," *North American Review* (February 1912), p. 152.
9. *New York World*, January 27, 1912.
10. Henry M. Hall, *New York World*, October 4, 1908.
11. See "Hearings on the Rainey Resolution—the Story of Panama," Report of the House Committee on Foreign Affairs, 62nd Congress, 2nd Session, Government Printing Office, Washington, D.C. (1913). The House took no final action on the resolution. The bulk of the material gathered by the committee and often spoken of as "The Rainey Report" is included in "The Panama Canal and Our Relations with Colombia," *Senate Document* #47, 63rd Congress, 2nd Session (1914). During the hearings the press carried extensive dispatches, particularly during the public testimony given on Jan. 26, 1912, and from February 9–20, 1912.

12. Mack, *The Land Divided*, p. 478.
13. Francisco J. Urrutia, *A Commentary on the Declaration on the Rights of Nations* (Washington, 1916; Bogotá, 1917), p. 55.
14. The Root-Cortes Treaty. See "Diplomatic History of the Panama Canal," *Senate Document #474*, vol. 15, serial 6582, 63rd Congress, 2nd Session (April 29, 1914).
15. *Foreign Relations of the United States*, vol. 1 (1914), pp. 146–69.
16. Theodore Roosevelt, "The Panama Blackmail Treaty," *Metropolitan Magazine* (February 1915), p. 71.
17. Joseph G. Freehoff, *America and the Canal Title* (New York, 1916), p. 15.
18. Lawrence Ealy, *The Republic of Panama in World Affairs, 1903–1950*, (Philadelphia, 1951), pp. 32–35.
19. *Messages and Papers of Woodrow Wilson*, vol. 1, pp. 559 et. seq.
20. Roosevelt, "Blackmail Treaty," *Metropolitan Magazine* (February 1915), p. 71.
21. Freehoff, *Canal Title*, p. 102.
22. Eugene H. Roseboom, *A History of Presidential Elections* (New York, 1957), pp. 382–83.
23. W. R. Thayer, *The Life and Letters of John Hay* (Boston, 1915), vol. 2, p. 327, quotes this letter of July 2, 1915.
24. J. F. Rippy, *The Capitalists and Colombia*, pp. 103–121; Bailey, *Diplomatic History*, p. 498.
25. Treaty Series #661, Department of State; *Congressional Record*, 67th Congress, 1st Session, p. 157–488; *Foreign Relations of the United States*, vol. 1, (1921), 638–45.
26. Act of August 24, 1912–37 Stat., L.560; *Congressional Record*, 62nd Congress, 2nd Session, vol. 48, p. 11069; vol. 11, p. 11218.
27. *Foreign Relations of the United States* (1912), pp. 467–89.
28. B. J. Hendrick, *The Life and Letters of Walter Hines Page*, vol. 1 (Garden City, N.Y., 1922), p. 249.
29. Richardson, *Papers of the Presidents*, vol. 17, p. 7933; *Congressional Record*, 63rd Congress, 2nd Session, vol. 51, pt. 5, p. 4313.
30. *New York American*, March 5–14, 1914.
31. *Congressional Record*, 63rd Congress, 2nd Session, vol. 51, pt. 10, p. 10247–342.
32. There have been efforts in Congress to legislate preferences for United States shipping. A bill offered by Republican Senator Borah of Idaho passed the Senate October 10, 1921, but died in the House. It would have given free passage to U.S. ships (*Congressional Record*, 67th Congress, 1st Session. vol. 51, pt. 6, pp. 6169, 6236). In 1938 Senator William G. McAdoo, Democrat of California, introduced a bill to give exemption to U.S. ships in the coastal trade. This was buried in a Senate committee and never came to vote (*Congressional Record*, 75th Congress, 3rd Session, vol. 83, pt. 1, p. 1095). A comprehensive account of these efforts is contained in William S. Coker, "The Panama Canal Tolls Controversy; A Different Perspective," *The Journal of American History*, vol. 55, no. 3 (December 1968).

A YANQUI MONUMENT IN LATIN AMERICA

1. John and Mavis Biesanz, *The People of Panama* (New York, 1955), pp. 308–13.
2. Laurence Duggan, *The Americas—the Search for Hemisphere Security* (New York, 1949), pp. 71–72.
3. Treaty Series #945, Department of State; *Senate Executive Report #5*, 76th Congress, 1st Session; *Documentos Fundamentales para la Historia de la Nación Panameña* (Panamá, R.P., 1953), pp. 455–71.
4. *Christian Century* (March 18, 1936), p. 251.
5. Ealy, *Panama in World Affairs*, pp. 171–73.
6. *U.S. Treaties and Other International Agreements* (Washington, D.C.: Government Printing Office, 1956), vol. 6, part 2, p. 2273.
7. Daniel James, "Demands from Panama," *Philadelphia Bulletin*, July 23, 1958; *New York Times* dispatches of July 14, 1958.
8. Biesanz, *People of Panama*, pp. 157, 163–64, 192–93; Ealy, *Panama in World Affairs*, pp. 168–71, 179, 182.
9. Padelford, *The Panama Canal*, p. 28.
10. "Plans of the Atomic Age for the Big Ditch," *Philadelphia Inquirer Sunday Magazine*, November 10, 1946.
11. Biesanz, *People of Panama*, pp. 59–60.
12. "The Panama Canal: The Sea Level Project and National Security," Report of the Special Committee on the Panama Canal of the National Rivers and Harbors Congress, (Government Printing Office, Washington, 1956). See also Hanson Baldwin, "New Currents in the Panama Canal," *New York Times Magazine*, May 26, 1957; "Vast Work Urged at Panama Canal," dispatch to *New York Times*, December 9, 1956, section L., p. 69.
13. Committee on Latin American Studies, University of California at Los Angeles, *Statistical Abstract of Latin America for 1956* (Los Angeles,   ), p. 16.
14. Ealy, *Panama in World Affairs*, pp. 107–8; 177–80.
15. "Panama to Check Vessels in Canal," *New York Times*, August 17, 1958.
16. "No Emparedados," *Time*, April 18, 1949.
17. "U.S. Aid Sought on Latin Highway," *New York Times*, July 21, 1957. For a discussion of the present status of the Pan American Highway with reference to its last uncompleted segment through the Darien region of Panama see Mario Barraco Marmol, "Darien," *Americas*, vol. 21, no. 7 (July 1969), pp. 23–31. *Americas* is the magazine of the Pan American Union.
18. George W. Goethals, *The Government of the Canal Zone* (Princeton, 1915). Also Harry N. Howard, *Military Government in the Panama Canal Zone* (Norman, Okla., 1931).
19. Marshall E. Dimock, *Government Operated Enterprises in the Panama Canal Zone* (Chicago, 1934); Clark H. Galloway, "Canal Zone Workers Like Their U.S. Shops," *U.S. News and World Report* (December 3, 1948). The issue of the U.S. commissaries was long a thorny one because the Panamanian merchants felt that the mighty U.S. Government was pitted

against them in economic competition. This tension has been somewhat eased by new restrictions on persons eligible to buy in the commissaries. See *New York Times* dispatches, "Panama Reaction to PX Curb Mixed," July 7, 1957, "Net Income Down on Panama Canal," November 17, 1957.

20. Lawrence Ealy, "The Development of an Anglo-American System of Law in the Panama Canal Zone," *American Journal of Legal History* (October, 1958), p. 283.

21. McCain, *United States and Panama*, p. 244.

22. Union officials, organizers, and troubleshooters maintain close contact with isthmian labor problems. For example, in February 1958, union advisers went to Panama to give guidance and assistance to the Printers' Union in their prolonged strike against newspapers and printshops. See "Printers in Panama get New Strike Aid," *New York Times*, February 23, 1958.

THE YANQUI LEGAL SYSTEM IN THE CANAL ZONE

1. Biesanz, *People of Panama*, pp. 55–56.

2. Isthmian Canal Convention of November 18, 1903, T.S. 431; 33 *Stat.* 2234, 2 Malloy 1349. Text is in *Senate Document* #474, 63rd Congress, 2nd Session, pp. 295–313.

3. 32 *Stat.* 481, 84 P. L. 183.

4. Goethals, *Government of the Zone*, p. 11.

5. Johnson, *Four Centuries*, p. 282.

6. Goethals, *Government of the Zone*, p. 13, n. 4.

7. Ibid., p. 17.

8. *Seven Commercial Laws of the World, Panama Canal Zone*, pp. 111–12; Hinckley, "Canal Zone Laws and Judiciary", 17 *Case and Comment*, pp. 220–22.

9. 33 Stat. 429. See also *Treaties and Acts of Congress Relating to the Panama Canal* (Mt. Hope, C.Z., 1917), pp. 27–29. (Annotated in supplements published in 1922, 1925, and 1926).

10. See historical discussion in *Documentos Fundamentales*.

11. Charles P. Sherman, *Roman Law in the Modern World* (New Haven, 1922), pp. 286–92.

12. Ibid., p. 292, n. 11.

13. Richard C. Backus and Phanor J. Eder, *A Guide to the Law and Legal Literature of Colombia* (Washington, D.C., 1943), p. 161.

14. Ibid., p. 162.

15. *Documentos Fundamentales*, p. 35, n. 10.

16. Backus and Eder, *Law of Colombia*, p. 33, n. 13.

17. Ibid., p. 181.

18. Ibid.

19. Ibid.

20. Ibid., pp. 33, 181.

21. *Foreign Relations of the United States*, vol. 1 (1904), pp. 582–83.

22. Goethals, *Government of the Zone*, p. 31, n. 4. The commerce, mining and admiralty codes of Panama were also adopted in toto by the Commission.

23. Frederic J. Haskin, *The Panama Canal* (Garden City, N.Y., 1913), p. 260; also Goethals, *Government of the Zone*, p. 38, n. 4.

24. *Panama, 50 Años de República Edición de la Junta Nacional del Cincuentenario* (Panamá, R.P., 1953), p. 509.

25. McCain, *United States and Panama*, pp. 78–85.

26. Goethals, *Government of the Zone*, p. 41, n. 4.

27. Ibid., p. 47.

28. The president's orders are executed as virtually the sole responsibility of the Governor of the Canal Zone. His authority, subject only to that of the president, is otherwise absolute. See 37 *Stat.* 560; 42 *Stat.* 1004; the case of *Cie Generale Transatlantique* v. *Governor of Canal Zone et al.*, 90 F. 2d 225. See also, *Final Report of the U.S. Isthmian Canal Commission*, (Government Printing Office, Washington, D.C., 1916).

29. Act of August 24, 1912, 37 *Stat.* 560.

30. 54 *Am. Jur.*, 922; 28 U.S.C. 225 (d).

31. In addition to the general jurisdiction of a regular U.S. District Court, the C.Z. District Court has been held analogous to a state court of unlimited jurisdiction. See *Arthur* v. *Compagnie Generale Transatlantique*, 72 F. 2d (C.A.A. 5) 662.

32. *McConaughey* v. *Morrow*, 3 C.Z. Sup. Ct. 377, 381.

33. Haskin, *The Panama Canal*, p. 258, n. 23; Goethals, *Government of the Zone*, p. 72, n. 4.

34. *Canal Zone* v. *Christian*, 1. C. Z. Sup. Ct. 12; *Government* v. *Diaz* 3 C. Z. Sup. Ct. 465; and *Dixon* v. *Goethals*, 3 C. Z. Sup. Ct. 23.

35. The Canal Zone courts took judicial notice of the law of the Republic of Panama existing Feb. 26, 1904, and, in the absence of evidence to the contrary, the law then prevailing was presumed to continue in force. *Panama Railroad Co.* v. *Toppin*, 252 U.S. 308.

36. *Kung Ching Chong* v. *Wing Chong*, 2 C. Z. Sup. Ct. 25–30.

37. Civil Code of Panama, Articles 2341, 2347, 2349.

38. See n. 35, above.

39. *The Panama Railroad Company* v. *Bosse*, 249 U.S. 41.

40. *Panama Electric Railroad Co.* v. *Moyers*, 249 Fed. 19 (C. C. A. 5); and *Theokistan* v. *Panama Railroad Co.*, 6 F. 2d 116 (C. C. A. 5).

41. *Fitzpatrick* v. *Panama Railroad* Co., 2 C. Z. Sup. Ct. 111, 121, 128; and *McKenzie* v. *McClintic-Marshall Construction Co.*, 2 C. Z. Sup. Ct. 181–82.

42. *Fitzpatrick* v. *Panama Railroad* Co., 2 C. Z. Sup. Ct. 111.

43. Act of Congress, August 24, 1912, 37 *Stat.* 560.

44. Act of Congress, June 19, 1934, 48 *Stat.* 1122.

45. Padelford, *Panama Canal*, p. 186.

46. Executive Orders, Proclamations, and Regulations in force as of June 1, 1938, are found in 35 C. F. R., "Panama Canal." Those issued since June 1, 1938, are in *The Federal Register*.

47. Equity jurisdiction is blended with Law and not exercised separately in the C. Z. courts. 48 U.S.C. 1357.

48. Before the establishment of the present District Court the Canal Zone was not treated as a U.S. Judicial District. (27 O.A.G. 136.)

49. 48 U.S.C. 1351.

50. 48 U.S.C. 1342.
51. 48 U.S.C. 1347. The question of U.S. citizenship was legally beclouded, as it concerned the growing number of persons born in the Canal Zone of alien parentage, until passage of legislation providing that if at least one parent is an American citizen, an individual born in the Zone is a citizen. (50 *Stat.* 558). Today all housing within the Zone is U.S. government-owned.
52. *Fullerton* v. *The Government of the Canal Zone*, 8 F. 2d 968 (C.C.A. 5).
53. Executive Order 6166 of June 10, 1933; Executive Order 6390 of November 3, 1933.
54. 48 U.S.C. 1342.
55. Appeals from the District Court of the Canal Zone lie to the 5th Circuit Court of Appeals, as heretofore (see note 30). The Governor is empowered to grant pardons and reprieves and remit fines and forfeitures for offenses against the laws of the Canal Zone. He may grant reprieves for offenses against the laws of the United States until the decision of the president is made known for appeals to executive clemency thereon. He appoints a "Pardons Board" to advise him in these matters.
56. 30 O.A.G. 220.
57. 20 *Am. J. Intl. L.* 120–122: "Whether there is at least titular sovereignty in the Republic of Panama is a question of diverging opinions." In *Huastua Petroleum Co.* v. *U.S.*, 14 F. 2d 495, the 5th Circuit Court of Appeals says that the Canal Zone is a possession but that it is not a "part of the United States." In *Vermilya-Brown Co.* v. *Connell*, 335 U.S. 377, J. Reed, *in obiter dicta*, makes reference to the Canal Zone as admittedly territory over which we do not have "sovereignty." In his dissenting opinion in the same case J. Jackson seems to take another viewpoint. An excellent presentation of the Panamanian position is given by the eminent international law authority, Ricardo J. Alfaro, in *Panamá, 50 Años de República*, p. 120, n. 24. The issue is also appraised in Ealy, *Panama in World Affairs*, 151–54.
58. 35 *Stat.* 65, p. 2; 45 U.S.C. p. 52 (1908).
59. Act of March 9, 1933, 48 *Stat.* 2, 12 U.S.C. 202 (1933).
60. 54 *Stat.* 795, as amended 15 U.S.C. 80a—2 (37).
61. A prime example of congressional vagueness is found in the application of the postal laws. The agreement with Panama to use their stamps overprinted (see note 71) was abrogated in 1924. The Canal Zone Code now provided that "postal service of the Canal Zone shall be governed . . . by such of the laws, rules, and regulations of the Postal Service of the United States as are not inapplicable to the conditions existing in the Canal Zone." 2 U.S.C. 271.
62. 52 *Stat.* 1040, sec. 201 (a); 21 U.S.C. 321 (a).
63. 48 *Stat.* 1064, 1065, sec. 3 (g) as amended; 47 U.S.C. 153 (g).
64. 54 *Stat.* 1137 sec. 101 (e); 8 U.S.C. 50 (e).
65. 56 *Stat.* 1035; 42 U.S.C. 1651.
66. 65 *Stat.* 174 sec. 2; 15 U.S.C. 606b-2 (a).
67. 40 *Stat.* 231 sec. 1; 18 U.S.C. 39. For a discussion of the application of U.S. Neutrality Acts of 1937 and 1939 to the Canal Zone see Padelford, *The Panama Canal*, pp. 158–82, n. 4.
68. In *Luckenbach Steamship Co.* v. *U.S.*, 280 U.S. 173 (1920), the court said

that the matter "depends upon long continued legislative and administrative construction of such statute."

69. For example, in 1955 the Panama-U.S. Treaty of Mutual Understanding and cooperation, Jan. 25, 1955, T.I.A.A. 3297, 6 U.S.T. 2273, contained an agreement by the United States to bring Panamanian nationals employed by the U.S. within the Canal Zone under the Civil Service Retirement Act on an equal basis with U.S. citizens already covered by the law.

70. *Panamá, 50 Años de República*, pp. 120–26, n. 24.

71. See note 61; McCain, *United States and Panama*, pp. 23–47.

72. Secretary Hughes to Panamanian Minister, Oct. 15, 1923, 2 *Hackworth Digest of International Law*, pp. 801–6. See also the joint statement by President Franklin D. Roosevelt and Panamanian President Arias, Oct. 17, 1933, General Treaty and Supplementary Convention of March 2, 1936, ratified July 26, 1939.

73. By the 1955 Treaty of Mutual Understanding and Cooperation (see note 69), the United States allows the Republic of Panama to impose and collect income taxes upon its own citizens who before that time were beyond its jurisdiction because they worked and lived within the Canal Zone. The republic is also given the right to levy import duties on goods landed for non-governmental purposes at Canal Zone piers and destined for ultimate delivery in Panamanian territory.

74. 204 U.S. 24.

75. 280 U.S. 173.

76. 335 U.S. 377.

EISENHOWER AND THE PANAMANIAN QUESTIONS

One of the best sources for information about Panama in the 1950's is Larry La Rae Pippin's dissertation, *The Remón Era, An Analysis of a Decade of Events in Panama 1947–1957,* which was published in 1964 by the Institute of Hispanic American and Luso-Brazilian Studies at Stanford University as a special issue of *The Hispanic American Report.* Dr. Pippin conducted extensive personal interviews on the isthmus in addition to making exhaustive use of all published sources. The bibliography published in this book is invaluable.

1. The Treaty of Mutual Understanding and Cooperation (Chapin-Fabrega Pact) of 1955, Article XII reads:

> The United States of America agrees that, effective December 31, 1956, there will be excluded from the privilege of making purchases in the commissaries and other sales stores in the Canal Zone as well as the privilege of making importations into the Canal Zone all those persons who are not citizens of the United States of America, except members of the Armed Forces of the United States, and who do not actually reside in the Canal Zone but who are included in the categories of persons authorized to reside in said Zone; it being understood nevertheless that all personnel of the agencies of

the United States of America will be permitted under adequate controls to purchase small articles such as meals, sweets, chewing gum, tobacco, and similar articles near the sites of their jobs.

The United States of America further agrees that, effective December 31, 1956, and notwithstanding the provisions of the first paragraph of Article IV of the General Treaty signed March 2, 1936, the Government of the Republic of Panama may impose duties and other charges upon goods destined or consigned to persons, other than citizens of the United States of America, included in class (a) in Section 2 of Article III of said Treaty, who reside or sojourn in territory under the jurisdiction of the Republic of Panama during the performance of their service with the United States of America or its agencies, even though such goods are intended for their own use and benefit.

See Vicente Saenz, *Nuestras vías Interoceanicas* (Mexico, D.F., 1957), pp. 64–67, 209–17.

2. *Area Handbook for Panama*, Special Operations Research Office of the American University operating under contract with Department of the Army, Washington, D.C. (OPS PL SP-4), p. 320.

3. Rollie Poppino, *International Communism in Latin America* (New York, 1964).

4. *Area Handbook for Panama*, pp. 320–21.

5. Sheldon B. Liss, *The Canal, Aspects of United States–Panamanian Relations* (South Bend, Ind., 1967), pp. 63–64. See also *New York Times*, November 22, 1959.

6. *Philadelphia Evening Bulletin*, September 17, 1960.

7. *Panama Star and Herald*, September 23, 1960.

8. The full text of Mr. Flood's remarks is found in *Congressional Record*, 86th Congress, 1st session (January 9, 1959). It is discussed in an article by Demaree Bess, "The Panama Danger Zone," *Saturday Evening Post* (May 9, 1959).

9. Lawrence O. Ealy, "Strategic Waterways," *U.S. Naval War College Review*, vol. 12, no. 7 (1960), pp. 40–51.

10. Saenz, *Nuestra vías Interoceanicas*, pp. 125–42.

11. *Area Handbook for Panama*, pp. 242, 246–48.

12. Liss, *The Canal, Aspects*, pp. 131–35.

13. *Area Handbook for Panama*, pp. 323–24. See also Liss, *The Canal, Aspects*, pp. 126–31.

14. Although Secretary of State Dean Rusk declared that Farland was given the customary debriefing, the former ambassador stated quite bluntly upon several subsequent occasions that he felt his treatment was due to a belief that he opposed the *Alianza* when in fact he disagreed only with its emphasis upon erroneous goals in Panama.

15. Jack Hood Vaughan was appointed ambassador when relations were resumed with Panama in the winter of 1964 but served only a few months before being replaced by Charles W. Adair. In an interview with The Associated Press quoted in the Trenton, New Jersey *Times-Advertiser* in

February, 1964, Mr. Farland charged that the White House had "passed the word" at the time of his return that he was to be ignored by top policy makers. He was not consulted, furthermore, by the State Department even after the isthmian riots of January, 1964.

PRESIDENT JOHNSON FAILS TO END THE PANAMA PROBLEM

1. Secondary sources remain the best available references for the great uprising of January, 1964. *Life* in its issue of January 24, 1964, vol. 56, no. 4, did an excellent job of written and photographic reporting. See also *U.S. News & World Report* for January 27, 1964; March 30, 1964; and June 22, 1964. Daily newspapers are also important, containing many background articles as well as factual reports.
2. "2 Die, 26 Hurt in Riots as Panamanian Mob Storms Canal Zone," *Philadelphia Inquirer*, January 9, 1964.
3. *Philadelphia Evening Bulletin*, September 17, 1960.
4. "Inside Story of Panama Riots," *U.S. News & World Report* (March 30, 1964), p. 48.
5. "Inside an Ugly Fight—Bullets Fly in Panama over the Right to Fly the Flag," *Life* (January 24, 1964), p. 22.
6. *New York Times*, January 17, 1964.
7. "Panama Agrees to Resume its Relations with U.S. and Discuss Differences Later," *Philadelphia Evening Bulletin*, January 15, 1964.
8. "Panama: Bluffs, Pressures, Impasse," *Newsweek* (January 27, 1964), p. 45.
9. "Who Incited Riot in Panama—Findings of Official Body," *U.S. News & World Report* (June 22, 1964), p. 37.
10. "U.S. Welcomes Exoneration in Panama Riots," *U.S. News & World Report* (June 22, 1964), p. 37; see also *Newsweek* (June 22, 1964), p. 48.
11. Sheldon B. Liss, *The Canal, Aspects*, p. 143, especially n. 8.
12. "Robles, New Panama Leader, Makes His Own Decisions," *Philadelphia Evening Bulletin*, May 13, 1964.
13. *New York Herald Tribune*, April 8, 1964; "Panama Flag Won't Mourn" (UPI), *Philadelphia Inquirer*, April 7, 1964.
14. "How Reds Inflamed Panama," *U.S. News & World Report* (February 10, 1964); Henry J. Taylor, "Cuban Guerillas Threaten Canal," *Philadelphia Evening Bulletin*, August 11, 1967; "Nixon says Castro Set Panama Off," *Trenton Times*, January 18, 1964.
15. *U.S. News & World Report* (September 5, 1966), p. 89.
16. "More Riots in Panama, More Trouble for U.S.," *U.S. News & World Report* (June 20, 1966).
17. "Panama Plan is Endorsed in Congress" (AP), *Philadelphia Evening Bulletin*, September 25, 1966.
18. "The Atom and the New Canal," *Philadelphia Sunday Bulletin*, January 31, 1965, section 2; see also "Is U.S. Facing Another Crisis Over the Panama Canal," *U.S. News & World Report* (March 27, 1967), p. 104.

19. "A Deal On Panama Canal: Rough Transit Ahead," *U.S. News & World Report* (July 10, 1967), p. 41.

20. "Young Flag Raiser Returns, Says He Did Right in Panama" (AP), *Philadelphia Evening Bulletin*, January 24, 1964.

21. "The Atom and the New Canal," *Philadelphia Sunday Bulletin*, January 31, 1965; Robert C. Albrook, "Panama Wants New Canal in Panama," *Philadelphia Evening Bulletin*, April 19, 1967.

22. "Soviet Backs Panama to Hilt in Canal Fight," *Philadelphia Sunday Bulletin*, January 12, 1964, cites the ever ready hopes of Russian profit from U.S.–Panamanian disputes.

23. August C. Miller, Jr., "To Build a Bigger Ditch," *U.S. Naval Institute Proceedings* (September 1967), pp. 26–34.

24. Carl T. Rowan, "U.S., Panama in Treaty Deal," *Philadelphia Evening Bulletin*, January 30, 1967.

25. "A Deal on Panama Canal: Rough Transit Ahead," *U.S. News & World Report* (July 10, 1967), p. 41.

26. James J. Kilpatrick, "Panama Canal Pact Called a Giveaway," *Philadelphia Evening Bulletin*, July 10, 1967.

27. "Opposition Grows to Canal Treaties," *Trenton Sunday Times*, August 20, 1967, p. 17.

28. "Is U.S. Facing Another Crisis over the Panama Canal?" *U.S. News & World Report* (March 27, 1967).

29. "Nixon's New Look at Latin America," *Vision Letter* (October 16, 1968).

WHAT OF THE 1970s?

1. See *Panama Star and Herald*, May 18–20, 1969, on Rockefeller visit; see also, "Panama Says Polite Hello to Rockefeller," *Philadelphia Evening Bulletin*, May 19, 1969.

2. "Panama Tells Rocky of Plan for 1970 Vote," *Trenton Evening Times*, May 19, 1969.

3. "Panama Junta Taken to Task by Rockefeller," *Philadelphia Evening Bulletin*, May 18, 1969.

4. *Miami* (Fla.) *Herald*, August 20, 1969.

5. *Congressional Record*, 91st Congress, 1st Session (August 7, 1969), p. H 7187.

6. *Philadelphia Evening Bulletin*, November 5, 1969.

7. For events of November 14–18, 1969, see the *New York Times*.

8. *Vision Letter* (November 19, 1969).

9. Ibid.

10. "Nixon Talks of Changes in Latin Policy," *New York Times*, June 12, 1969.

11. *Panama Star and Herald*, September 27, 1969.

12. John C. Briggs, "The Sea Level Canal: Potential Biological Castastrophe," *BioScience* (January 1969), p. 44.

13. *Congressional Record*, 91st Congress, 1st Session (July 31, 1969), p. S 129; (August 4, 1969), p. H 6845–H 6848.

14. *BioScience* (April 1969), p. 301.
15. H. H. Gibbs, "A Southwest Passage?", *U.S. Naval Institute Proceedings* (April 1969), pp. 64–73. See also George D. Saunders, "Land Bridge from Sea to Shining Sea," *U.S. Naval Institute Proceedings* (July 1969), pp. 45–51.
16. It is interesting to note that a "Republican Party Citizen's Council," headed by Dr. Milton Eisenhower, in 1964 suggested a seven point program to revitalize U.S.–Panamanian relations including construction of a new sea level canal in Panama within twenty-five years. Mr. Nixon has never been as specific as the party leaders who served on this council, including the following members of President Eisenhower's cabinet: Thomas S. Gates, ex-secretary of defense; Marion B. Folsom, ex-secretary of health, education, and welfare; Oveta Culp Hobby, ex-secretary of health, education and welfare; and James P. Mitchell, ex-secretary of labor. See "G. O. P. Urges Second Panama Canal as Solution to Issues," *New York Herald Tribune*, April 7, 1964.
17. The closing of the Suez Canal has resulted in an undoubted increase in traffic through the Panama Canal. See "Panama Canal Breaks Tonnage and Toll Records," special dispatch from Balboa, Canal Zone, June 28, 1969, *New York Times*, June 29, 1969.
18. See remarks by Senator S. Thurmond, *Congressional Record*, 91st Congress, 1st Session, June 17, 1969, p. S 6653, quoting *Chicago Tribune* editorial of June 7, "No Sea Level Canal."
19. Carl T. Rowan, "Panama's Student Groups," *Philadelphia Evening Bulletin*, February 1, 1967; see also Karl Abraham, "Agitators Are Threatened by President of Panama," *Philadelphia Bulletin*, January 16, 1965. For an appraisal of Panamanians' attitudes toward the United States, see "Panama, Link Between Oceans and Continents," *National Geographic Magazine*, vol. 137, no. 3 (March 1970), pp. 402–40.
20. Since the advent of Castro there has been much liaison between Panamanian leftists and Cuba. See Henry J. Taylor, "Cuban Guerillas Threaten Canal," *Philadelphia Evening Bulletin*, August 11, 1967.
21. The Red Chinese have become a most significant psychological influence on Latin America's left wing forces. See William E. Ratliff, "Chinese Communist Cultural Diplomacy toward Latin America, 1949–1960," *Hispanic American Historical Review*, vol. 49, no. 1 (February 1969), pp. 53–79.
22. C. R. Vosburgh, *Panama Star and Herald*, June 2, 1965. An interesting appraisal of the Junta, the Panamanian National Guard's role in Isthmian politics, and General Omar Torrijos is contained in an article by Georgie Ann Geyer of the *Chicago Daily News* Service, "Oligarchy is Enemy of Latin Armies," *Trenton Evening Times*, July 9, 1969.

Bibliography

I would like to thank the *American Journal of Legal History* for its cooperation in giving me permission to use much of the material contained in my article in the October, 1958, issue of that publication.

I would also like to thank both Hon. Daniel J. Flood and the *U.S. Naval Institute Proceedings* for their kind permission to reproduce Congressman Flood's statement contained in the Appendix of this book.

Of particular value in my research for this study were *Vision Letter*, a biweekly analysis of Latin American affairs published by Vision, Incorporated, New York, and *Latin American Digest*, a bimonthly letter from the Center for Latin American Studies at Arizona State University.

MANUSCRIPTS

All are located in the Division of Manuscripts, Library of Congress Annex, Washington, D.C. unless otherwise designated.

John Barrett papers.

Edward Everett papers, Massachusetts Historical Society, Boston.

Abraham Lincoln papers in Robert Todd Lincoln Collection.

James Monroe papers.

John T. Morgan papers.

Theodore Roosevelt papers and correspondence.

Elihu Root papers.

Notes, Dispatches, and Instructions to United States Ministers and Consuls in Panama. The later years are in the State Dept. Division of Historical Policy Research; the earlier years at the National Archives.

OFFICIAL AND SEMI-OFFICIAL SOURCES (UNITED STATES)

Abridgement of the Annual Message of President McKinley, December, 1898, with Annexes and Reports, 2 vols., Government Printing Office, Washington, D.C., 1899.

The Annual Reports of the Governor of the Canal Zone 1914–1965, Government Printing Office, Washington, D.C., 1915–1966.

Area Handbook of Panama, prepared by Special Operations Research Office, The American University, for the Department of the Army (OPS PLSP-4), 1962.

Diplomatic Correspondence of the United States Concerning the Independence of the Latin American Nations, ed. W. R. Manning, 3 vols., New York, 1925.

The First International American Conference; Reports of Committees and Discussions Thereon, 4 vols., Government Printing Office, Washington, D.C., 1890.

"Hearings on the Rainey Resolution before the Committee on Foreign Affairs of the House of Representatives," *House of Representatives Report* #32, 62nd Congress, 2nd Session, 1913.

The Panama Canal–50th Anniversary, Panama Canal Information Office, Balboa, 1964.

Papers Relating to the Foreign Relations of the United States 1861–1946, Government Printing Office, Washington, D.C., published annually from 1902, covering the years 1861–1946. (The years 1861–1899 have been republished by the Kraus Reprint Corp., New York, N.Y., 1966–1968.)

Report of the Special Committee on the Panama Canal, of the National Rivers and Harbors Congress, Government Printing Office, Washington, D.C., 1956.

"Report of the U.S. Isthmian Canal Commission, 1899–1902," *Senate Document* #222, 58th Congress, 2nd Session, parts 1 and 2.

Reports of the Isthmian Canal Commission, 1905–1914, 4 vols., Government Printing Office, Washington, D.C., 1915.

Final Report of the Isthmian Canal Commission, Government Printing Office, Washington, D.C., 1916.

Treaties and Other International Acts of the United States of America, ed. Hunter Miller, Government Printing Office, Washington, D.C. (Published from 1931, covering 1776 onward.)

U.S. Treaties and Other International Agreements, 17 vols., Government Printing Office, Washington, D.C. (Published from 1950 through 1966.)

Department of State Bulletins and House and Senate Reports and Documents cited in the notes are not listed here.

OFFICIAL AND SEMI-OFFICIAL SOURCES (PANAMA)

Documentos Fundamentales Para la Historia de la Nación Panameña, Panamá, R.P., 1953.

Ministerio de Relaciones Exteriores, Documentos Relacionados con los Estados Unidos 1903–1965.

Panamá, 50 Años de República Edición de la Junta Nacional del Cincuentenario, Panamá, R.P., 1953.

Compilación de Ciertos Tradados y Convenciones Relacionados con la Zona del Canal (1903–1950), Panamá, R.P., 1952.

GENERAL REFERENCES

Committee on Latin American Studies, *Statistical Abstract of Latin America for 1956*, Los Angeles, 1957.

Jefferson, Thomas, *Writings, Official and Private*, ed. H.S. Washington. 9 vols., Washington, D.C., 1854.

Moore, John Bassett, *Digest of International Law as Embodied in Diplomatic Discussions and Treaties*, 8 vols., Washington, D.C., 1906.

Porter, Kirk H., and Johnson, Donald B., eds., *National Party Platforms, 1840–1964*, Urbana, Illinois, 1965. All quotations from party platforms contained in the text are taken from this source.

Ramirez, José F., ed., *Memorias para servir a la Historia de la Communicación Interoceanica por el istmo de Tehuantepec*, Mexico, 1853.

Richardson, James D., ed., *Compilation of the Messages and Papers of the Presidents*, 20 vols., Washington, D.C., 1899, 1915.

Roosevelt, Theodore, *State Papers as Governor and President*, H. Hagedorn, ed., 20 vols., New York, 1926.

Sullivan, George H. and Cromwell, William N., eds., *Compilation of Executive Documents and Diplomatic Correspondence Relative to a Trans-Isthmian Canal in Central America*, 3 vols., New York, 1905.

Wilson, Woodrow, *The Messages and Papers of Woodrow Wilson*, New York, 1924.

SECONDARY WORKS

Alfaro, Ricardo J., *Los Acuerdos entre Panamá y los Estados Unidos*, Panamá R.P., 1943.

———, *Los canales internacionales Panamá*, Panamá, Escuela de Temporado Universidad de Panamá, 1957.

American Enterprise Institute for Public Policy Research, *The Panama Canal— Its Past and Future*, Washington, D.C., 1964.

Arias, Harmodio, *El canal de Panamá, un estudio en derecho internacional y diplomacia*, Panamá R.P., Editora Panamá América, 1957.

Backenhus, Reuben E., Knapp, Harry S., and Johnson, Emory R., *The Panama Canal*, New York, 1915.

Backus, Richard C., and Eder, Phanon J., *A Guide to the Law and Legal Literature of Colombia*, Washington, D.C., 1943.

Bailey, Thomas A., *A Diplomatic History of the American People*, 6th ed., New York, 1958.

Ballesteros, Marto, ed., *Fiscal Survey of Panama*, Baltimore, 1964.

Bemis, Samuel F., *The Latin American Policy of the United States*, New York, 1943.

Biesanz, John and Mavis, *The People of Panama*, New York, 1955.

Bishop, Joseph B., *The Panama Gateway*, New York, 1913 and 1915.

———, *Theodore Roosevelt and His Time*, 3 vols., New York, 1920.

Bunau-Varilla, Philippe, *The Great Adventure of Panama*, New York, 1920.

————, *Panama, the Creation, Destruction, and Resurrection*, New York, 1914.

————, *From Panama to Verdun*, Philadelphia, 1940.

Castillero Reyes, Ernesto J., *La Causa Imediata de la Emancipación de Panamá*, Panamá, R.P., 1933.

Core, Sue Pearl, *Panama, Yesterday and Today*, New York, 1945.

Dimock, Marshall E., *Government Operated Enterprises in the Panama Canal Zone*, Chicago, 1934.

Duggan, Laurence, *The Americas—The Search for Hemispheric Security*, New York, 1949.

DuVal, Miles P., *Cadiz to Cathay, The Story of the Long Struggle for a Waterway Across the American Isthmus*, Palo Alto, 1940.

Ealy, Lawrence O., *The Republic of Panama in World Affairs, 1903–1950*, Philadelphia, 1951; reprint ed., Westport, Conn., 1970.

Franck, Harry A., *The Pan American Highway from the Rio Grande to the Canal Zone*, New York, 1940.

Freehoff, Joseph C., *America and the Canal Title*, New York, 1916.

Fuller, John D. F., *The Movement for the Acquisition of All Mexico, 1846–1848*, Baltimore, 1936; reprint ed., New York, 1969.

Gargáz, Pierre-André, *A Project of Universal and Perpetual Peace*, ed. and trans. George S. Eddy, New York, 1922.

Goethals, George W., *Government of the Canal Zone*, Princeton, 1915.

Goldrich, Daniel, *Sons of the Establishment: Elite Youth in Panama and Costa Rica*, Chicago, 1966.

Harding, Earl, *In Justice to the United States—A Settlement with Colombia*, New York, 1914.

————, *Untold Story of Panama*, New York, 1959.

Haskin, Frederick J., *The Panama Canal*, Garden City, New York, 1913.

Hendrick, B.J., *The Life and Letters of Walter Hines Page*, 3 vols., Garden City, N.Y., 1922.

Howard, Harry N., *Military Government in the Panama Canal Zone*, Norman, Okla. 1931.

Humboldt, Alexander von, *Political Essay on the Kingdom of New Spain*, 4 vols., London, 1822.

Ireland, Gordon, *Boundaries, Possessions, and Conflicts in Central and North America and the Caribbean*, Cambridge, Mass. 1941.

James, Preston, *Latin America*, New York, 1942.

Johnson, Willis F., *Four Centuries of the Panama Canal*, New York, 1906.

Klette, Immanuel J., *From Atlantic to Pacific: A New Interocean Canal*, New York, 1955.

Korngold, Ralph, *Thaddeus Stevens: A Being Darkly Wise and Rudely Great*, New York, 1967.

Lane, Wheaton Jr., *Commodore Vanderbilt, An Epic of the Steam Age*, New York, 1942.

Lee, W. Storrs, *The Strength to Move a Mountain*, New York, 1958.

Liss, Sheldon B., *The Canal, Aspects of U.S.–Panamanian Relations*, South Bend, Ind., 1967.

Mack, Gerstle, *The Land Divided, A History of the Panama Canal and Other Isthmian Projects*, New York, 1944.

Mansfield, Michael J., *The Panama Bases, Report of an Inquiry into Rejection of an Agreement on*, Washington, 1948.

McCain, William D., *The United States and the Republic of Panama*, Durham, N.C., 1937; reprint ed., New York, 1965.

Medina, Leandro, *Limité Oriental de Panamá*, Bogotá, 1913.

Mendez, Pereira Octavio, ed., *Antologia del Canal, 1914–1939*, Panamá, R.P., 1939.

Miner, Dwight C., *The Fight for the Panama Route*, New York, 1940.

Minter, John E., *The Chagres, River of Westward Passage*, New York, 1948.

Miró, Rodrigo, *La emprenta y el periodismo en Panamá durante el periodo de la Gran Colombia*, Panamá, R.P., 1963.

Moon, Parker T., *Imperialism and World Politics*, New York, 1932.

Moore, John Bassett, *Digest of International Law as Embodied in Diplomatic Discussions and Treaties*, 8 vols., Washington, D.C., 1906.

Moore, J. Hampton, *With Speaker Cannon Through the Tropics*, Philadelphia, 1907.

Miller, Hugh G., *The Isthmian Highway*, New York, 1932.

Nichols, Roy F., *Disruption of the American Democracy*, New York, 1948.

Niemeier, Jean Gilbreath, *The Panama Story*, Portland, Oregon, 1968.

Oppenheim, Lassa F., *The Panama Canal Conflict between Great Britain and the U.S.A.*, Cambridge, England, 1913.

Padelford, Norman J., *The Panama Canal in Peace and War*, New York, 1942.

Parks, E. Taylor, *Colombia and the United States*, Durham, N.C., 1935.

Perkins, Dexter, *The United States and the Caribbean*, Cambridge, Mass., 1947.

————, *A History of the Monroe Doctrine*, New York, 1955.

————, *The Monroe Doctrine, 1823–1826*, Cambridge, Mass., 1932.

————, *The Monroe Doctrine, 1867–1907*, Baltimore, 1937.

Pierce, Clyde, *The Roosevelt Panama Libel Cases*, New York, 1959.

Pippin, Larry LaRae, *The Remón Era, An Analysis of a Decade of Events in Panama, 1947–1957*, Hispanic American Report, Stanford University, 1964.

Poppino, Rollie, *International Communism in Latin America*, New York, 1964.

Pratt, Julius W., *A History of United States Foreign Policy*, New York, 1955.

Quintanilla, Luis, *A Latin American Speaks*, New York, 1943.

Radler, D. H., *El Gringo, Yankee Image in Latin America*, Philadelphia, 1962.

Rippy, J. Fred, *Latin America and the Industrial Age*, New York, 1947.

————, *Latin America in World Politics*, New York, 1938.

Robertson, William S., *The Life of Miranda*, 2 vols., Chapel Hill, 1929.

Rodman, Selden, *The Road to Panama*, New York, 1966.

Roosevelt, Theodore, *Autobiography*, New York, 1913.

Roseboom, Eugene H., *A History of Presidential Elections*, New York, 1957.

Saenz, Vicente, *Nuestras Vias Interoceanicas*, México, D.F., 1957.

Schuster, Edward, *Guide to the Law and Legal Literature of the Central American Republic*, New York, 1937.

Shaw, Felix Fernandez, *Panamá Y Sus Relaciones Centroamericanas*, Ediciones Cultura Hispanica, Madrid, 1964.

Sherman, Charles P., *Roman Law in the Modern World*, 3 vols., New Haven, 1922.

Siegfried, André, *Suez and Panama*, London, 1940.

Smith, Darrell H., *The Panama Canal, Its History, Activities, and Organization*, Baltimore, 1927.

Stephens, H. M., and Bolton, H. E., *The Panama Congress—A Collection of Papers and Addresses on the Pacific Ocean in History*, New York, 1917.

Susto, Juan Antonio, and Castillero Reyes, Ernesto J., and Mendez, Pereira Octavio, *Panamá en la Gran Colombia*, Panamá, R.P., 1939.

Teeters, Negley K., *Penology from Panama to Cape Horn*, Philadelphia, 1946.

Thayer, William R., *The Life and Letters of John Hay*, 2 vols., Boston, 1915.

Tomlinson, Edward, *The Other Americans*, New York, 1943.

Valdes, Ramon M., *La Independencia del Istmo de Panamá; sus antecedentes, sus causas, y su justificación*, Panama, R.P., 1903.

Velarde, Fabian, *Analises de Nuevo Tratado*, Panamá, R.P., 1927.

Whitaker, Arthur P., *The United States and the Independence of Latin America*, Baltimore, 1941.

———, *The United States and South America, the Northern Republics*, Cambridge, 1948.

———, *The Western Hemisphere Idea*, Ithaca, N.Y., 1954.

Williams, Mary W., *Anglo-American Isthmian Diplomacy*, London, 1916.

ARTICLES

Allan, Donald A., and Sherman, George, "Panama: Distrust and Delay," *The Reporter*, vol. 30 (February 27, 1965), pp. 28–29.

Allen, Cyril, "Felix Belly, Nicaraguan Canal Promoter," *Hispanic American Historical Review*, vol. 37, no. 1 (February 1957), pp. 46–59.

Ameringer, Charles D., "The Panama Canal Lobby of Philippe Bunau-Varilla and William Nelson Cromwell," *American Historical Review*, vol. 68, no. 2 (January 1963), p. 346.

———, "Philippe Bunau-Varilla: New Light on the Panama Canal Treaty," *Hispanic American Historical Review*, vol. 46, no. 1 (February 1966), pp. 28–52.

Baldwin, Hanson, "New Currents in the Panama Canal," *The New York Times Magazine*, (May 26, 1957), p. 14.

Beichman, Arnold, "Red 'Phantom Fleet' Sails Under Panama Flag: Boycott War Looms," *New Leader* (April 15, 1950).

Berguido, Carlos, Jr., "The Rights of a Seaman on a Ship under Panamanian Registry," *Temple University Law Quarterly*, vol. 19, no. 4 (April 1946).

Billard, Jules B., "Panama, Link Between Oceans and Continents," *National Geographic Magazine*, vol. 137, no. 31 (March 1970), pp. 402–40.

Breece, Laurence M., "R.P. Merchant Marine is a Real Asset," *The Panama Star and Herald* (March 2, 1950).

Briggs, John C., "The Sea Level Canal: Potential Biological Catastrophe," *Bio-Science* (January 1969).

Chamberlain, Leander, "A Chapter of National Dishonor," *North American Review* (February 1912), p. 152.

Coker, William S., "The Panama Canal Tolls Controversy," *Journal of American History*, vol. 55, no. 3 (December 1968), p. 555.

Crowell, Jackson, "The U.S. and a Central American Canal, 1869–1877," *Hispanic American Historical Review*, vol. 49, no. 1 (February 1969), p. 27.

DuVal, Miles P., "Isthmian Canal Policy—An Evaluation," *U.S. Naval Institute Proceedings*, vol. 81, no. 3 (March, 1955), p. 263.

Ealy, Lawrence O., "The Development of an Anglo-American System of Law in the Panama Canal Zone," *American Journal of Legal History*, vol. 2 October 1958), p. 283.

———, "The Monroe Doctrine in International Law," *Social Science Magazine*, vol. 38, no. 1 (January 1963), p. 3.

———, "Strategic Waterways," *Naval War College Review*, vol. 7 (1960), p. 40.

Fenwick, C. G., "Legal Aspects of the Panama Case," *American Journal of International Law* (April 1964), pp. 436–41.

Galloway, Clark H., "Canal Zone Workers Like Their U.S. Shops," *U.S. News & World Report* (December 3, 1948).

Gibbs, R. H., "A Southwest Passage?" *U.S. Naval Institute Proceedings*, vol. 95, no. 4 (April, 1969), p. 64.

Grant, Ulysses S., "The Nicaragua Canal," *North American Review*, (February 1881), p. 107.

Hyde, Charles C., "The Significance of the Hay-Pauncefote Treaty," *Harvard Law Review*, vol. 15, (1900), p. 52.

James, Daniel, "Demands from Panama," *Philadelphia Bulletin* (July 23, 1958).

Llano, Antonio, "A Colombian View of the Treaty," *New York Times* (March 13, 1917).

Miller, August C., Jr., "Prognosis for the Panama Canal," *U.S. Naval Institute Proceedings*, vol. 90, no. 3 (March 1964), pp. 64–73.

———, "To Build a Bigger Ditch," *U.S. Naval Institute Proceedings*, vol. 93, no. 9 (September, 1967), 26–34.

Munro, Dana G., "Dollar Diplomacy in Nicaragua, 1909–1913," *Hispanic American Historical Review*, vol. 38, no. 2 (May 1958), 209.

Marden, Luis, "Panama, Bridge of the World," *National Geographic Magazine*, vol. 80, no. 5 (November 1941), pp. 591–630.

Mason, Carol Y., and Rowlands, Adagrace, "Panama Canal Traffic," *Economic Geography*, vol. 14 (1938), pp. 325–37.

Price, A. Grenfell, "White Settlement in the Canal Zone," *Geographic Review*, vol. 25 (1935).

Ratliff, William E., "Chinese Communist Cultural Diplomacy toward Latin America," *Hispanic American Historical Review*, vol. 49, no. 1 (February 1969), p. 53.

Rippy, J. Fred, "Political Issues in Panama Today," *Current History*, vol. 28 (1928).

———, "The United States and Panama: The High Cost of Appeasement," *Inter-American Economic Affairs* (Spring 1964), 87–94.

Scheips, Paul J., "Gabriel LaFond and Ambrose W. Thompson: Neglected Isthmian Promoters," *Hispanic American Historical Review*, vol. 37, no. 1 (February 1958), p. 34.

———, "Lincoln and the Chiriqui Colonization Project," *The Journal of Negro History*, vol. 37 (October 1952), p. 428.

Stanford, N., "Last Days of the Panama Canal," *Science Digest*, vol. 54, no. 1 (July 1963), pp. 29–31.

Steinberg, Morton C., "Sea Level Canal a Vital Defense Need," *Philadelphia Sunday Inquirer*, December 26, 1948.

Stratton, James H., "Sea Level Canal: How and Where," *Foreign Affairs*, vol. 43, no. 3 (April 1965), pp. 513–18.

Magazines and newspapers appropriately cited in the notes to each chapter are not listed here. An unusual number of by-lined articles and stories about Panama have appeared in recent years in the *U.S. News & World Report*—more than in almost any other periodical. These articles have been informative and useful in researching recent years for which governmental publications and original sources are seldom available.

Index